ByDesign

A Journey to Excellence through Science

SEVENTH-DAY ADVENTIST CHURCH

Kendall Hunt Religious Publishing
A Division of Kendall Hunt Publishing

Developed in Collaboration with the
Seventh-day Adventist NAD Office of Education and
Kendall Hunt Religious Publishing
A Division of Kendall Hunt Publishing Company

Acknowledgments

SDA/NAD Office of Education
Larry Blackmer, Executive Editor/Vice-President of Education
Carol Campbell, Director of Elementary Education
Debra Fryson, Director of Education, Southern Union

Program Development and Publisher
Kendall Hunt Religious Publishing, a Division of Kendall Hunt Publishing

Program Consultants Lead Team I
Dan Wyrick, Director of Nature by Design
Lee Davidson, Associate Professor of Teacher Education/Dept. Chair, Andrews University
Jerrell Gilkeson, Associate Director of Education, Atlantic Union
Ed Zinke, Biblical Researcher
Tim Standish, Geoscience Research Institute

Associates Representing Lead Team II
Betty Bayer, Associate Director of Education, SDA Church in Canada
Diane Ruff, Associate Director of Education, Southern Union
Eunice Warfield, Superintendent of Schools in the South Central Conference
Ileana Espinosa, Associate Director of Education, Columbia Union
James Martz, Associate Director of Education, Lake Union
Keith Waters, Associate Director of Education, North Pacific Union
LouAnn Howard, Associate Director of Education, Mid-America Union
Martha Havens, Associate Director of Education, Pacific Union
Mike Furr, Associate Director of Education, Southwestern Union
Patti Revolinski, Associate Director of Education, North Pacific Union

Contributing Writers and Reviewers
Karen Reinke, Freelance Writer
Katia Reinert, NAD Director of Health Ministries
Alayne Thorpe, President of Griggs University
David A. Steen, Ph.D. Professor Emeritus, Department of Biology, Andrews University

Contributing Multi-Grade Classroom Writers and Reviewers
Karen Reinke, Freelance Writer
Mark Mirek
Heidi Jorgenson
LaVona Gillham
Cindy French Puterbaugh

www.kendallhunt.com
Send all inquiries to:
4050 Westmark Drive
Dubuque, IA 52004-1840
1-800-542-6657

Copyright © 2012 by Seventh-day Adventists/North American Division Office of Education

ISBN 978-1-4652-0092-1

Kendall Hunt Publishing Company has the exclusive rights to reproduce this work, to prepare derivative works from this work, to publicly distribute this work, to publicly perform this work and to publicly display this work.

All rights reserved. No part of this publication may be reproduced, stored in a retrieval system, or transmitted, in any form or by any means, electronic, mechanical, photocopying, recording, or otherwise, without the prior written permission of the copyright owner.
Printed in the United States of America

1 2 3 4 5 6 7 8 9 10 17 16 15 14 13 12

A Prayer of Blessing

By Design: A Journey to Excellence through Science

Leader: Genesis 1:1 says, "In the beginning God created the heaven and the earth." This year we will learn about the world God created for us.

All: On the first day of Creation week, God created light.

Reader: Genesis 1:2–5

All: On the second day, God created air, or the firmament.

Reader: Genesis 1:6–8

All: On the third day, God created dry land and plants such as grass, flowers, and trees.

Reader: Genesis 1:9–13

All: On the fourth day, God created the Sun and the Moon with the stars.

Reader: Genesis 1:14–19

All: On the fifth day, God created air and water animals, such as fish and birds.

Reader: Genesis 1:20–23

All: On the sixth day, God created land animals and He created Adam and Eve.

Reader: Genesis 1:24–31

All: On the seventh day, God rested from His work and blessed the seventh day of each week as the Sabbath, a special day for us to worship the Creator and praise Him for all that He created for us.

Reader: Genesis 2:1–3

All: Thanks be to God for the world that He created for us.

Leader: Let us ask for God's blessing as we study His perfect Creation this year.

All: God, help us to discover and appreciate the wonders of your world as we use the Bible to study your Creation and bless our *Journey to Excellence through Science.* Amen!

Scavenger Hunt

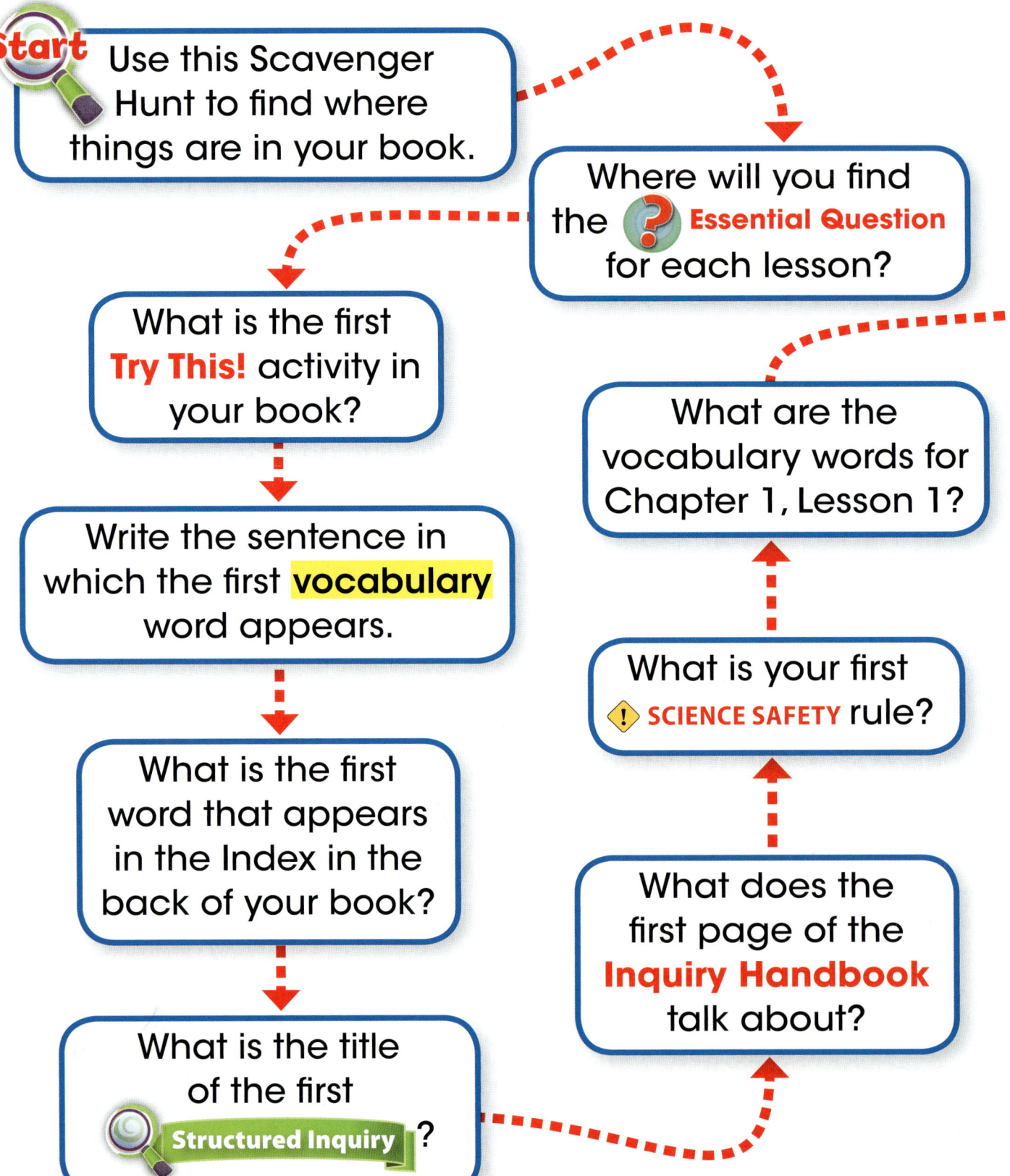

Start Use this Scavenger Hunt to find where things are in your book.

Where will you find the ❓ **Essential Question** for each lesson?

What is the first **Try This!** activity in your book?

Write the sentence in which the first **vocabulary** word appears.

What is the first word that appears in the Index in the back of your book?

What is the title of the first **Structured Inquiry**?

What are the vocabulary words for Chapter 1, Lesson 1?

What is your first ⚠️ **SCIENCE SAFETY** rule?

What does the first page of the **Inquiry Handbook** talk about?

iv

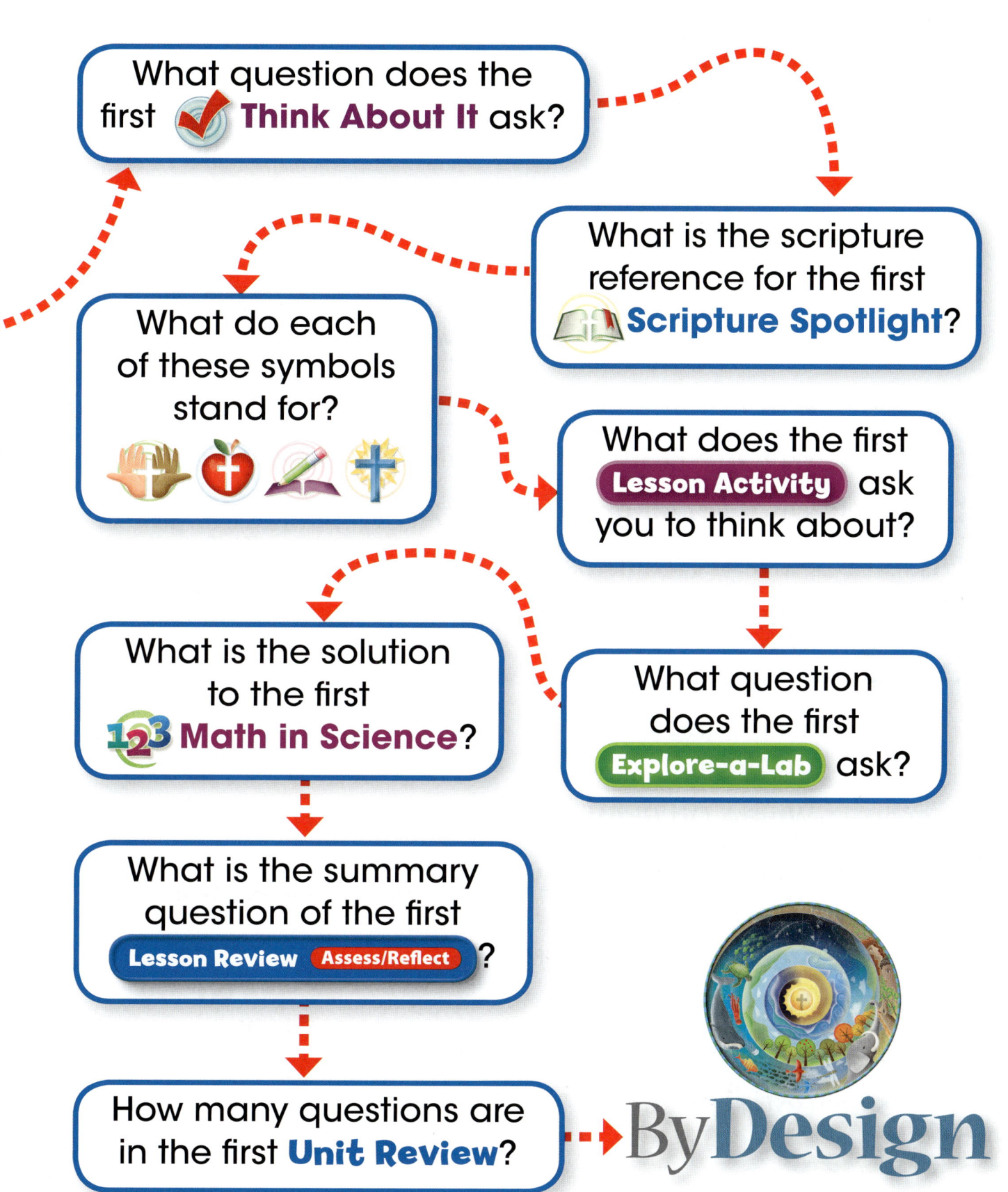

Table of Contents

Science Skills .... **SS 0**

Unit 1: Life Science 12

Chapter 1: Plants and Animals 14

    Lesson 1: What Do All Plants Need? 16

    Lesson 2: What Do the Parts of a Plant Do? 26

    Lesson 3: Why Are Plants Important? 36

    Lesson 4: What Do All Animals Need? 46

    Lesson 5: How Are Animals Different? 56

    Chapter Feature: People in Science 68

    Chapter Feature: Careers in Science 69

Chapter 2: Plants and Animals Live Together 70

    Lesson 1: Where Do Plants and Animals Live? ... 72

    Lesson 2: What Are Food Chains and Food Webs? 82

    Lesson 3: How Do People Affect the Environment? 90

    Chapter Feature: People in Science 102

    Chapter Feature: Careers in Science 103

Unit 1 Review 104

Unit 2: The Human Body 106

Chapter 3: Food and Your Body 108
- Lesson 1: What Is Your Digestive System? 110
- Lesson 2: What Are Some Types of Food? 120
- Lesson 3: What Is Good Nutrition? 128
- Chapter Feature: People in Science 136
- Chapter Feature: Careers in Science 137

Chapter 4: Body and Mind 138
- Lesson 1: How Does Your Nervous System Work? 140
- Lesson 2: How Do You Communicate? 150
- Lesson 3: What Is Mental Health? 160
- Chapter Feature: Science and Technology 170
- Chapter Feature: Careers in Science 171

Chapter 5: Keeping Your Body Safe and Healthy 172
- Lesson 1: How Can You Avoid Germs? 174
- Lesson 2: Why Is Hygiene Important? 184
- Lesson 3: What Are Common Safety Hazards? .. 194
- Chapter Feature: People in Science 204
- Chapter Feature: Careers in Science 205

Unit 2 Review 206

Unit 3: Earth and Space Science 208

Chapter 6: Earth's Land, Air, and Water 210

- Lesson 1: What Features Are on Earth's Surface? 212
- Lesson 2: What Are Rocks and Minerals? 226
- Lesson 3: How Does Earth's Surface Change? .. 236
- Lesson 4: What Can We Learn from Fossils? 246
- Chapter Feature: Careers in Science 254
- Chapter Feature: Science and Technology 255

Chapter 7: Weather and Seasons 256

- Lesson 1: How Is the Weather Predicted? 258
- Lesson 2: What Is the Water Cycle? 268
- Lesson 3: What Causes the Seasons? 276
- Chapter Feature: Careers in Science 284
- Chapter Feature: Science and Technology 285

Chapter 8: Space Science 286

- Lesson 1: What Makes Up Our Solar System? ... 288
- Lesson 2: What Is the Universe? 298
- Lesson 3: How Do We Explore Space? 304
- Chapter Feature: People in Science 310
- Chapter Feature: Careers in Science 311

Unit 3 Review 312

Unit 4: Physical Science **314**

Chapter 9: Properties of Matter **316**

- **Lesson 1:** What Is Matter? **318**
- **Lesson 2:** What Are Solids, Liquids, and Gases? **328**
- **Lesson 3:** How Does Matter Change? **338**
- **Chapter Feature:** People in Science **346**
- **Chapter Feature:** Careers in Science **347**

Chapter 10: Energy and Machines **348**

- **Lesson 1:** What Is Energy? **350**
- **Lesson 2:** What Is Thermal Energy? **360**
- **Lesson 3:** What Are Sound and Light? **370**
- **Lesson 4:** What Are Simple Machines? **380**
- **Chapter Feature:** Careers in Science **390**
- **Chapter Feature:** Science and Technology **391**

Unit 4 Review **392**

- Glossary **394**
- Index **407**

Science Skills

God and Science

God made all things—He is the Creator. He knows all things. Knowing God can help you understand the world He created. We do not understand everything God did when He created the world. But science helps us understand the laws God put into place to control things that happens in the natural world. Scientists are always learning about the laws God created to make the world go on and on as it does. There are many examples of science in the Bible. Science and the Bible go hand in hand.

God's designs can be seen in the largest things—in galaxies, in black holes, and in supernovas. They can also be seen in the tiniest things we can imagine. Everything that exists shows some kind of design. For example, the parts that make up a flower in Bermuda are the same as the parts that make up a similar flower in China. Everything in the world has its own design created by God. God created the laws by which the world works. People across the world get the same results when they do the same investigations. As you study science this year, you will discover things about the laws of nature that God created.

What Is Science?

Science is knowledge. The word *science* comes from the Latin word *scientia,* which means "knowledge." Science is much more than facts in a book. Actually, science is more about the *way* we learn. We learn science through questioning, observing, and investigating. We find out more about our world, our Universe, ourselves, and our Creator.

Science is fun. It can be exciting to perform investigations. You can learn how things work. You can watch things grow. It is exciting to see and figure out things for yourself. You get to test all kinds of ideas. You get to make interesting projects. You get to learn some amazing facts, too!

Science is useful. Science is very powerful. It is used to make new inventions. It is used to treat illness. It is used to explore new worlds. It can even help us learn about plants and animals.

Science is always changing. Scientists are always learning new things. They find new ways to study things. Your study of science never ends. You will always be asking questions. You will always be exploring. You will always be sharing what you have learned with others.

Who Are Scientists?

People started asking questions about the world a long time ago. The methods they used followed a similar pattern. It all began with questions. Scientists use those same methods today.

Scientists ask questions. They explore. They study the results. Then they tell what they have learned. Scientists are curious. They try to find patterns or rules. They try to explain how things work. Scientists might study things like plants and animals. They might study volcanoes. They might study the human body. Scientists use what they learn to predict what will happen next.

Science Skills

Perform an Investigation

Scientists can find answers to their questions in many different ways. One way is to use the **scientific method**.

Suppose Lilly and her family plant beans in a garden. Lilly would like the plants to grow as many beans as possible. She could use the scientific method to perform an investigation.

Step 1 Observe the plants. Lilly could ask *how, what, when, who, which, why,* or *where* about the things she sees. She asks the question, "How can I make these plants grow more beans?"

Step 2 Form a hypothesis, or a good guess, about how things work. A hypothesis tells what you think will happen in an investigation. Lilly could think, "If I do _____, then _____ will happen." The hypothesis should help Lilly answer her question. It should also be something that can be measured. Lilly forms this hypothesis: "If I give the plants some plant food, then they will grow faster."

Step 3 Test the hypothesis. Lilly learns about good food for bean plants. She feeds the plants in one row. She does not feed the plants in the other row. That way, Lilly can compare the plants that get fed to those that do not.

Scientists make sure that their investigations are fair. They change only one thing at a time. They may do an investigation more than one time. This helps the scientists to be sure the results are true.

Step 4 Measure the results. Lilly keeps a record of how many beans each plant grows. Then she finds the total number of beans grown by each row of plants.

Step 5 Create explanations. The data show that the plants Lilly fed grew more beans than the plants she did not feed. The data show that her hypothesis about feeding bean plants is true.

Lilly also shares her results. She uses words, pictures, numbers, and a table to share her results with her family and her classmates.

Sometimes, scientists find that their guesses are false. When this happens, they form new hypotheses. Then they conduct new investigations.

Science Skills

How Scientists Think

When scientists perform an investigation, they rely on **inquiry practices**. You learned some of these practices in Grade 1. The table below summarizes those practices for you.

Observe	Use one or more of your senses and available tools to study something closely.
Compare	Look for ways things are the same and ways they are different.
Predict	Use what you already know to figure out what might happen.
Use or Make Models	Make a representation of something real to show how it happens or how it works.
Measure	Find out the size, length, or quantity of something by using a measuring tool.

In Grade 2, you will learn more inquiry practices. These practices include how to infer, order, classify, and communicate scientific information.

Scientists **infer** information. They draw conclusions based on what they observe. Lilly observed that plant food helps bean plants grow more beans. She might infer that plant food will also help other plants grow more, too.

Scientists **order** things. Putting things in order helps them to see patterns. You could order the life cycle of a bean plant. You could draw a seed and then a sprouting seed. Next, you could draw the plant and the plant with beans. Finally, you could draw the plant spreading its seeds and dying.

Scientists **classify** things. They group objects to show how they are alike. You could classify beans by type, size, shape, or color.

Scientists also **communicate**. They share their thoughts, ideas, and observations. You will use words, pictures, numbers, and charts or tables to communicate what you learn with your teacher and your classmates.

Science Skills

Science Tools

Scientists have many tools to help them. You will learn to use some of these tools this year.

Thermometer

1. A thermometer is a science tool that measures temperature. It is made of a long, thin glass tube with a bulb at the bottom. There is a liquid inside the tube that is usually colored red. Most thermometers have two temperature scales printed on them: Celsius and Fahrenheit. Scientists use Celsius.

2. Do not hold the thermometer in your hand. Heat moves from your hand and changes the temperature.

3. To read the temperature on a thermometer, your eyes should be level with the top of the liquid in the tube.

4. Record the temperature in degrees Celsius.

Balance

1. A balance is a science tool that measures an object's mass, or the amount of matter in it. Make sure the pan is empty. Place the object you wish to measure in the pan on the left.

2. Add standard masses to the other pan. The pointer should move as you add masses. The pans are balanced when the pointer is at the middle mark.

3. Add the numbers on the masses you used. Record the total for the object you measured.

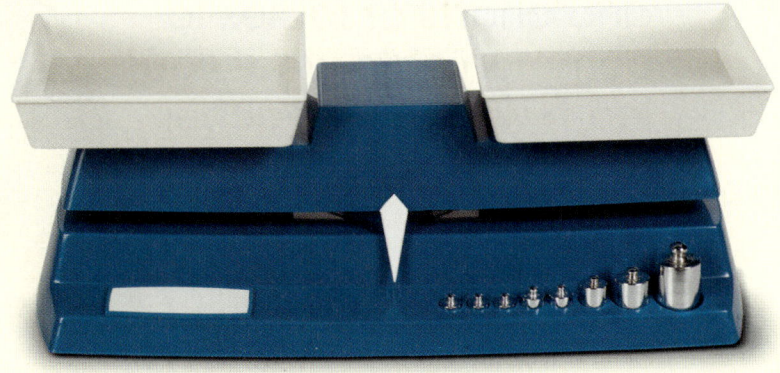

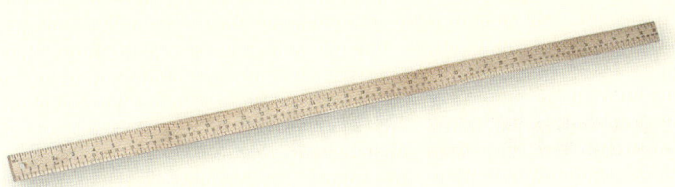

Meterstick (or Ruler)

1. A meterstick measures length.
2. Find the 0 mark on the meterstick.
3. Line up one end of the object with the 0 mark.
4. Read the number on the meterstick that is closest to the other end of the object.
5. Record the number and the unit of measurement.
6. A meterstick is 100 centimeters long.

Graduated Cylinder

1. A graduated cylinder measures volume.
2. Pour the liquid into the graduated cylinder.
3. Look level at the flat top of the liquid.
4. Read the number measurement closest to top of the liquid.
5. Record the number and the unit of measurement.
6. A graduated cylinder is marked in milliliters (mL).

Stopwatch

1. A stopwatch is used to measure time. Make sure the stopwatch is set at zero. Reset it if needed.
2. Hold it in one hand with your thumb on the *Start* button.
3. Press the button when you want to start timing.
4. Press the *Stop* button to stop timing.
5. Read the numbers to find how much time has passed.
6. Record the time in minutes and seconds.

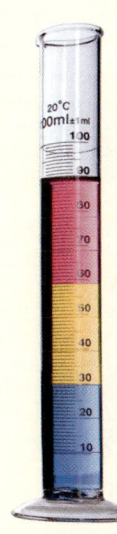

How to Record Data

Scientists collect information. There are many ways to record information. Charts and tables can help you compare things.

First, write a title for your table. It should tell what your table is about. Then write a label for the left column. It should tell what is being compared. List each item in the rows below the label.

In the right column, write a label that tells what the values mean. As you collect the data, fill in the rows of the second column.

Number of Beans	
Bean Plant	Number
Plant 1	26
Plant 2	32
Plant 3	18
Plant 4	14

Each type of chart or graph has a certain use. A bar graph can show how many items are in each group. It also shows how the items compare. It has a title and labels that tell about the data.

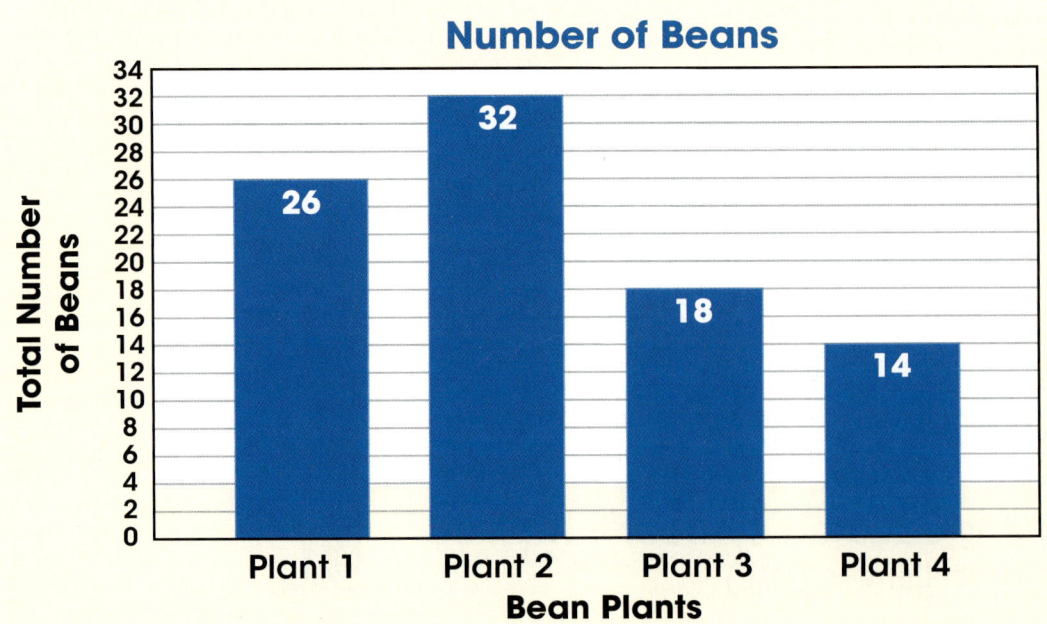

Be Safe!

It's important to be safe when you perform hands-on investigations. Always look for the safety symbol in your textbook. It tells you how to be safe as you perform your investigations. Below are some important safety rules to follow for most investigations. Remember to be alert and listen to your teacher for any additional safety rules.

SAFETY:

- Carefully listen to and follow any instructions.
- Do not touch any materials unless your teacher says you may.
- Look around you before moving materials, and do not run in the classroom.
- Wear safety goggles, gloves, and other protective clothing when needed.
- Keep your hands away from your eyes and mouth.
- Do not taste any materials, unless it is part of the activity.
- Tell your teacher right away about any accident.
- Keep your work area clean and neat.
- Wash your hands and work area after the activity.

Unit 1
Life Science

Chapter 1 14
Plants and Animals

Chapter 2 70
Plants and Animals Live Together

Unit 1 Review ... 104

Life science is the study of living things. In this unit, you will learn about the plants and animals God created. God created plants and animals to adapt to the environments they live in.

- What do plants and animals need to live?
- What are some ways plants and animals are different?
- How do plants and animals need each other?
- How does God care for living things?

Boing! Boing! A kangaroo uses its two large legs to hop. It uses its tail to balance when it stands up.

Your teacher may assign an Open Inquiry lab and a Lifestyle Challenge activity. Use your *Science Journal* to record your work.

Chapter 1
Plants and Animals

Lesson 1
What Do All Plants Need?............ 16

Lesson 2
What Do the Parts of a Plant Do? .. 26

Lesson 3
Why Are Plants Important? 36

Lesson 4
What Do All Animals Need? 46

Lesson 5
How Are Animals Different? 56

Scripture Spotlight

The Bible tells how God created all Earth's plants and animals. You can read about plants and animals in the Bible. You will read these passages in this chapter.

Genesis 1:11–13 (p. 20)   Genesis 2:8–9 (p. 33)
Mark 4:26–29 (p. 31)   Luke 12:22–31 (p. 48)

The Big Idea

God made many kinds of plants and animals. They have parts that help them live and grow.

How is this animal using its tongue?

Lesson 1

Vocabulary
living thing   p. 18
plant   p. 21
basic need   p. 22
nutrient   p. 23
drought   p. 24

Find out what these words mean as you study this lesson.

? **Essential Question**

What Do All Plants Need? Engage

Get Ready to Learn What differences do you see in the plants shown here? God made plants in all sizes and colors. Even though they might look different, all plants have the same basic needs.

Try This! What kinds of plants have you heard of? See how many kinds of plants you can list in two minutes.

Structured Inquiry — Discover

Record your work for this inquiry. Your teacher may also assign the related Guided Inquiry.

Water Me
What is one thing plants need to grow?

Your Group Needs
- two plants
- container to hold water
- water

Step 1 Label one plant *A* and the other plant *B*. **Observe** the two plants. Draw or write down your observations.

Step 2 Water plant A according to your teacher's instructions. Do not water plant B. **Predict** how each plant will look after a week.

Step 3 **Compare** both plants each day. **Record** your observations.

Step 4 **Communicate** your observations from Step 3 with a classmate.

Create Explanations

1. What is one thing plants need to grow?
2. How did your observations compare with your classmates'?

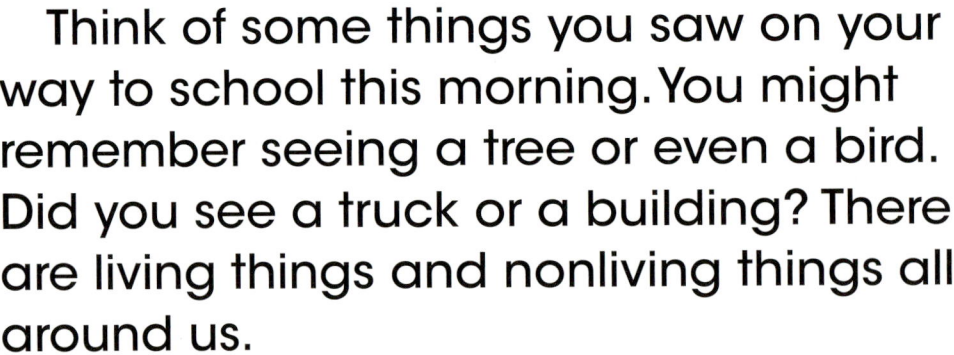

Plants and animals are living things. Nonliving things include air, water, sunlight, rocks, and soil.

Living Things Explain

Think of some things you saw on your way to school this morning. You might remember seeing a tree or even a bird. Did you see a truck or a building? There are living things and nonliving things all around us.

All **living things** grow and change. They make more living things like themselves. Living things respond to conditions around them.

Think About It

How can you tell if an object is living or nonliving?

In the Bible, the Creation story tells that God created the living things in six days and rested on the Sabbath. Plants are living things. God created them on the third day of Creation. Animals are living things. They were created on the fifth and sixth days of Creation. A pet fish is a living thing. The bowl the fish swims in is a nonliving thing.

Think About It

Can you name something that has most of the characteristics of a living thing but is not alive?

? What are some living things in this picture? What are some nonliving things?

Plants Explain

Scripture Spotlight

Read **Genesis 1:11–13**. When did God create plants?

You might know that an oak tree is a kind of plant. But did you know that grass and a rose bush are also plants? When God created plants, He made many kinds.

A <mark>plant</mark> is a kind of living thing. Most plants make their own food inside their leaves. Just like people, plants can look very different. Some plants have small leaves. Other plants have leaves that are larger than your hand. There are very tall plants and plants that smell sweet.

Math in Science

Tom has a plant that should be watered every 24 hours. The plant was watered Monday at 8:00 A.M. When should the plant be watered next?

Giant sequoia trees live in California. They can grow to be more than 75 meters (246 feet) tall!

Basic Needs Explain

air

light

All living things have basic needs. **Basic needs** are what a living thing must have to stay alive. Needs are different from wants. You might want a new game to play. But you do not need a game to stay alive.

Plants are living things, so they have basic needs. The basic needs of a plant are water, air, nutrients, and light. Plants must get their basic needs to stay alive.

water

nutrients

God provides for the basic needs of plants in many ways. Seeds get water when it rains. This helps the seeds grow. Plants that live on land get air from the area around them. **Nutrients** are substances living things need to grow. Plants get nutrients from the soil. Most plants get light from the Sun. A plant in your house can get it from a light bulb.

Think About It

Why do you think most plants live outside?

These plants are getting their basic needs.

What are the four basic needs of a plant?

Basic Needs Are Important Explain

Think About It

What would happen to a plant if it was left in a dark closet? Draw a picture of what the plant would look like.

Living things must meet all their basic needs to grow and stay alive. A plant cannot move. It must get its basic needs from the place where it lives. God designed plants so they could get the things they need without moving.

Sometimes the place a plant lives changes. A **drought** is a very long time without rain. During a drought, a plant might wilt. Its leaves will begin to droop and turn brown. If it does not get water soon, it will die.

Explore-a-Lab
Structured Inquiry

 How does blocking sunlight affect plant leaves?

Cover part of a leaf with foil. Place it in sunlight. Record your observations of the leaf after a week. What effect did the foil have on the leaf? Explain.

Make a Connection Extend

Suppose you are going on vacation. You ask a friend to take care of your plant. Make a detailed list. Explain how to care for your plant.

Lesson Review Assess/Reflect

Summary: What do all plants need? Plants are one kind of living thing. All plants have basic needs. They must have these things to grow and stay alive.

1. **Graphic Organizer** Use *Basic Needs of Plants* as the main idea. Write the details that go with it.

2. **Vocabulary** How can you tell if something is a living thing?

3. **Test Prep** Which does not help a plant meet its basic needs?
   A. sunlight   C. air
   B. rain   D. music

4. Describe what a plant might look like if it did not have its basic need for water met.

5. What did God create that provides light to plants?

Family Link Go on a walk with your family. Have each family member make a list of plants he or she sees. Did everyone see the same plants? Which plant was your favorite?

Lesson 2

Vocabulary

life cycle p. 30
seed p. 31
germinate p. 31
seedling p. 31
flower p. 32
pollen p. 32

Find out what these words mean as you study this lesson.

Essential Question

What Do the Parts of a Plant Do? Engage

Get Ready to Learn How do its flowers help a plant grow and change? Flowers can be colorful and beautiful. Many flowers smell sweet. Flowers are an important part of a plant. They help plants make seeds.

Try This! Can you name all the parts of a plant? Try it. Then make a model or drawing of a plant. Try to label all the parts.

26

Structured Inquiry
Discover

Record your work for this inquiry. Your teacher may also assign the related Guided Inquiry.

Growing Roots
How does the root system of a plant grow?

Your Group Needs
- two bean seeds
- two clear plastic cups
- two paper towels
- water

Step 1 Wet the paper towels with water until damp. Stuff them into the cups.

Step 2 Slip a bean seed between each paper towel and the side of each plastic cup. Put them about halfway down.

Step 3 **Observe** both seeds for two to three days, watching for roots. Keep the towels damp.

Step 4 After the roots start to grow, turn one cup on its side. Repeat Step 3 and compare the direction each root system grows. Make a drawing to record your findings.

Create Explanations
1. How does the root system of a plant grow?
2. Do you think it matters if you plant a seed upside-down? Explain.

Parts of a Plant Explain

Think about what you would do if you were hungry. You might ask for a snack. People and other animals must find food and eat it. Plants do not eat like you do. They do something you cannot. They make their own food inside their leaves.

God designed all the parts of a plant to work together. Each part of the plant is important. The *roots* take nutrients and water from the soil. The *stem* carries the nutrients and water to the leaves. The *leaves* use water with air and sunlight to make food. Then the stem carries the food to the rest of the plant. The nutrients are used to build plant parts. The food supplies energy for growth and for other life activities.

Bamboo grows very quickly.

? Why do the stems of the bamboo have this shape?

Math in Science

Sara planted a bean seed. On Monday it had 4 leaves. By Friday it had 11 leaves. How many leaves grew between Monday and Friday?

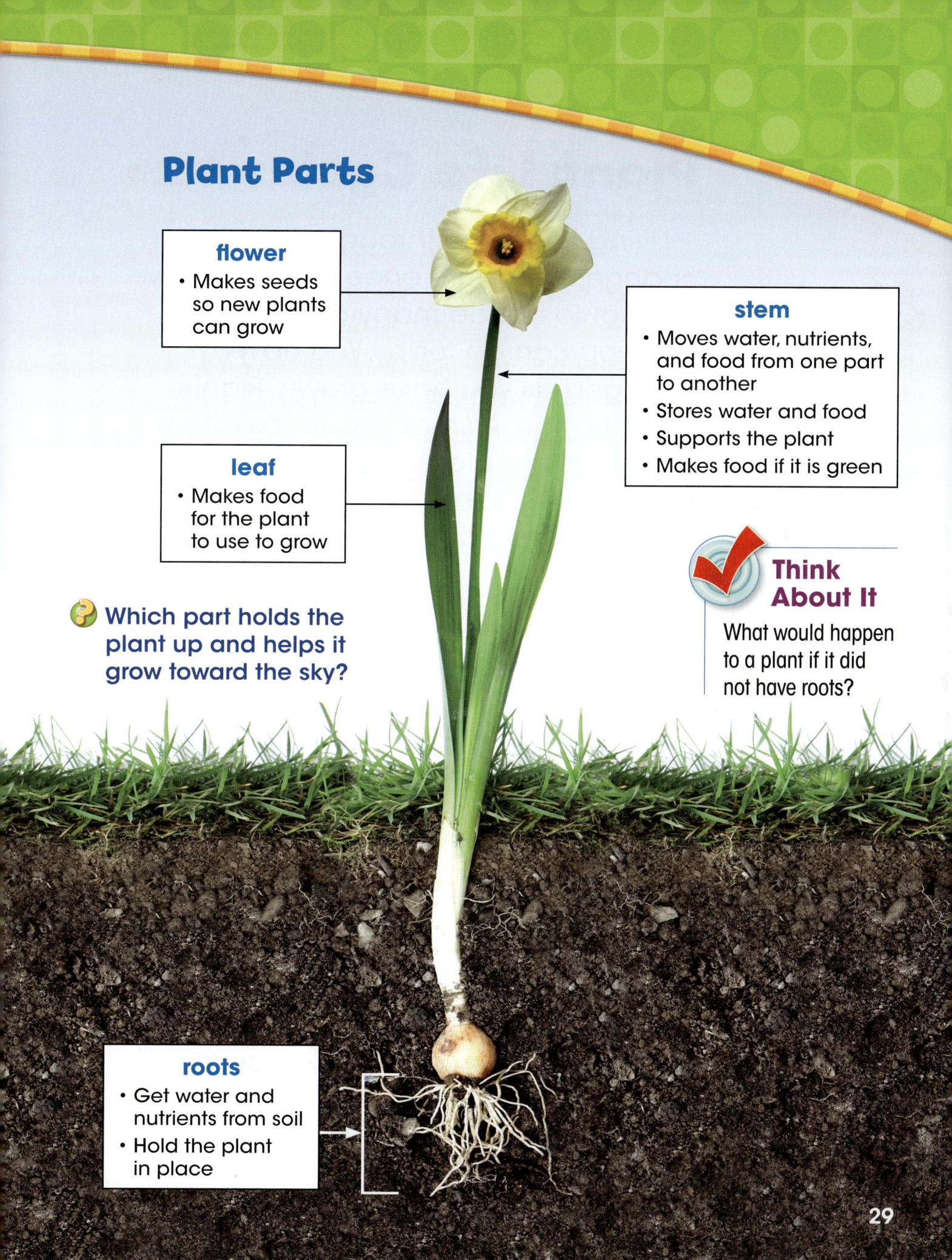

Plant Life Cycles Explain

Think About It

How have you changed since you were born?

Living things go through many changes. You were once a small baby. You could not do many of the things that you can do today. You have changed as you have grown. Plants also change. A small plant has a few leaves. As the plant grows, it will grow more leaves. Some leaves will even grow larger as the plant gets older.

A **life cycle** is all the stages a living thing goes through during its lifetime. Many plant life cycles begin with a seed.

The seed of an oak tree is an acorn. It takes many years for an acorn to grow into a tall tree.

Explore-a-Lab
Structured Inquiry

What will you find if you open up a seed?

Soak a bean seed for a few hours. Carefully split the seed in half. Observe the inside of the seed. Draw the parts you see. What could you see inside the seed?

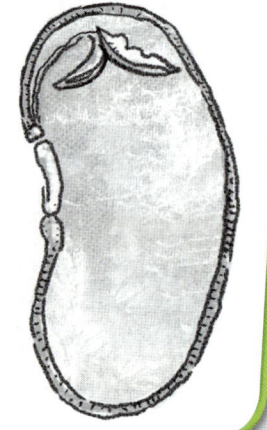

A **seed** is the first stage of the life cycle for most plants. A seed has stored food and a tiny plant inside. When a seed gets water and the right temperature, it will germinate. To **germinate** is to sprout, or start to grow.

A young plant that has just started to grow is called a **seedling**. Stems sense light and grow toward it. The roots sense gravity and grow downward. The seedling will keep growing if its basic needs are met. It will grow into an adult plant.

Scripture Spotlight

Read **Mark 4: 26–29**. What is being described in this passage?

This seed is germinating.

This seedling will grow into an adult plant.

Plants with Flowers Explain

God designed all living things to make more living things like themselves. Making more plants is part of a plant's life cycle. Many adult plants make seeds. Seeds are one way plants make more plants.

Some plants have flowers. **Flowers** are parts of a plant that have petals and help make seeds. Flowers have male parts and female parts. **Pollen** is a powder made by the male parts of a flower. A flower can make seeds when pollen lands on the female part of a flower.

Pollen is carried from flower to flower in many ways.

? What is helping to move pollen in this picture?

Flowers turn into fruit. The fruit of a plant protects the new seeds. If a seed is planted, it can start its own life cycle and make a new plant. The new plant will look like the plant the seed came from.

Think About It

Think about where most seeds are found in a fruit. Why do you think this is so?

Scripture Spotlight

Read **Genesis 2:8–9**. It describes the Garden of Eden. The Garden was filled with trees that provided fruit for Adam and Eve. They lived in the Garden until they disobeyed God by eating fruit from a tree that God had asked them not to eat from.

 What type of plants can grow from these seeds?

A female part of a flower is what turns into a fruit. An apple is a fruit.

Plants with Cones Explain

Think About It

Look at the plants on this page. What plant parts do you think these plants will not have?

Not all plants use flowers to make seeds. Some plants have cones. Cones have scales instead of petals. The cones make and protect the seeds. Plants with cones do not have fruit.

One plant you might know about that has cones is a pine tree. A pine tree starts its life cycle as a seed. It then grows into a seedling. The seedling will continue to grow throughout its life cycle. But instead of having flowers and fruit, it will have cones.

▼ This is the male cone of a pine tree. It makes pollen.

This pine cone is a female ▲ cone. God designed the pine cone to protect the seeds that grow inside.

34

Make a Connection Extend

Farmers need to know about the life cycles of the plants they grow. Choose several fruits or vegetables. Draw what the plants look like. Make sure you include the flowers and the fruit. When do farmers plant the seeds? When do they harvest the crop?

Lesson Review Assess/Reflect

Summary: What do the parts of a plant do? The parts of a plant work together. They make food. They supply energy for life activities. Plant parts also help the plant make more plants like itself.

1. **Graphic Organizer** Make a list comparing and contrasting plants with flowers and plants with cones.

2. **Vocabulary** Explain what a seed needs to germinate.

3. **Test Prep** Which part of a plant gets water and nutrients from the soil?
    A. roots	B. leaves	C. pollen	D. stems

4. Explain how plants make food.

5. What did God design fruit for?

Family Link With your family, research the size and shape of five different seeds. Make a poster to show your findings. Be sure to include drawings.

Lesson 3

Vocabulary
edible p. 38
resource p. 40

Find out what these words mean as you study this lesson.

❓ Essential Question
Why Are Plants Important? *Engage*

Get Ready to Learn What plant roots do you eat? People eat the roots of the carrot plant. Carrots are full of vitamins and minerals. They are very good for you. What other plant roots do you eat?

Try This! What would you plant in your own garden? Make a list. Draw a plan for your garden.

Structured Inquiry — Discover

Record your work for this inquiry. Your teacher may also assign the related Guided Inquiry.

Saving Paper, Saving Trees

How can using less paper help save trees?

Your Group Needs
- large container
- chart paper
- markers
- bathroom scale

Step 1 **Predict** how much paper your class uses in one week.

Step 2 Use a large container to collect all the paper for an entire week

Step 3 Use the scale to **gather data**. Find the mass of the paper that was collected each day. **Record** the data in the table in your ***Science Journal*** and on a class chart.

Step 4 Make a bar graph to show your data.

Create Explanations

1. How can using less paper help save trees?

2. List three ways you could use less paper.

3. Suppose the same amount of paper was collected each week. How much paper will the class use in a month? Add the class totals from the chart.

Plants Are Food Explain

Do you have a favorite food? Many of the foods you eat come from plants. You can get all of the things your body needs to stay healthy by eating plants. The parts of a plant that people can eat are called **edible** parts.

People eat all parts of plants. Lettuce is a leaf. Carrots and beets are roots. Celery is part of a stem. Corn and beans are seeds. You can even eat some flowers, such as honeysuckles.

Focus on Health

Scientists have studied what people eat and how long they live. People who eat a lot of plants usually live longer.

Explore-a-Lab Structured Inquiry

Which plants do you eat most often?

List all the food and drinks you have in one day. Do not forget about snacks! Circle each item that comes from a plant.

All of these plants are edible.

Not all foods come directly from a plant. Parts of a plant can be changed or used with other items to make a type of food. Apples come from a tree. Apple juice and applesauce are made from apples.

When you eat bread, you are eating part of a plant. Bread is made from flour. Flour is made by grinding seeds. Flour might be made from wheat, corn, or even almonds. The bread has a part of a plant in it, but it did not come directly from a plant.

Called to Serve

Why is it important to help people in places where there is not enough food?

Think About It

Name three foods that are eaten directly from a plant. Then name three foods that are made from parts of plants.

Wheat flour is one of the ingredients in this bread.

Which part of the wheat plant was used?

Plant Resources Explain

Think About It
What resource could a shirt come from?

We use plants in many ways. They are an important resource. A **resource** is a material found in nature that people use. Food is one way we use plants as a resource. Another use of plants is for the fibers used in making cloth. Examples of these natural resources from plants are cotton and linen.

Trees are important natural resources. They are used to make many products. Houses, desks, and pencils can be made from wood. Even books are made from plants. That is because ground-up trees are used to make paper. Recall the Structured Inquiry. You can help save a tree if you use less paper and recycle products made from trees.

A log cabin is made of tree trunks. The wood being used to make this house came from trees, too.

Math in Science

There are 100 sheets of paper in a package. Betsy used 30 sheets of paper for an art project. How many sheets of paper are left in the package?

There are many kinds of resources. Sunlight is an example of a resource that will not run out. It does not matter how much sunlight is used. The sunlight cannot be used up. Some resources can get used up. Coal and oil are examples of resources that can get used up.

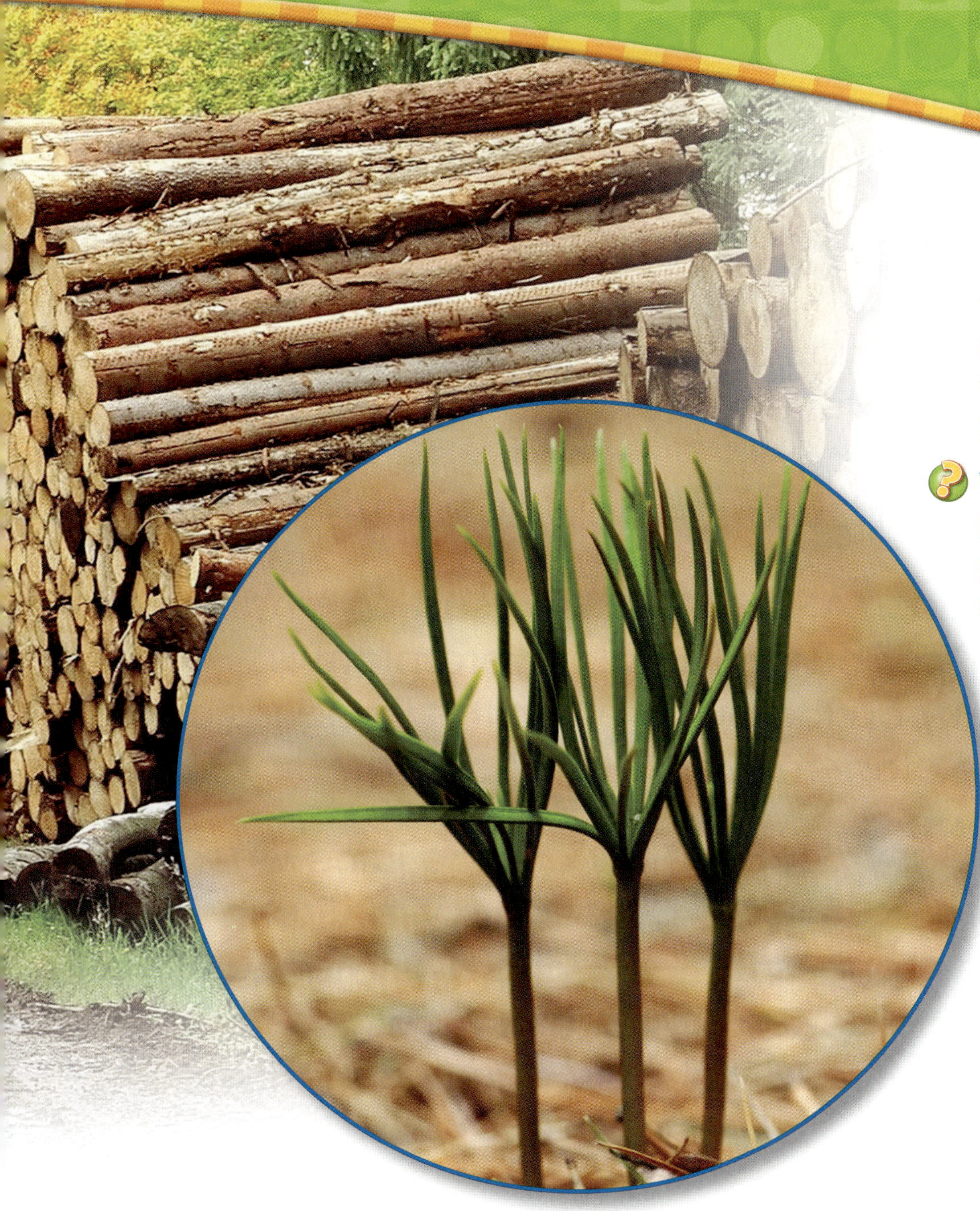

Trees are an important resource. We use them to make lumber and paper.

❓ What might happen if new trees were not planted when trees are cut down?

Check out your *Science Journal* for a Structured Inquiry about tree rings.
Discover

It is important to care for the things God created. A forest ranger works to help forests grow. Tree seedlings are planted when old trees are cut down. This way we can use trees as a renewable resource for a long time.

Think About It

Are there more or fewer trees in the United States today than in the past?

Other Uses of Plants Explain

Think About It
Other than as food, how have you used a plant this week?

Have you ever had a cold or stomach ache? Have you ever gotten a small cut on your hand? Plants have been used for many years to help us feel better.

Aloe (AL•oh) can be used on small cuts or burns. The aloe vera plant is spiky on the outside. But the liquid inside the plant may help heal a burn.

Many people drink orange juice when they have a cold. There are vitamins in the oranges that help the body fight off the cold. Many important medicines were discovered by people studying plants.

Aloe vera plants grow in dry places. Farmers grow them in fields. They are a resource people use. Aloe is the gel inside the plant.

Make a Connection — Extend

When you recycle paper, it is turned into new paper. Trees do not have to be cut down. Find out what things can be recycled where you live. Make a poster. Write instructions for recycling things instead of throwing them away.

Lesson Review — Assess/Reflect

Summary: Why are plants important? Plants are important to people and to other animals. Plants are used as food, medicines, and resources.

1. **Graphic Organizer** Use *Plants* as the main idea. Make a web showing at least five items that come from plants or can be made from plants.

2. **Vocabulary** What does it mean if a plant is edible?

3. **Test Prep** Which food comes directly from a plant?
   - **A.** bread
   - **B.** lemonade
   - **C.** pasta noodle
   - **D.** tomato

4. Chris ate a grilled cheese sandwich, applesauce, a banana, and milk. Which foods came from plants?

5. What are some things you can do to care for the resources God provided?

Family Link Find out the favorite foods of each family member that come from plants. Draw the foods and the plants they come from.

Lesson 4

Vocabulary
oxygen   p. 49
gill   p. 50
shelter p. 52

Find out what these words mean as you study this lesson.

Essential Question

What Do All Animals Need? Engage

Get Ready to Learn How are the basic needs of plants and animals alike? You learned about the basic needs of plants in Lesson 1. Can you remember what those needs are? In this lesson, you will learn about animals and their basic needs.

Try This! Where do wild animals that you know of live? Trees are a good home for some animals. Other animals make their homes underground. Find out what the home of your favorite animal looks like. Draw a picture of the home.

Structured Inquiry
Discover

Record your work for this inquiry. Your teacher may also assign the related Guided Inquiry.

Build a Nest
How do the shapes of birds' nests help protect their young?

Your Group Needs
- three sheets of paper
- tape and a tray
- nine marbles
- scissors

Step 1 Use paper to **make a model** of three different nests. Make the first one flat and the second one in the shape of a U. Make the last nest in a bowl shape.

Step 2 **Predict** which nest shape will keep bird eggs safest.

Step 3 Tape each nest to the tray. Place three marbles in each nest.

Step 4 Gently move the tray back and forth. **Observe** and **record** how the marbles move.

Create Explanations
1. How do the shapes of birds' nests help protect their young?
2. Research the shapes of nests for three birds from your area. Which nest shape do you think most birds make? Why?

Basic Needs of Animals Explain

Scripture Spotlight

Read **Luke 12:22–31**. What needs does God promise to provide for us?

God created plants and animals. He also created all the things they would need to live. Like plants, animals have basic needs. Animals must get all their basic needs met to stay alive. The basic needs of an animal are water, food, shelter, and oxygen.

Animals find water and food in the places they live. Sheep nibble on grass in a field. Horses go to a stream to drink water. People give their pets food and water.

Oxygen is a gas found in air. Land animals breathe in oxygen from the air around them. Many land animals use lungs to breathe. You also have lungs to breathe in oxygen from the air. Animals can only live as long as all their basic needs are met.

All animals have the same basic needs.

What are the basic needs of this dog?

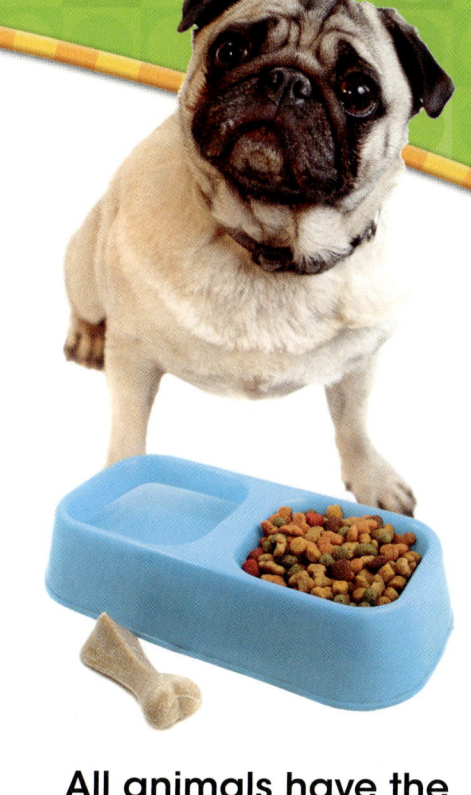

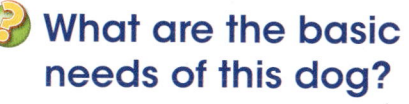

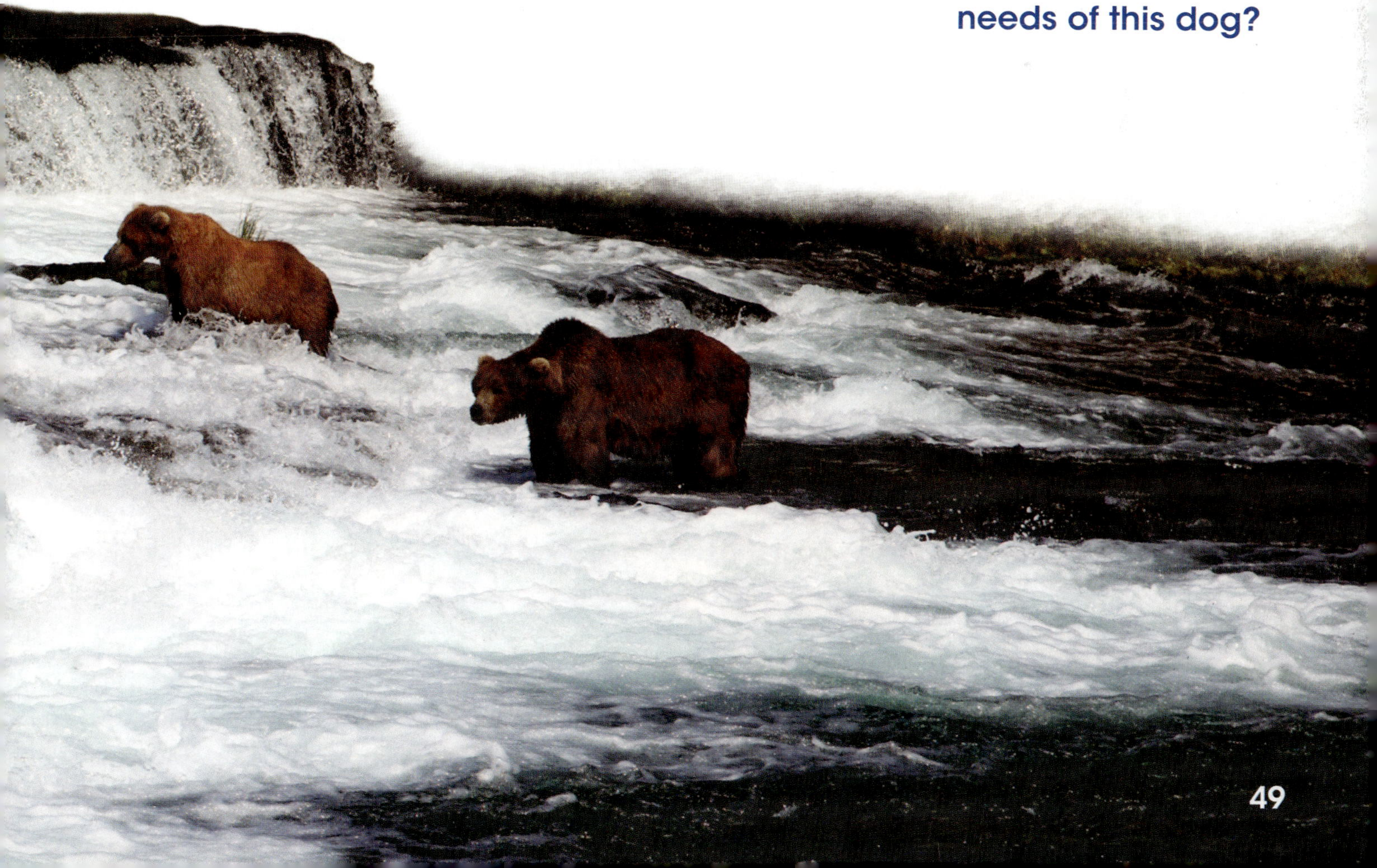

Think About It

How are the basic needs of a fish in a tank met?

How do you think fish get the oxygen they need? God designed gills for fish. **Gills** are body parts that a fish uses to take in oxygen from water.

You use lungs to breathe. Fish do not have lungs. They have gills that can take in oxygen from the water.

gills

Some animals that live in water do not have gills. Turtles, alligators, whales, and dolphins have lungs. They must swim to the surface to breathe air.

Faith Connection

When you pray, you may ask God for certain things. What are some things you ask for? Are any of them basic needs? Is prayer a basic need of spiritual life?

Explore-a-Lab

Guided Inquiry

How do different animals meet their basic needs?

Choose an animal with unusual body parts or abilities. Research and find out about how the animal you picked meets its basic needs for air, water, food, and shelter. For example, the walking catfish can still meet its needs when the pools of water it lives in dry up.

Hiding Places: Another Basic Need Explain

Think About It

Make a list of some materials a bird could use to make a nest. Explain why you picked the materials you did. Find out what your three favorite birds use to make their nests.

Many animals find or build shelters. A **shelter** is a place where an animal can go to be safe. Think about the bird nests you built. A nest helps keep eggs and young birds safe.

There are many types of shelters used by animals. Some bees build large beehives. Foxes dig holes called dens. Beavers build lodges out of sticks. Some bats find shelter in caves. Clams close their shells and dig into the sand.

Woodpeckers build shelters by carving out holes in trees.

What happens if loggers cut down all the trees in an area where these birds live?

Some animals use shelters to keep their eggs or babies safe. Sea turtles dig nests in the sand to lay eggs. But the sea turtle does not stay in the nest. Other animals use shelters to stay out of bad weather. A snake might find shelter under a rock to keep cool in a hot desert.

Math in Science

Scientists studying green sea turtles recorded the following numbers.

- Female turtles lay between 100 and 200 eggs.
- The eggs take between 45 and 75 days to hatch.
- An adult green sea turtle can weigh 80 kilograms (176 pounds)!

Write the number names for each of the numbers above.

Faith Connection

Read **Psalm 61:3**. God has promised to shelter us. He provides us with safety and security. What does God shelter us from?

Why is this sea turtle digging in the sand?

Helpful Body Parts Explain

Think About It

Giant anteaters eat insects from inside trees and in tunnels under ground. Why do you think a giant anteater has a tongue that is 58 cm (23 in.) long?

Birds can fly because they have wings. Horses can run fast because they have long, strong legs. God designed body parts that help all animals meet their needs and stay alive.

Beavers are large animals. They use their sharp front teeth to chew tree bark. They use their front paws for digging. Beaver lodges can only be reached from underwater. Beavers move quickly through the water. They use their webbed hind feet like swim fins and broad paddle-like tails to steer. Their thick fur and body fat keep them warm and dry in the coldest water.

Make a Connection Extend

Find out about animals with interesting body parts. Draw a picture of how one of the animals uses the body part to meet a basic need.

Lesson Review Assess/Reflect

Summary: What do all animals need? All animals have basic needs for oxygen, water, food, and shelter. They must meet these needs to stay alive. Animals have body parts that help them meet their basic needs.

1. **Graphic Organizer** Use *Basic Needs of Animals* as the main idea. Write details to go along with the main idea.

2. **Vocabulary** Why do fish have gills?

3. **Test Prep** Which is not a reason a bird finds or builds shelter?
    A. to lay eggs
    B. to stay safe during storms
    C. to hide from other animals
    D. to help plants survive

4. What will happen to an animal that cannot get enough food?

5. How has God provided for your needs?

Family Link Choose an animal you and your family like. Research, or find out about, the animal. Make a model of the shelter the animal uses.

Lesson 5

Vocabulary

invertebrate p. 58
vertebrate p. 58
behavior p. 60
migrate p. 60
larva p. 64
pupa p. 64

Find out what these words mean as you study this lesson.

Essential Question

How Are Animals Different? Engage

Get Ready to Learn How does this fish differ from land animals you know of? Animals move and act in many different ways. Some fly. Others crawl, run, or swim. Animals grow and change in many ways.

Try This! How does a house cat look and act? Choose an animal and act like it. See if your classmates can guess what animal you chose.

God designed the salmon with amazing abilities. Even after years in the sea, it can find its way back to the river where it was born to lay its eggs.

Record your work for this inquiry. Your teacher may also assign the related Guided Inquiry.

Animals Move
Why does the mealworm move the way it does?

SAFETY: Do not use the hand lens to concentrate heat from sunlight.

Your Group Needs
- mealworm
- hand lens
- paper

Step 1 Predict how a mealworm moves. Write your prediction.

Step 2 Place a mealworm on a clean sheet of paper. Use your hand lens to **observe** how the mealworm moves. Draw or describe what you observe.

Step 3 Compare how the mealworm moves to the way you move.

Step 4 Communicate your comparisons with a classmate.

Create Explanations
1. Why does the mealworm move the way it does?
2. Did all the mealworms move the same? Why or why not?

Kinds of Animals Explain

Think About It

Make a list of ten different kinds of animals that live in your area.

How would you describe the mammal?

God created animals on the fifth and sixth days of Creation. Animals looked like they do today. Some animals are **invertebrates**. They do not have a backbone. Other animals God created have a backbone like you do. These animals are called **vertebrates**.

	Types of Vertebrates	
Fish	• live in the water • lay eggs in the water • have gills to breathe • have scales	
Amphibians	• live in the water and on land • lay eggs in water • young live in water • adults live in water or on land • have smooth skin	
Reptiles	• live in water and on land • lay eggs on land • have lungs to breathe • have dry, scaly skin	
Birds	• live on land • lay eggs • have lungs to breathe • have feathers	
Mammals	• live in the water and on land • give birth to live young (usually) • have lungs to breathe • nurse the young • have fur	

Animals live in certain places. Polar bears live within the Arctic Circle. Other kinds of bears live in other parts of the world.

Genesis 1 is the Creation story. It tells how God created all things. First, He created heaven and Earth, and day and night. Then He created oceans and land. Next, He created plants. On the fifth day, God made birds and sea creatures. On the sixth day, God made land animals and people. Finally, on the seventh day He created the Sabbath as a memorial of His Creation.

Think About It

Make a list of ten kinds of animals that do not live in your area. Describe the types of environments they live in.

Lesson Activity

Choose an animal. Write its name on an index card. List some facts about the animal on the back of the card. Switch cards with a classmate. Now try to guess the animal by reading the facts.

List three new animal facts you learned.

Animal Behaviors Explain

You know animals differ in how they look and where they live. Animals also differ in their actions, or behaviors. A **behavior** is something an animal does or a way it acts. Singing songs is a behavior of some birds.

Most animals live in the same area their entire lives. Other animals **migrate**, or travel back and forth between two places. Many birds travel north in spring. They build nests and lay eggs. Then they migrate south in fall. The birds spend winter in warmer places where there is plenty of food. In spring, they return north.

A mallard is a duck that migrates. Many mallards breed in Canada in spring and summer and then fly south in fall. They return again the next spring.

Most owls rest and sleep during the day.

❓ Why do animals need to sleep?

Sleep is another type of behavior. There are animals that sleep during the day and are awake at night. Most owls and bats are actively hunting food at night, so they sleep during the day.

Behaviors help animals meet their basic needs. Different animals use different behaviors to find food. Lions sneak up on their food and chase after it. Some spiders spin webs and wait for their food to get trapped.

Faith Connection

God designed animals and gave them a world to meet their needs. We do not know what behaviors He gave them before sin entered the world. We do know that some animals, such as the kangaroo, nurture their young. What other examples of behaviors show God's design?

Think About It

What are some characteristics of animals that hunt at night?

Animal Life Cycles Explain

Think About It

Where are some different places animals lay their eggs?

Like plants, animals have life cycles. Not all animals have the same life cycle. All animal life cycles begin when a living thing is born or hatched. The last part of every life cycle is when a living thing dies.

Some animals hatch from eggs. Adult animals such as birds and frogs lay eggs. Some animals protect their eggs. Others lay the eggs and leave.

These Nile crocodile hatchlings live in Africa. Adult crocodiles may grow to 3.5–5 meters (11.5–16 feet) in length.

Many animals do not hatch from eggs. These animals start life inside their mother and are born. People are born in this way. Some animals have just one baby at a time. Some have many.

Some animals live for a long time. Others live for just a few days.

How Long Animals Live	
Animal	**Life Span**
human	78 years
African elephant	70 years
Canada goose	25 years
North Pacific giant octopus	4 years
monarch butterfly	2 months
honey bee	1 month
mosquito	3 weeks

How does the life span of the African elephant compare with that of people?

Life Cycle of a Butterfly Explain

A butterfly goes through big changes during its life cycle.

Think About It

How are the life cycles of a butterfly and a flowering plant the same? How are they different?

1. The *egg* is the first part of the life cycle. A female butterfly lays eggs on a plant.

2. After a few days, a caterpillar hatches from the egg. A caterpillar is called a larva (LAR•vuh). A **larva** is a young animal that does not look like the adult. Caterpillars eat leaves and grow larger.

3. A caterpillar attaches itself to a plant. It becomes a pupa (PYOO•puh). A **pupa** is the stage of an insect that is changing from a larva to an adult.

4. The change is complete! The adult butterfly has wings. It feeds on the sweet liquid that flowers make.

1 egg

2 larva

 **Math in Science**

Butterflies have symmetry. They have two equal sides. Look at the left wing of this butterfly. Now look at the right wing. The halves look very similar. Draw one half of a butterfly. Switch papers with a classmate. Draw the other half of your classmate's butterfly.

3 pupa

4 adult butterfly

The Great Butterfly Migration [Explain]

Think About It
What are some reasons why monarch butterflies migrate so far from where they hatch?

The migration of the monarch butterfly is a wonderful example of God's design in nature. Each fall, millions of these insects migrate from Canada. They nearly block out the sky. They fly to a place they have never been before in the mountains of Mexico. They even fly to the same trees their ancestors stayed in. They spend the winter hibernating.

They leave Mexico in the spring. The butterflies make it far enough to lay their eggs. Then several generations of their offspring complete the journey north.

Scientists believe that monarch butterflies use clues such as Earth's magnetic pull and the Sun to find their way.

? **What would happen to these butterflies if they stayed in the North during the winter?**

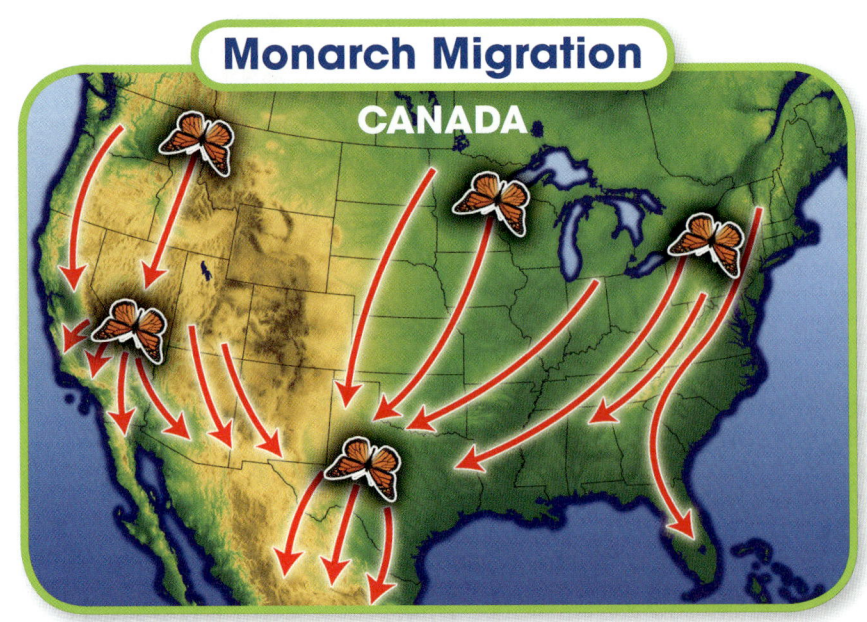
Monarch Migration

Make a Connection Extend

Choose an animal that lives in a hot, dry part of the world. Research the behaviors of the animal. How does it meet its basic needs? What behaviors help it survive? Write one or two sentences to tell what you learned.

Lesson Review Assess/Reflect

Summary: How are animals different? Animals have many differences. They have different life cycles and different behaviors that help them stay alive.

1. **Graphic Organizer** Draw and label the life cycle of a butterfly.

2. **Vocabulary** What are two reasons animals might migrate?

3. **Test Prep** Which animal lays eggs?
   A. cat   C. chicken
   B. dog   D. elephant

4. Explain why an animal might be awake at night and sleep during the day.

5. When were animals created?

 **Family Link** Choose a bird you and your family like. Research the life cycle of the bird you picked. Make a mobile showing the life cycle.

67

People in Science

Extend

Get to Know
Luther Burbank

Luther Burbank was born in Lancaster, Massachusetts. He studied the science of growing fruits, vegetables, and flowers. This science is called horticulture.

Mr. Burbank hoped he could use plants to increase the world's food supply. He experimented with plants at his home in Santa Rosa, California.

He introduced over 800 kinds of plants, including more than 200 types of vegetables, fruits, nuts, and grains. The Shasta daisy, the fire poppy, the freestone peach, and the Burbank potato are just a few examples.

Fun Fact
People in California celebrate Luther Burbank's birthday on Arbor Day. People plant trees in his memory.

Concept Check

1. How do you think the science of horticulture helped Luther Burbank reach his goal?
2. How did Luther Burbank improve people's lives?

Careers in Science
Extend

Botanist

Botany is the study of plants. Botanists study how plants grow. They study how plants affect people. They find new ways to use plants in medicine. Botanists learn new ways to use plants to make things. They also study which plants make good food.

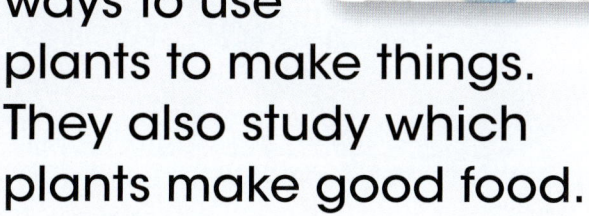

Botanists use scientific tools and methods to study plants. Some botanists do research. Others work in national parks, in rain forests, and on farms.

Botanical Illustrator

A botanical illustrator draws flowers and trees. The drawings show many details. They show how plants look in real life. Some drawings show how plants grow. Others show what the inside of a plant looks like.

Concept Check
1. How do botanists help people?
2. Why does a botanical illustrator need to study botany?

69

Chapter 2

Plants and Animals Live Together

Lesson 1
Where Do Plants and
Animals Live? 72

Lesson 2
What Are Food Chains and
Food Webs? 82

Lesson 3
How Do People Affect the
Environment? 90

Scripture Spotlight

Evidence of God's activity is everywhere! He created plants and animals that live in many different places.

You will read the following passages in this chapter.

Isaiah 11:6–9 (p. 75)   Psalm 104:10–35 (p. 86)

The Big Idea

Plants and animals affect one another and are affected by changes in the places they live. God cares for the living things He created, and we should do the same.

🔎 **How is removing litter helpful to living things?**

Lesson 1

Vocabulary

habitat   p. 74
desert   p. 76
grassland   p. 78
forest   p. 79
wetland   p. 80

Find out what these words mean as you study this lesson.

Essential Question

Where Do Plants and Animals Live?

Engage

Get Ready to Learn What do animals use for grocery stores? Where do they get their food? Our world is home to many plants and animals. They live in places where they can find the things they need to live. The otter is a good swimmer. It lives near water, where it gets most of its food.

Try This! How does an animal's home help meet its needs? Make a diorama showing a wild animal's home. It must show all the things the animal needs to live.

Structured Inquiry
Discover

Record your work for this inquiry. Your teacher may also assign the related Guided Inquiry.

Animal Homes
How many animals and plants live here?

SAFETY: Do not handle any animals you see.

Your Group Needs
- a plot of land
- measuring tape
- string
- magnifying lens

Step 1 Measure a piece of land that is one meter square. Mark it with the string.

Step 2 Observe what is living there. Use the magnifying lens to see details.

Step 3 Draw what you see. Label the plants and animals. Tell what they are doing.

Step 4 Compare what you discovered with what the other groups found.

Create Explanations

1. How many animals and plants live here?

2. Suppose you observed land in a different place. Do you think you would find the same plants and animals? Explain.

Many Places to Live Explain

Think About It

Can one environment have more than one habitat?

Many places are similar to one another. But no two places are exactly the same. Some places are hot. Others are very cold. A place may get a lot of rain, or it may be very dry. There may be tall trees, short grasses, or bare rock and sand. God created plants and animals that live in each of these places.

A pond has many places for plants and animals to live. Each living thing uses a different part of the pond. A **habitat** is the place where a plant or an animal finds the things it needs to live.

A pond has many habitats. Ducks float on top of the pond. Reeds grow on the pond's edges. Frogs rest on water lilies, and turtles spend much of their time on the bottom of the pond. What other animals might live in and around this woodland pond?

Plants and animals have lived together since God created the world. All the living things in a place need each other. For example, all the things in a pond are connected. If one part changes, it affects the other parts.

Scripture Spotlight

Read **Isaiah 11:6–9**. How does the verse describe animals? How are animals different today?

Explore-a-Lab

Guided Inquiry

What happens if houseplants get too much light?

Some houseplants grow well in shade. What happens if you put them under direct light? Compare how shade plants grow in direct light and in the shade.

◀ Some plants and animals live in the deep water of the pond. Other plants and animals live near the pond's edges.

75

Different Spaces (Explain)

Some plants and animals live on land. Others live in or near water. Each place where a plant or an animal lives is different. Some places have many living things. Other places have just a few.

A **desert** is a very dry place. Plants and animals that live there have special designs. They must live with a lot of Sun and very little water. Many deserts are hot, but some are cold.

Think About It

What kind of weather would you expect to find in a cold desert?

Many plants have ways to store water for a long time. Desert animals are able to live in the heat. They may dig into the ground to get out of the Sun. They move around at night when it is cooler. They often get water from the food they eat.

A cactus has a thick stem that stores water.

? How do desert animals benefit from the ability of desert plants to store water?

desert

The kangaroo rat gets the water it needs from the seeds it eats.

A **grassland** is a natural area that is filled with grasses. Grasslands do not get much rain, but they are not as dry as deserts. Fires often burn the grasses when they are dry. The soil is deep and full of nutrients.

Many animals live in grasslands. Bison, grasshoppers, rabbits, and sparrows eat grasses and seeds. Foxes eat other animals.

Grasslands are home to bison.

❓ Why do you think many grasslands are used to raise cows or grow crops?

grassland

forest

Bears use many parts of a forest.

A **forest** is a place with many tall trees. Forests get enough rain to support many animals. It rains almost every day in the rain forests of Africa and South America.

Forests have many different habitats for plants and animals. Birds and squirrels live in the trees. Deer and skunks live on the forest floor.

Wet Places Explain

Faith Connection

It is important to care for the living things God created.

Most of Earth is covered with oceans. Oceans are deep and filled with saltwater. There are many living things in oceans. Dolphins, squid, and fish swim in the water. Clams and corals live on the ocean floor.

Some parts of the land are covered with shallow water. A **wetland** is an area of land that is usually wet. Swamps, marshes, and bogs are wetlands.

Think About It

Why is it important to care for all wetland animals, even insects?

People have drained many wetland areas. This has harmed plants and animals that need wetlands in order to survive. Ducks, frogs, and beavers need wetlands. So do herons, other birds, alligators, and many insects.

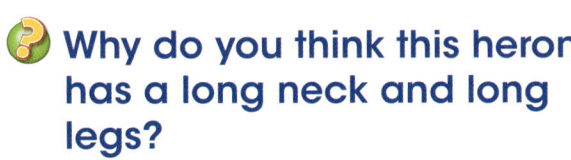

wetland

Why do you think this heron has a long neck and long legs?

Make a Connection Extend

Learn about the official animal of your state, province, or country. Where does it live? Write a description of its habitat.

Lesson Review Assess/Reflect

Summary: Where do plants and animals live? Plants and animals live in many places. Deserts, grasslands, forests, oceans, and wetlands have many habitats. A habitat is a home for a plant or an animal.

1. **Graphic Organizer** Make a diagram. Compare and contrast a forest and a desert.

2. **Vocabulary** Describe a bear's habitat.

3. **Test Prep** Which of these places gets the least amount of rain?
   - A. desert
   - B. forest
   - C. wetland
   - D. grassland

4. How are oceans and wetlands different?

5. God created many places for plants and animals to live. Why is it important to care for Earth?

Family Link Search for animal habitats in and around your home. List what you found, and compare your list with the group.

Lesson 2

Vocabulary
food chain p. 86
food web p. 88

Find out what these words mean as you study this lesson.

Essential Question

What Are Food Chains and Food Webs?

Engage

Get Ready to Learn What are your favorite things to eat? Our bodies get energy from the food we eat. We need energy to play, grow, and live. But where do we get food? We may go to the store to get food. Where does the food come from that we buy at the store?

Try This! What food have you seen an animal eat? Draw a picture of what you saw. What else does the animal eat? Share your picture with the class.

Structured Inquiry Discover

Record your work for this inquiry. Your teacher may also assign the related Guided Inquiry.

Links in a Chain
Where do living things get food?

Your Group Needs
- set of index cards from your teacher
- yarn

Step 1 Discuss with your group how the living thing on each card gets food.

Step 2 **Order** the cards. Start with the thing that makes its own food. The next card should eat what is on the first card. Continue until you use all the cards.

Step 3 Use yarn to tie the cards together in order. This represents a food chain.

Step 4 Show your chain to other groups. Look for things on other chains that eat things on your chain. Tie these cards together. This represents a food web.

Create Explanations

1. Where do living things get food?
2. Why must a food chain start with a plant?

Food for Life Explain

Think About It

How was the world different before Adam and Eve ate the fruit God told them not to eat?

What did you eat today? You ate food! It could have been hot or cold. It might have been spicy or sweet. We all need food. It gives us energy to play games and to learn.

In the beginning, when God created everything, He did so with a purpose. All living things were at peace. The world was a different place. When God created Adam and Eve, He provided food for them in the Garden of Eden. Animals lived in peace. Lions did not eat lambs.

Sin came into the world when Adam and Eve ate fruit that God asked them not to eat. As a result of sin, it became harder for people to get the food they needed. People had to work to get food. Animals no longer lived in peace. Lions ate lambs.

In the beginning, lions did not eat lambs. When Adam and Eve sinned, the world changed. Then lions began to eat other animals.

All living things need food. But where do they get food? Where does the energy in food come from?

Plants can use energy from sunlight to make their own food. The energy from the Sun is stored in the food they make.

Animals need to find food to live. An animal gets energy from the food it eats. It uses most of the energy to stay alive. Some of the energy is stored.

Some animals eat only plants. Some animals eat mostly other animals. Some animals eat both plants and animals.

What does this chimpanzee get when it eats a banana?

Lesson Activity

Draw or cut out pictures of living things. Sort the pictures into the following groups.

- makes its own food
- eats only plants
- eats both plants and animals
- eats only animals

Are there any animals that can be sorted into more than one group? Why?

Food Chains Explain

Scripture Spotlight

Read **Psalm 104:10–35**. What would happen if God did not provide food for animals?

Think about a forest environment. There are many plants and animals in a forest. Plants store energy in the food they make. Animals get that energy when they eat plants.

A **food chain** shows how food energy goes from one living thing to another. Food chains show the order in which animals eat plants and other animals.

There are many food chains in a forest. Look at the diagram on the bottom of the page. It shows one food chain.

A Forest Food Chain

This food chain begins with a tree. The tree makes its own food. It changes energy from the Sun into energy stored in food.

The bark beetle eats tree trunks. It gets energy by eating parts of the tree. It uses the energy to live.

A food chain has to be in the right order. A food chain always starts with a living thing that can make its own food. All plants make their own food. Some other living things can make their own food too.

The arrows in a food chain point in the direction that energy flows. Animals that eat plants get energy from the plants. So the arrows always point away from the thing being eaten.

Think About It

What is an example of a smaller animal that eats a larger animal?

 **Math in Science**

Suppose an owl eats 10 mice every day. How many mice does it eat in 7 days?

This woodpecker eats the bark beetle. It must eat many bark beetles to get enough energy.

A Cooper's hawk eats the woodpecker. Many food chains end with a large animal.

Food Webs Explain

A food chain shows one path that food energy takes. Most living things eat more than one kind of food. A bear might eat berries, fish, nuts, and leaves.

When a food chain links to other food chains, it becomes a food web. A **food web** links all of the different food sources for each member of the web.

In a food web, arrows can point to more than one animal. One plant or animal might be eaten by more than one animal.

Think About It
How is a food web different from a food chain?

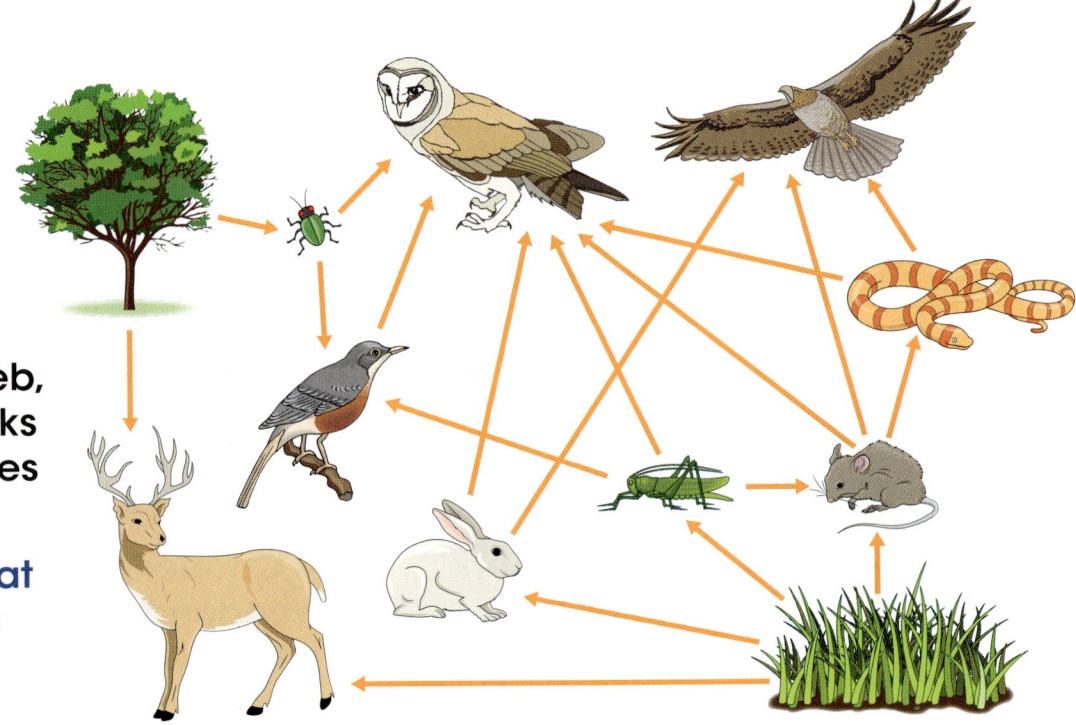

In this food web, owls and hawks eat both snakes and rabbits.

What things eat grasses in this food web?

Make a Connection Extend

Find out about plants and animals that live in a location your teacher assigns. Draw a food web for that location.

Lesson Review Assess/Reflect

Summary: What are food chains and food webs?
All living things need food to live. Plants make their own food. Animals eat plants or other animals. Food chains and food webs show how food energy flows among living things.

1. **Graphic Organizer** Make a diagram that shows a food chain.

2. **Vocabulary** Fill in the blanks in the sentence.
   One food ____ has many food ____ in it.

3. **Test Prep** Which of these should not be part of a food chain?
   A. plant   C. rock
   B. bird   D. fish

4. What would happen if all of the plants died and there were none left?

5. How do you think food chains were different in the Garden of Eden?

Family Link Help a family member draw a food chain that includes a food he or she ate today.

Lesson 3

Vocabulary
pollution p. 95
acid rain p. 96
litter p. 98
endangered p. 100

Find out what these words mean as you study this lesson.

Essential Question
How Do People Affect the Environment?
Engage

Get Ready to Learn How have people affected the habitat of the giant panda? There are not as many pandas today as there used to be. People have changed the land where they live. Now there are only a few areas where the animals can live.

Try This! How can people help wild animals that are in danger of becoming extinct? Choose an animal that is losing its habitat and needs our help. Make a poster telling what you can do.

Record your work for this inquiry. Your teacher may also assign the related Guided Inquiry.

Effects of Pollution

How will acid rain or an oil spill affect plant growth?

Your Group Needs
- three seedlings
- clean water
- "acid rain" water
- "oil spill" water
- measuring cup

Step 1 Measure the height of the seedlings. Label the three pots.
- Clean Water
- Acid Rain
- Oil Spill

Step 2 Give each plant the same amount of water. Make sure you use the type of water on the label. **Record** your observations every day for five days.

Step 3 Measure the seedlings again. **Record** any other observations.

Create Explanations

1. How will acid rain or an oil spill affect plant growth?
2. In what ways did the plant that was watered with polluted water differ from the one grown in clean water?

Changes Affect Living Things Explain

There are many resources we use from our environment. God has provided these resources. We dig and drill into the ground to get oil, gas, and coal. We use these resources to make electricity and to run our cars. We cut down trees to build our houses and to make paper. We use water to flush the toilet and to clean things.

Dams are built to stop or control water flow. A dam floods the land behind it. As a result, large areas of land that provide habitats for many plants and animals may be covered with water.

God wants us to be wise in our use of the resources He has provided. When we use resources, we change the environment. The changes can be good for some living things. It can harm others.

People may put up a dam on a river to make electricity. Water stopped by the dam can make a lake. The lake may be good for some fish or animals and not good for others. Some plants and animals may die. Others may find habitats in new areas.

Think About It

What living things are harmed when a dam is built? What living things are helped?

❓ Compare this water with the river the dam was built to control. How will this change affect the living things?

People may want to build houses where there are trees. They cut down the trees. They change the environment. The change was good for the people. They can live there. It may be bad for the plants and animals that needed the trees.

God has provided us with resources that we should be thankful for. God also wants us to take care of our home on Earth. We may damage the environment when we obtain resources. This is why we need to use resources from our environment wisely. When we cut down trees, we should plant new ones. We must not waste resources.

What are some reasons that people cut down trees?

Air and Water Pollution [Explain]

One type of change that is always bad is pollution. **Pollution** occurs when substances are added to the air, water, or ground that can harm living things.

Sometimes you can tell when there is air pollution. The air smells bad. It looks like a brown fog. Most of the time, you cannot see or smell air pollution. But your body knows. Air pollution can make it hard to breathe. It can make you cough.

Laws have been passed to help stop pollution. A factory must control the pollutants in the smoke it makes.

When acid rain falls in a forest, it runs down through the plant leaves. It enters the soil and finds its way into rivers and streams.

🌐 How do you think acid rain might harm the animals and plants in this forest?

Air pollution comes from many things. It comes from burning the gas we put in our cars. It also comes from burning coal to give us electricity. Air pollution hurts us, and it hurts the environment.

Think About It

Are there things you do that contribute to acid rain? Explain.

Some gases in air pollution can mix with water in the air. The water falls to Earth as **acid rain**. This acid rain will not burn your skin. But when it falls on the land, the acid rain pollutes the soil. It changes the soil and harms the plants. Acid rain falls into rivers and streams. It pollutes the water and can kill fish. It even damages some buildings.

An oil spill is another type of water pollution. Oil spills can happen when oil leaks from a ship, a pipeline, or an oil well into the ocean or other bodies of water, such as rivers and lakes. Chemicals in oil kill living things. Birds covered with oil cannot fly. When they try to clean their feathers, the oil gets inside them and makes them sick. They may die.

Check out your *Science Journal* for a Structured Inquiry that explores oil spill clean-up.
Discover

Oil is a kind of chemical. When some chemicals are spilled, they harm the land and water and make water unsafe to drink. Some spills can kill many living things.

Land Pollution Explain

Do you know where garbage goes when you throw it away? It goes into landfills where it is buried in the ground. Garbage builds up like a mountain.

Garbage is a type of land pollution. Litter is garbage that is thrown away outside. It is not recycled. It is not sent to a landfill. Paper in streets and bottles in parking lots are litter. Plastic bags blowing across the grass are litter too.

Chemicals can also cause land pollution. People may use too many chemicals. They put them on farm fields, lawns, and gardens. The chemicals can hurt the land and the things that live there. Chemicals can wash into streams and rivers. This affects plants and animals that live there.

Think About It

Why do people have events to clean up litter?

This picture is a good illustration of pollution we can do something about.

What kind of pollution do you see in this photograph?

Habitat Loss

You have read about many ways that people affect the environment. You also know that many plants and animals can live only in a certain habitat.

Some plants and animals lose their habitats when their environment is changed. This is called habitat loss. Some changes that cause habitat loss are caused by people. Other changes, such as forest fires, are natural.

Think About It

What kind of habitat loss is most permanent? Explain.

Math in Science

A forest is 15 square kilometers (about 6 square miles). People cut down 5 square kilometers (about 2 square miles) of the forest. How much forest habitat is left?

People dig strip mines to get resources. This changes the land. Plants and animals cannot live there anymore. U.S. mining companies are required to restore the land after mining is done.

Gone Forever Explain

Habitat loss has caused some kinds of living things to become endangered. **Endangered** describes plants or animals that may die out. There are very few of their kind left. They need to be protected or they may all die. Once they are gone, they are gone forever. That type of plant or animal will never live again.

Whooping cranes are endangered. There are very few of these birds left. Scientists help raise their young. The band on this bird's leg helps scientists tell the birds apart.

Explore-a-Lab

Guided Inquiry

How does cutting down trees affect bobcats?

Set 20 pennies on a table. Each penny stands for a square kilometer of forest land. A bobcat needs 4 square kilometers of forest to get the food it needs to survive. List reasons why people cut down trees. Take away a penny for each reason on your list. Make a bar graph. Show how the number of bobcats changes when the amount of forest land changes.

Make a Connection Extend

Think about how life would be without the resources God has provided. Research a plant or animal that is endangered. Color an outline map showing where it lives today and where it once lived. Share what you learned with your class.

Lesson Review Assess/Reflect

Summary: How do people affect the environment?
People can cause pollution. Pollution can damage habitats and cause some plants and animals to become endangered. People can restore the land, clean up pollution, and protect wildlife.

1. **Graphic Organizer** Make a cause-and-effect graphic organizer. Show what happens when people pollute the environment.

2. **Vocabulary** Which vocabulary word refers to plants or animals that are in danger of dying out?

3. **Test Prep** Which term names pollution that mixes with water in the air and falls from the sky?
   A. litter   **B.** oil spills   **C.** acid rain   **D.** endangered

4. Suggest one way you can help the environment.

5. How does God want you to treat your environment?

Family Link Ask your family to help you pick up litter around your yard or block. List the things you picked up, and compare your list with other students' lists.

People in Science

Extend

Get to Know
Dr. Nancy M. Darrall

Dr. Nancy Darrall is a botanist. She is a scientist and a Christian. Dr. Darrall's faith is part of her everyday life. She believes science and God go together.

Dr. Darrall studies the environment. She wants to know how making electricity affects life on Earth. Making electricity creates air pollution. She wants to know how air pollution harms plants and trees.

Dr. Darrall says we use our faith and information to think. Then we know God better. Dr. Darrall sees God in His Creation. Creation shows who God is. There is order and beauty in God's Creation.

Called to Serve

Dr. Darrall uses her faith to help her find better ways to take care of plants and trees.

Concept Check

1. In what ways do you see beauty in God's Creation?
2. How do God and science go together?

Careers in Science
Extend

Entomologist

An entomologist is a scientist who studies insects. Entomologists study how insects affect living things and the environment. They teach us which insects are helpful to humans. They teach us which insects harm our food crops and carry disease.

Most entomologists work in a science lab some of the time. Some entomologists work with farmers. Others work outside looking for new kinds of insects.

Herpetologist

Herpetologists are scientists who study frogs, snakes, lizards, and turtles. They study how these animals live and act. They also study their bodies.

Herpetologists can work in zoos, museums, and in wildlife habitats. They watch for changes in animals. These changes might mean the environment is changing.

Concept Check
1. Why should we learn about harmful insects?
2. How do herpetologists help take care of Earth?

Unit 1 Review — Assess/Reflect

Vocabulary

Use the words to complete the sentences.

basic needs	seedling	food chain
life cycle	pollen	shelter
germinate	resource	endangered

1. The flow of food energy from one living thing to another is shown in a(n) _____ _____.

2. All of the stages a living thing goes through is a(n) _____ _____.

3. An animal is _____ if there are very few left.

4. Bats use a cave as their _____.

5. A yellow powder made by a flower is called _____.

6. Trees are a(n) _____ that people use almost every day.

7. Water, light, nutrients, and air are a plant's _____ _____.

8. A young plant that has just started to grow is a(n) _____.

9. When seeds get water and warmth, they will _____, or start to grow.

Describe What You See

10. Look at the plant. Label its parts. Tell what each part does.

104

Use Science Practices

11. Suppose you **observe** deer, woodpeckers, and trees. What type of environment can you **infer** you are in?

Multiple Choice

12. Which of the following is not a wetland?
    - **A.** bog
    - **B.** marsh
    - **C.** forest
    - **D.** swamp
13. Which is a root that you eat?
    - **A.** carrot
    - **B.** lettuce
    - **C.** orange
    - **D.** tomato

Short Answer

14. How are a food chain and a food web different?
15. Tell how interactions between living things in the world were different before Adam and Eve sinned.
16. Draw the life cycle of a butterfly. Label the different stages.
17. Name an animal that migrates. Tell why it migrates.
18. How does God provide plants and animals with the things they need?
19. Explain how people cause air pollution.
20. Name one thing you could do today to help the environment.
21. Suppose you have a pet dog. What are its basic needs?
22. Explain how fish breathe.

Unit 2 The Human Body

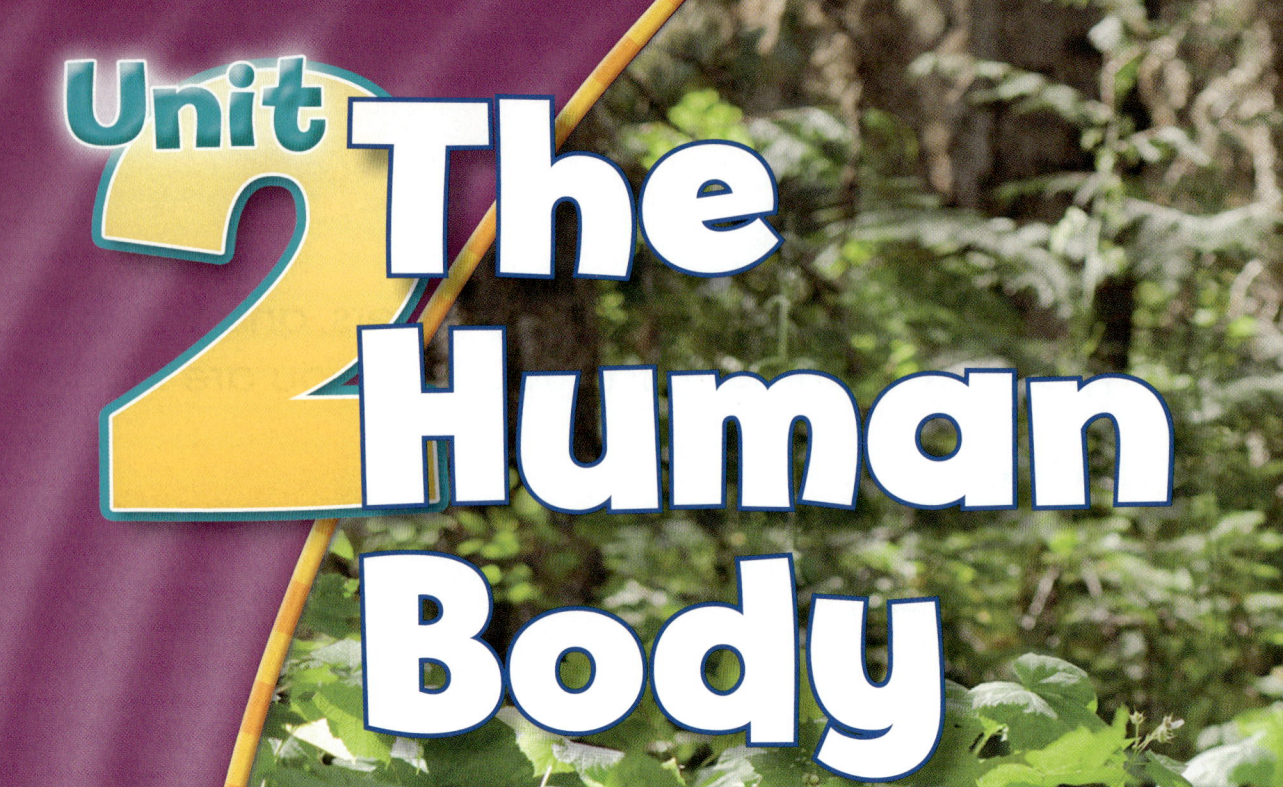

Chapter 3 108
Food and Your Body

Chapter 4 138
Body and Mind

Chapter 5 172
Keeping Your Body Safe and Healthy

Unit 2 Review ... 206

You will learn about parts of the human body. God designed the body to meet all our needs. You honor God by taking care of your body. Many questions about your body will be answered in this unit.

- How does your body use the food you eat?
- Why is it important to keep your mind healthy?
- How does following safety rules keep you and others safe?
- How does God want you to care for and use your body?

Chapter 3
Food and Your Body

Lesson 1
What Is Your Digestive System?..110

Lesson 2
What Are Some Types of Food? ..120

Lesson 3
What Is Good Nutrition?............128

Scripture Spotlight

When God created Adam and Eve, he created foods for them to eat and enjoy. In the Garden of Eden, there was plenty of healthy plant-based food. After Adam and Eve sinned, people had to dig up the soil and work harder to get their food. In this chapter you will learn about healthy foods and how your body uses food. You will read the following passages in this chapter.

Leviticus 11 (p. 112)   Genesis 1:29 (p. 122)

The Big Idea

Your body gets energy and nutrients from the foods you eat. A healthy body and mind helps you do better work for God.

❓ Have you ever eaten too much food at one time? How do you decide when you have had enough to eat?

Lesson 1

Vocabulary

nutrient p. 112
cell p. 112
digestive system p. 112
saliva p. 113
esophagus p. 116
stomach p. 116
intestine p. 116
waste p. 117

Find out what these words mean as you study this lesson.

Essential Question
What Is Your Digestive System?
Engage

Get Ready to Learn What does your favorite food taste like? Have you ever thought what it would be like if you didn't have a tongue? Some foods taste very good. But you don't eat food just because it tastes good. You eat food because you need it to survive and thrive.

Try This! What happens to food once you place it in your mouth? Discuss what happens when eating a soda cracker. Place a soda cracker on your tongue. Let it sit on your tongue for 30 seconds. What happens to the cracker?

Structured Inquiry — Discover

Record your work for this inquiry. Your teacher may also assign the related Guided Inquiry.

Your Digestive System

How does your food move from your mouth to your stomach?

Your Group Needs
- mirror
- scissors
- marble
- long balloon
- petroleum jelly

Step 1 Use a mirror to look at your mouth and throat. What do you **observe**?

Step 2 Cut the ends off the balloon. It is a **model** of the tube that carries food from your mouth to your stomach.

Step 3 The marble is like a piece of food. Insert the marble coated with petroleum jelly in one end of the balloon.

Step 4 Gently squeeze the balloon so the marble moves through it. This is what happens after you swallow.

Create Explanations

1. How does your food move from your mouth to your stomach?

2. What could happen if you swallowed a cracker that had not been completely chewed?

111

Food and Your Body

Scripture Spotlight

Read **Leviticus 11** with your teacher. Talk about why Jesus prohibited eating certain foods.

Food is important to your health. It contains nutrients. **Nutrients** are substances that you need to live and grow. Vitamins, minerals, proteins, and carbohydrates are some nutrients found in foods. You use certain nutrients to repair cells and to build new cells. **Cells** are the small parts that make up the bigger parts of your body.

Some nutrients are used by your body for energy. You use energy to ride a bike, go for a walk, and even read a book. Many things happen inside your body that need energy.

The food you eat must be changed before your body can use it. The Creator designed the digestive system to do this job for us. The **digestive system** is all the parts of your body that break down food and absorb the nutrients that come from this food.

We buy food at grocery stores, restaurants, and farmer's markets. We grow food in our gardens.

What different types of fruit do you see in this photo?

Your mouth is the first part of your digestive system. When you chew your food, your teeth crush and grind food into smaller pieces. Small pieces of food can be broken down faster than large pieces of food. Chewing also makes it easier for you to swallow the food.

Your digestive system gets ready before you even take a bite of food. When you smell food, saliva starts to form. **Saliva** is the liquid in your mouth. Chewing mixes saliva with the food to make it easier to swallow. Saliva has chemicals that start to break down the food.

Think About It

Why is it important to eat a wide variety of healthy foods?

What happens to the corn inside the girl's mouth?

113

Your Teeth Explain

Think About It

Think about the location of your incisors and molars. Why are incisors in the front of your mouth and not in the back with the molars?

Why do small babies eat soft food or food that has been ground into a paste? You use your teeth to cut, tear, and grind the food you eat. Without your teeth, many kinds of food would be hard to eat.

Not all of your teeth are alike. Just like the other parts of your digestive system, your teeth have jobs or roles.

Incisors—These teeth are flat and located in the front. They bite into food and are able to cut through the food.

Canines—The canine teeth are next to the incisors. They are sharper than the other teeth in your mouth. Canines help tear the food into smaller pieces.

Premolars—Premolars are on the other side of your canines. These teeth have a different shape from your incisors and canines. Premolars help grind the food.

Molars—Molars are wide and strong. They are located in the back of your mouth and help crush food even more before you swallow it.

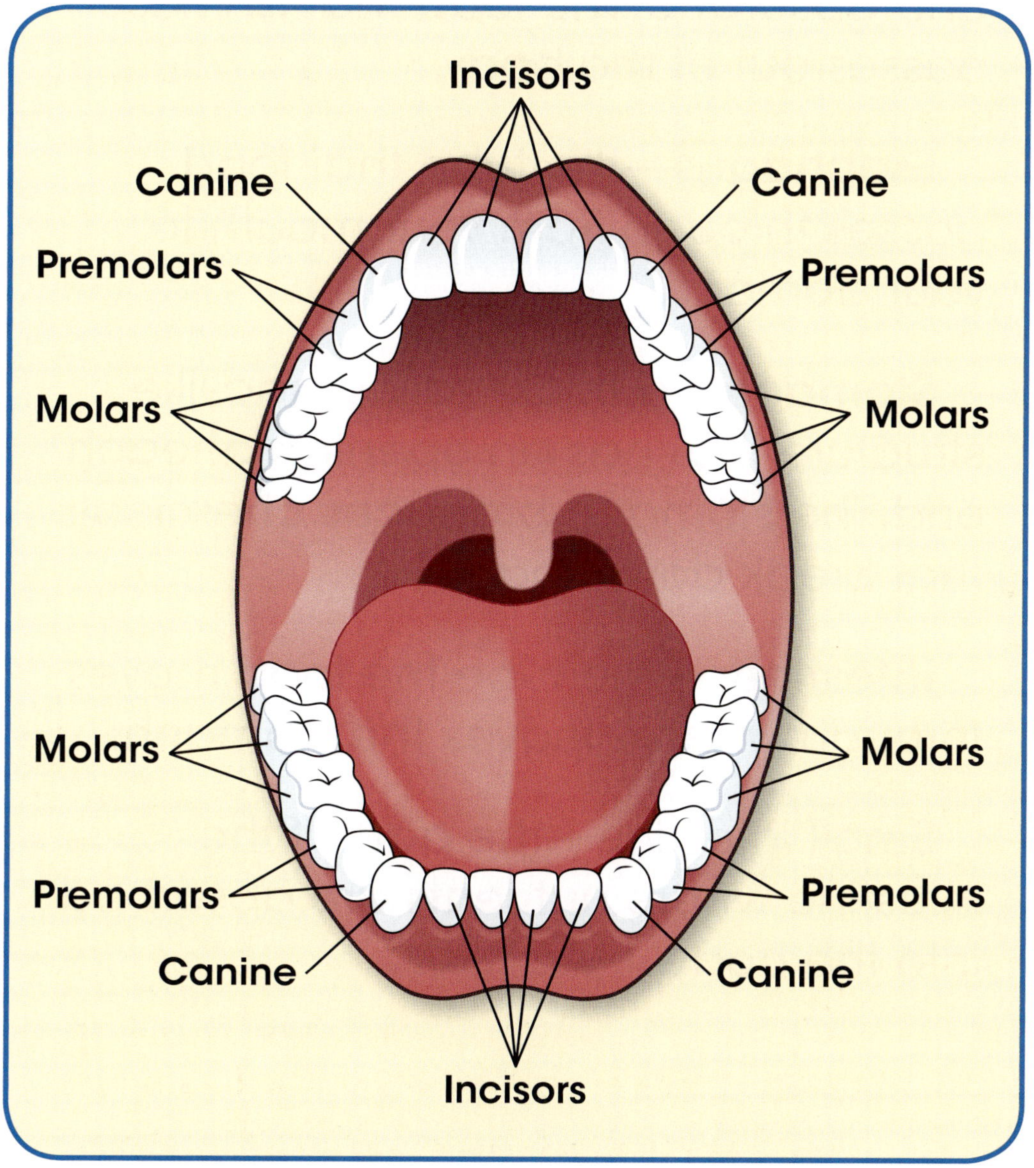

Check out your *Science Journal* for a Structured Inquiry that explores what happens in digestion.
Discover

Touch each type of tooth on the diagram.

Why do you think the molars at the top and bottom of the mouth match up when the mouth is closed?

Digesting Food Explain

When food leaves your mouth it passes through the rest of your digestive system. There it is digested and absorbed. The food that isn't used passes out of the body.

Esophagus—the tube that food passes through from your mouth to your stomach.

Stomach—a thick-walled, sac-like structure that has an opening at each end. The stomach produces chemicals that break down food.

Intestines—the tube the food moves through when it leaves the stomach.

Small intestine—the part of the intestine where nutrients are absorbed into the body.

Think About It

What might happen if the stomach's lining becomes damaged?

Large intestine—the part of the intestine where water in the food is absorbed. The food not used by the body is called <mark>waste</mark>. The waste moves to the rectum and is pushed out of the body.

Digestive System

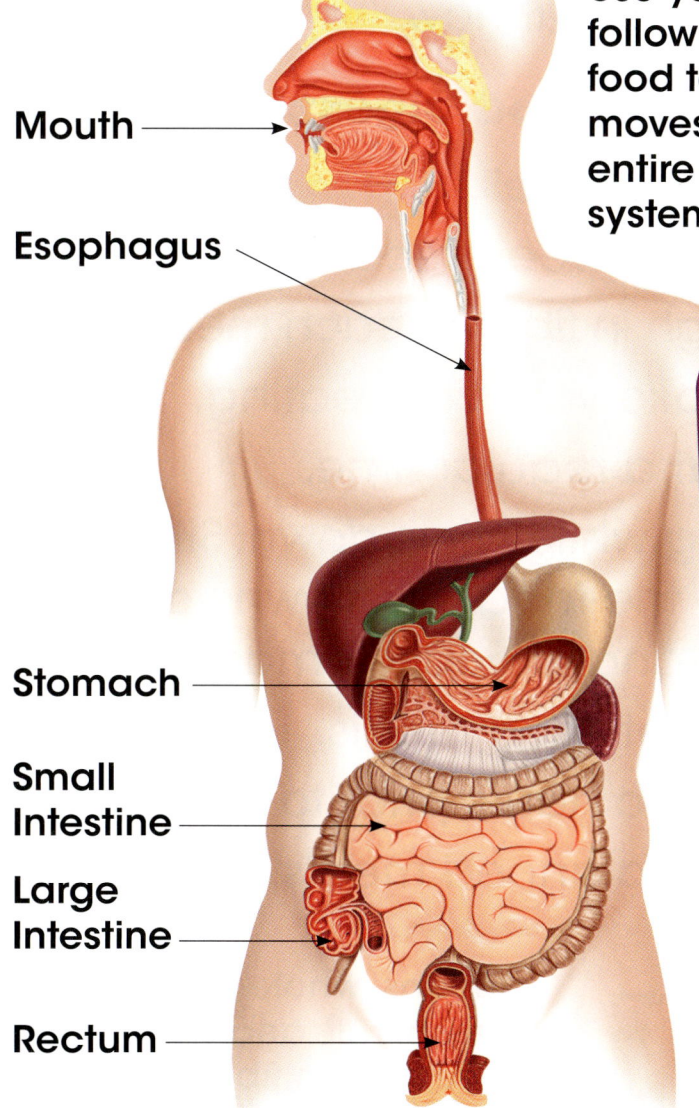

- Mouth
- Esophagus
- Stomach
- Small Intestine
- Large Intestine
- Rectum

Use your finger to follow the path that food takes. Food moves through the entire digestive system in 24–72 hours.

Faith Connection

The digestive system has many parts that must work together. It is evidence that God carefully designed our bodies.

Lesson Activity

The digestive process can begin even before you take that first bite. Picture a slice of lemon in your mind. Now think about biting the lemon.

- **How did your body respond to the thought of biting a lemon? Explain how your body began preparing for digestion without you having to take a single bite of food.**

117

Taking Care of Your Digestive System Explain

Chew your food! You might have heard someone tell you this before. Chewing makes it easier for your digestive system to digest food. There are other ways you can help your digestive system. Read the tips below to find out how.

Tips for Good Digestion

1. Chew your food well.
2. Drink water between meals.
3. Eat foods high in fiber at each meal.
4. Eat slowly. Take your time eating.
5. Eat meals at a regular time.
6. Avoid eating while lying down. Sitting up will help the food get down your esophagus and to your stomach.
7. Do not eat between meals.
8. Do not eat two hours prior to bedtime.
9. Eat healthy, balanced meals.

Think About It

Choose one of the tips. Explain why you think the tip is important.

Beans, whole grains, nuts, fresh fruit, and vegetables are high in fiber. Fiber helps food move through your digestive system.

Make a Connection Extend

Two other organs of your body work with your digestive system. They work with the small intestine to digest food. Research to find out these two organs, and write what each does.

Lesson Review Assess/Reflect

Summary: What is your digestive system? God designed the digestive system to break down food so the body can use it. Your digestive system has several organs with different jobs. All the parts work together to keep our bodies healthy.

1. **Graphic Organizer** Make a graphic organizer. Compare and contrast the small intestine and the large intestine.

2. **Vocabulary** What is the job of your digestive system?

3. **Test Prep** Which part of your digestive system makes an acid and turns food to liquid?
   - A. stomach
   - B. esophagus
   - C. large intestine
   - D. small intestine

4. Describe the path that a bite of food passes through as it moves through the digestive system.

Family Link Make a digestive system poster. Use arrows to show the path food takes. Make sure to label each body part.

Lesson 2

Vocabulary
diet   p. 122
vitamin   p. 123
mineral   p. 123
edible   p. 123
nonedible   p. 123
food guide   p. 124
food group   p. 124

Find out what these words mean as you study this lesson.

Essential Question
What Are Some Types of Food? Engage

Get Ready to Learn Why are things sorted into groups? Scientists sort plants and animals into groups based on common traits, or characteristics. Sorting helps scientists better understand how different groups work together. You can sort foods into groups in the same way. Some foods have a lot of fat. Some have a lot of protein. Others have a lot of sugar.

Try This! What food groups are good for your health? What food would you put into each group? Cut out pictures from a newspaper. Sort the foods into two groups—healthy and unhealthy. Compare your pictures with a classmate, explaining why you put them into the healthy or unhealthy group.

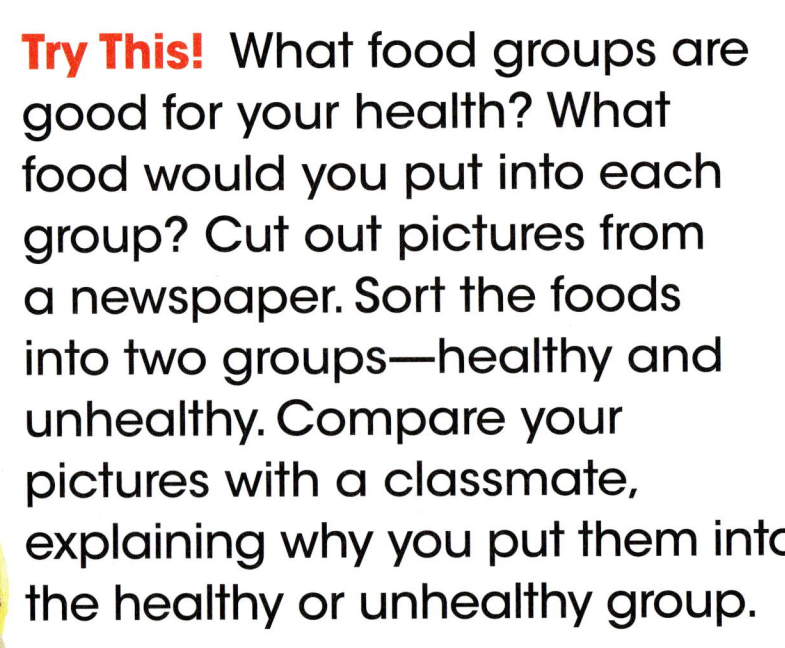

Structured Inquiry Discover

Record your work for this inquiry. Your teacher may also assign the related Guided Inquiry.

The Food Groups
What foods are in the food groups?

Your Group Needs
- pictures of food
- poster board
- scissors
- glue

Step 1 Look at the food guide on page 125. Identify the main food groups.

Step 2 Sort the pictures of food into the groups you see in the food guide. Do not include pictures that show more than one food group.

Step 3 Draw the food guide on the poster board. Label the sections. Glue each picture into the correct section.

Step 4 Glue foods that belong in more than one group on the bottom. Below each picture, list its food groups.

Create Explanations

1. What foods are in the food groups?
2. Which group from the MyPlate food guide has the foods you like best?

Food Is Important Explain

Scripture Spotlight

Read **Genesis 1:29**. What foods were part of the diet in God's original plan?

Think of some of your favorite foods. Why do you like these foods over other foods? What do you think would happen if you only ate your favorite foods? Do you think your body could work the way it should? A variety of foods is needed to keep your body healthy.

Eating food is a way to get the nutrients your body needs. There is not one food that has all the things your body needs to grow and stay healthy. Your **diet** is all the types and kinds of food you eat. A healthy diet includes many different foods. It is fun to try a variety of foods. You might even find a new favorite one.

You can get all the nutrients your body needs by eating the right kinds of food.

Vitamins and minerals are important nutrients. Your body needs vitamins and minerals in order to be healthy. You get most vitamins and minerals from the food you eat. Some people take a pill to make sure they get enough vitamins and minerals. Most people do not need to take vitamin pills if they eat a balanced healthy diet.

Think About It
What do you think would happen if you ate only candy? Why?

Vitamins are nutrients made by living things. **Minerals** are nutrients not made by living things. Plants get minerals from the soil. We get vitamins and minerals when we eat plants. Vitamins and minerals help keep our bodies well and help us grow.

The vitamins and minerals your body needs are edible. If an item is **edible**, it means it is safe to eat. If something is not fit to be eaten it is **nonedible**.

What are the names of the vitamins and minerals in strawberries?

Nutrition Facts
Serving Size: 8 medium strawberries (147g)

Amount per serving	
Calories 50	Calories from Fat 0

	% Daily Value
Total Fat 0g	1%
Saturated Fat 0g	0%
Trans Fat 0g	
Cholesterol 0g	0%
Sodium 1mg	0%
Total Carbohydrate 11g	4%
Dietary Fiber 2g	8%
Sugars 8g	
Protein 1g	

Vitamin A	0%	Vitamin C	160%
Calcium	2%	Iron	2%

A Helpful Guide Explain

God has created a wide variety of foods for us to eat. If you eat a variety of foods every day, your body gets all the nutrients it needs to stay healthy and strong. A **food guide** is an eating plan that helps people eat a balanced diet. Food guides are divided into parts with different kinds of food called **food groups**.

The food groups are shown at different sizes on the food guide. If the food group is a large size in the guide, you should eat more of that kind of food. If the food group is a small size, you should eat less of that kind of food.

Wheat and rice are part of the "grains" food group.

❓ What are some foods that are made with grain?

Lesson Activity

Write ten different foods, two from each food group, on ten pieces of paper. Place them in a bag. Pull five pieces of paper from the bag. Make a list of the foods you picked and which group each one belongs to.

❓ Would the five foods you picked make a nutritious meal? Explain.

Many food guides list a variety of food choices, but you can eat other foods from those groups also. Candy and sweets are not on this guide because they are not healthy foods. They do not supply many of the nutrients that your body needs.

Water is also a very important part of your diet. You should drink 6–8 glasses of water each day.

Think About It

How might the MyPlate diagram help you when you eat meals? Why do you think a plate and cup were used for the diagram?

Recommendations for a Healthy Plate	
Food Guide	Foods
USDA MyPlate 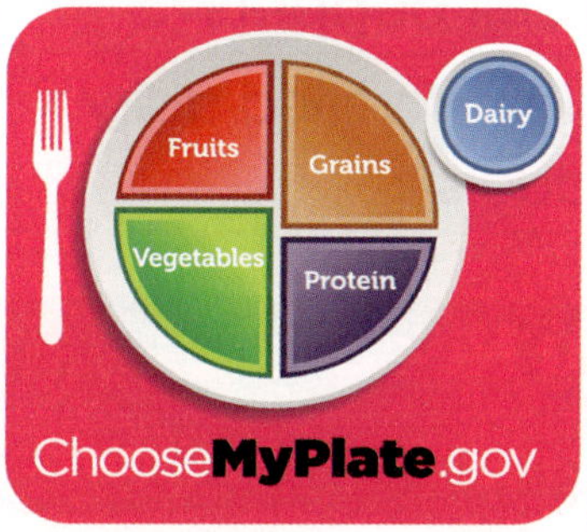	**Fruits:** berries, apples, bananas, melons **Vegetables:** greens, broccoli, tomatoes, corn **Grains:** bread, cereal, pasta, rice **Protein:** eggs, be... **Dairy:** yogurt, che...
My Vegetarian Plate 	**Fruits:** dried apric... **Vegetables:** spin... **Grains:** whole-wh... **Protein:** beans, n... **Dairy:** milk produ...
My Vegan Plate 	**Fruits:** blueberries... **Vegetables:** carr... **Grains:** whole-wheat bread, pita, pasta **Protein:** kidney beans, peanuts, black beans, tofu **Dairy:** leafy greens, calcium-fortified soy milk and juices

125

Nutrients Explain

Some foods are good sources of certain vitamins and minerals. Read the table below to see some foods that contain common vitamins and minerals.

Some Nutrients You Need		
Vitamins	**One Thing It Does**	**Some Good Sources**
Vitamin A	Promotes healthy vision	carrots, sweet potatoes, mangos
Vitamin B_{12}	Helps make red blood cells	cheese, eggs, milk, fortified cereals
Vitamin C	Promotes healthy teeth, bones, gums	broccoli, tomatoes, oranges, green and red bell peppers
Vitamin D	Helps keep bones strong	sunlight, fortified dairy products

Some Minerals You Need		
Minerals	**One Thing It Does**	**Some Good Sources**
Calcium	Promotes strong bones and teeth	broccoli, cabbage, mustard greens, nuts
Iron	Production of red blood cells	spinach, raisins, soybeans, apricots, nuts
Potassium	Promotes proper cell function	bananas, potatoes, plums, avocados
Magnesium	Promotes energy	nuts, spinach, whole grains

Vitamin D is added to milk and most soy milk. Make sure to read the labels.

Think About It

Carrots, sweet potatoes, and mangos are all good sources of vitamin A. What characteristic that you can see is common to all of these?

Called to Serve

What can you and your family do to help people in your community who don't have enough food?

Make a Connection (Extend)

Find out about some foods that are common in a different culture. List the food groups to which they belong.

Lesson Review (Assess/Reflect)

Summary: What are some types of food? A healthy diet includes a variety of foods. Vitamins and minerals help your body grow and work properly. A food guide such as MyPlate can help you make healthy food choices.

1. **Graphic Organizer** Make a graphic organizer. Show details about each of the food groups discussed in this lesson.

2. **Vocabulary** Which foods are normally part of your diet?

3. **Test Prep** Which food group does bread belong to?
    A. grains C. fruits
    B. dairy   D. vegetables

4. Why is it important to eat many different foods?

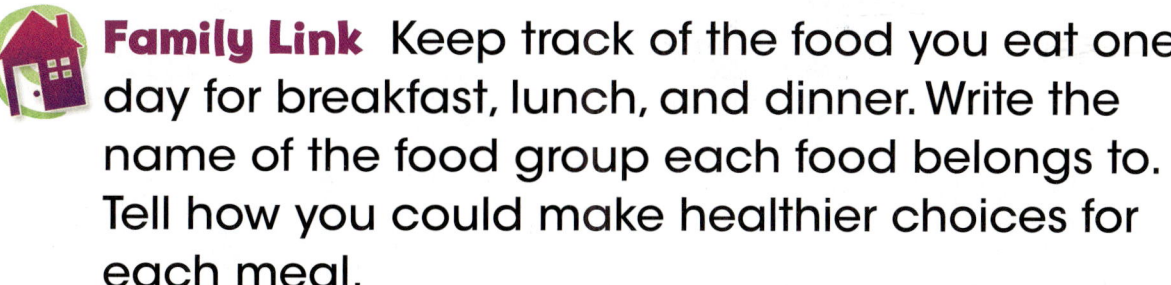 **Family Link** Keep track of the food you eat one day for breakfast, lunch, and dinner. Write the name of the food group each food belongs to. Tell how you could make healthier choices for each meal.

Lesson 3

Vocabulary

snack	p. 130
obese	p. 131
diabetes	p. 131
food ad	p. 131
food label	p. 132
serving	p. 133

Find out what these words mean as you study this lesson.

Essential Question

What Is Good Nutrition? Engage

Get Ready to Learn You hear the word *diet* used by many people. What do you think it means? In this lesson, you will learn how to make good choices about your diet. You will also find out what can happen if you don't.

Try This! How much food is enough? Fill a small bowl with the amount of a snack food you normally eat. Use a measuring cup to find out the actual amount. How does it compare with the serving size for your snack?

 **Structured Inquiry** Discover

Record your work for this inquiry. Your teacher may also assign the related Guided Inquiry.

Fatty Foods

How can you determine if a food contains fat?

Your Group Needs
- brown paper bag
- scissors
- food samples
- marker
- ruler

Step 1 Cut open the bag so it lays flat.

Step 2 Draw equal circles on the bag, one for each food sample. Label each circle. Place an equal-sized sample of each food in its circle.

Step 3 Let the foods sit for one hour. Remove the foods and let the paper dry.

Step 4 Use a ruler to measure each spot. Record the measures. **Compare** the sizes of the grease spots.

Create Explanations

1. How can you observe fat in some foods?
2. Rank the foods based on the size of the grease spot. What does the grease spot tell you about the amount of fat in the food?

Nutrition and Good Habits [Explain]

Focus on Health

A person who does not eat meat is a vegetarian. Many Seventh-day Adventists are vegetarians. Scientists think this is one of the reasons that Seventh-day Adventists live longer than other groups of people.

Your body was designed to be active and healthy. If you do not get the nutrition you need, you may feel tired, uncomfortable, or even sick.

Making good decisions about food can help you get the nutrition you need. Eat well-balanced meals at the same time each day.

People who are very active may use the nutrients from food more quickly, so they may need to eat between meals. A **snack** is a small amount of food or drink between meals. Snacks should always be small. Fruits and vegetables are good snack choices.

Make healthful food choices. Eat slowly. Stop eating when you are no longer hungry.

Eating more than your body needs will cause you to become obese. An **obese** person is over a healthy weight. Obesity can affect your health and activities. It can also cause heart disease.

Diabetes is a disease when the sugar level in the blood is too high. Some people are born with type I diabetes. Type II diabetes can develop if you eat too many foods high in sugar, are obese, or do not get regular exercise. A healthy diet and exercise may prevent diabetes.

A **food ad** is a way companies try to get people to buy their food. Be careful! Some food ads try to make unhealthy food look healthy.

Think About It

Name a good nutritional choice you have made today. Name a bad nutritional choice you have made in the last week.

Look at this food ad. Explain why you think this cereal would be a healthy or unhealthy food to eat.

131

Reading Labels Explain

You have learned that you should eat healthy foods and eat less sugar and fat. But how do you know what is in the foods you eat? You can find out by reading the food label. A **food label** lists information about the food. Some foods, such as fresh fruits and vegetables, may not come with labels. You can get information about these foods from books or on the Internet.

Math in Science

There are 2 servings in a bag of dried apples. You want to eat 1 serving. How much of the bag should you eat at one time?

Reading food labels helps you make healthy choices about your diet.

A food label tells you what nutrients are in the food. It also tells you what ingredients are added. The serving size is also listed on a food label. A **serving** is the amount of food in one portion of the food. If the serving is 24 pretzels, then all the amounts of nutrients listed on the food label are in 24 pretzels.

Think About It

Why is it important to look at the serving size?

❓ What can you learn by reading this food label?

The serving size is usually at the top.

The nutrients are usually listed in the middle.

The ingredients are usually listed at the bottom.

133

Junk Foods Explain

Think About It

Why are there a lot of food ads for junk foods?

Junk foods are not healthy compared to other foods. They do not supply many of the nutrients that your body needs. Many packaged snacks are junk food. Chips and soda are two other examples.

Junk foods taste good because they have a lot of fat, salt, or sugar. Some people learn to like junk foods and consider them treats. It is better to choose healthy foods over junk foods.

? Which of these foods are healthy food choices?

Lesson Activity

Record the number of food ads you see on TV for one day or in one magazine. Make a tally chart showing the number of junk food ads and the number of ads for healthy food you see.

? **Which kind of ad did you see most often?**

Why do you think there are more of these kinds of ads?

Make a Connection **Extend**

Choose three food labels. Look at the nutritional values for one serving of each food. Compare the following information: calories, salt (sodium), carbohydrates, and fats. Which food is the best nutritional choice? Explain why.

Lesson Review **Assess/Reflect**

Summary: What is good nutrition? Good nutrition comes from an understanding of what different foods contain. Knowing the nutritional value of foods helps you establish good food habits and avoid junk foods. Reading food labels and picking the proper serving sizes help you make good food choices to keep you healthy.

1. **Graphic Organizer** Make a cause-and-effect graphic organizer. Show the effects of an unhealthy diet.

2. **Vocabulary** Why is it important to read food labels?

3. **Test Prep** What is the amount of food in one portion of the food called?
   - **A.** a food label
   - **B.** ingredients
   - **C.** nutrients
   - **D.** a serving

4. Why is eating junk food a poor food choice?

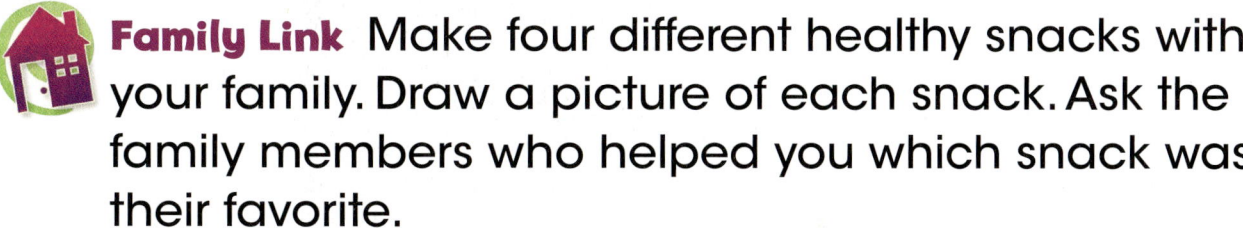 **Family Link** Make four different healthy snacks with your family. Draw a picture of each snack. Ask the family members who helped you which snack was their favorite.

People in Science

Extend

Get to Know
Will Keith Kellogg

Will Keith Kellogg believed God wants people to take good care of their bodies. Mr. Kellogg wanted to help sick people get healthier by feeding them better food. So, he made a healthy cereal that people liked.

Will Kellogg started selling his popular cereal. He made the cereal flakes out of corn. Later, his company began making many other breakfast foods.

Mr. Kellogg wanted to use the money he earned to help others. He started the W.K. Kellogg Foundation. He helped children stay healthy. He also helped build schools. Mr. Kellogg's foundation still helps children today.

 **Called to Serve**
Will Kellogg believed in teaching young people how to help themselves.

 Concept Check

1. Why did Will Kellogg invent cereal flakes?
2. How did Will Kellogg show his love for God?

Careers in Science

Extend

Nutritionist

Nutritionists help people make good food choices. They know what good foods children should eat to be healthy. They also know what good foods adults should eat. Good nutrition helps keep people from getting sick.

Nutritionists help other people plan healthy diets. This helps those people reach their fitness goals. They also work in hospitals. Nutritionists make sure patients get the best food to help them get better.

Food Scientist

Food scientists study the nutrition in foods. They find out how much sugar is in different foods. They also study the amount of vitamins and fat a food has. A food scientist finds the information that is put on food labels.

Some food scientists work on better ways to keep food fresh. They find ways to package food to keep it nutritious.

 Concept Check

1. How does a nutritionist help children?
2. Why is a food scientist's job important?

Chapter 4
Body and Mind

Lesson 1
How Does Your Nervous System Work? 140

Lesson 2
How Do You Communicate? 150

Lesson 3
What Is Mental Health? 160

Scripture Spotlight

God carefully designed the body and mind to work together. You use them to sense and understand the world around you. They allow you to worship God and communicate with other people. As we see how complex our bodies are, our faith in the wisdom of our God our Creator can grow. You will read the following passages in this chapter.

Proverbs 15:1 (p. 155)   Genesis 27 (p. 158)
Matthew 7:20–21 (p. 156)   Romans 12:2 (p. 168)

The Big Idea

Your body and your mind are affected by your thoughts, beliefs, emotions, diet, and exercise.

Your mental health affects how you view the world and care for the things God has created.

❓ What can you do to help keep your body and mind healthy?

Lesson 1

Vocabulary

nervous system p. 142
brain p. 142
nerve p. 145
spinal cord p. 146
reflex p. 146

Find out what these words mean as you study this lesson.

? Essential Question

How Does Your Nervous System Work? *Engage*

Get Ready to Learn Close your eyes. Can you still tell what is happening around you when you close your eyes? Some parts of your body sense what is around you. Other parts send messages and tell your body what to do. You will learn about these body parts in this lesson.

Try This! How are your sense of taste and your sense of smell connected? Put on a blindfold. Smell two pieces of food that your teacher gives you. Can you tell what they are? Then try tasting the food. Did you change your mind? Discuss which body parts you used.

Structured Inquiry

Discover

Record your work for this inquiry. Your teacher may also assign the related Guided Inquiry.

Get the Message

How do messages travel between your eyes and your muscles?

Your Group Needs

- messages from your teacher

Step 1 **Model** how your nervous system passes messages. Get into two teams of four. With your partners, form a line starting with your teacher (the brain).

Step 2 Student 1 **models** an "eye" at the end of one line. Students 2, 3, and 4 next in line after the "eye" **model** "nerves."

Step 3 The "eye" passes a message to the "nerves" until it reaches the "brain."

Step 4 The "brain" decides what to do and passes a message down the second chain of 3 students (nerves) to the 4th student who models the "leg muscle" at the end. The "leg muscle" reacts.

Step 5 Draw pictures to **communicate** how the "leg muscle" reacts.

Create Explanations

1. How do messages travel between your eyes and your muscles?
2. Why is the brain important?

The Nervous System (Explain)

Focus on Health

Eat the right foods to keep your nervous system healthy. Fruits and vegetables and healthy fats like those found in nuts support normal brain growth. Drink plenty of water to increase alertness.

Your body has many different systems. A system is a group of parts that are connected and work together. Each system has a job to do. The **nervous system** is the system that controls the body. It senses what is happening inside and outside the body.

The **brain** is the control center of the nervous system. It tells other body parts what to do. It directs your muscles to move. Your brain uses information it gets from other parts of the body.

 **Math in Science**

You use your brain to answer math questions. It helps you decide if something makes sense. Which estimate of the length of a kitten makes sense?

15 centimeters (6 inches) long,
150 centimeters (5 feet) long,
15 meters (49 feet) long

142

The brain helps you learn and remember things. It also helps you know right from wrong. Notice the different areas of the brain. Each area has a different job. But all the areas must communicate and work together.

The brain is surrounded by bones called the skull.

❓ **What might happen to your brain if your skull was damaged?**

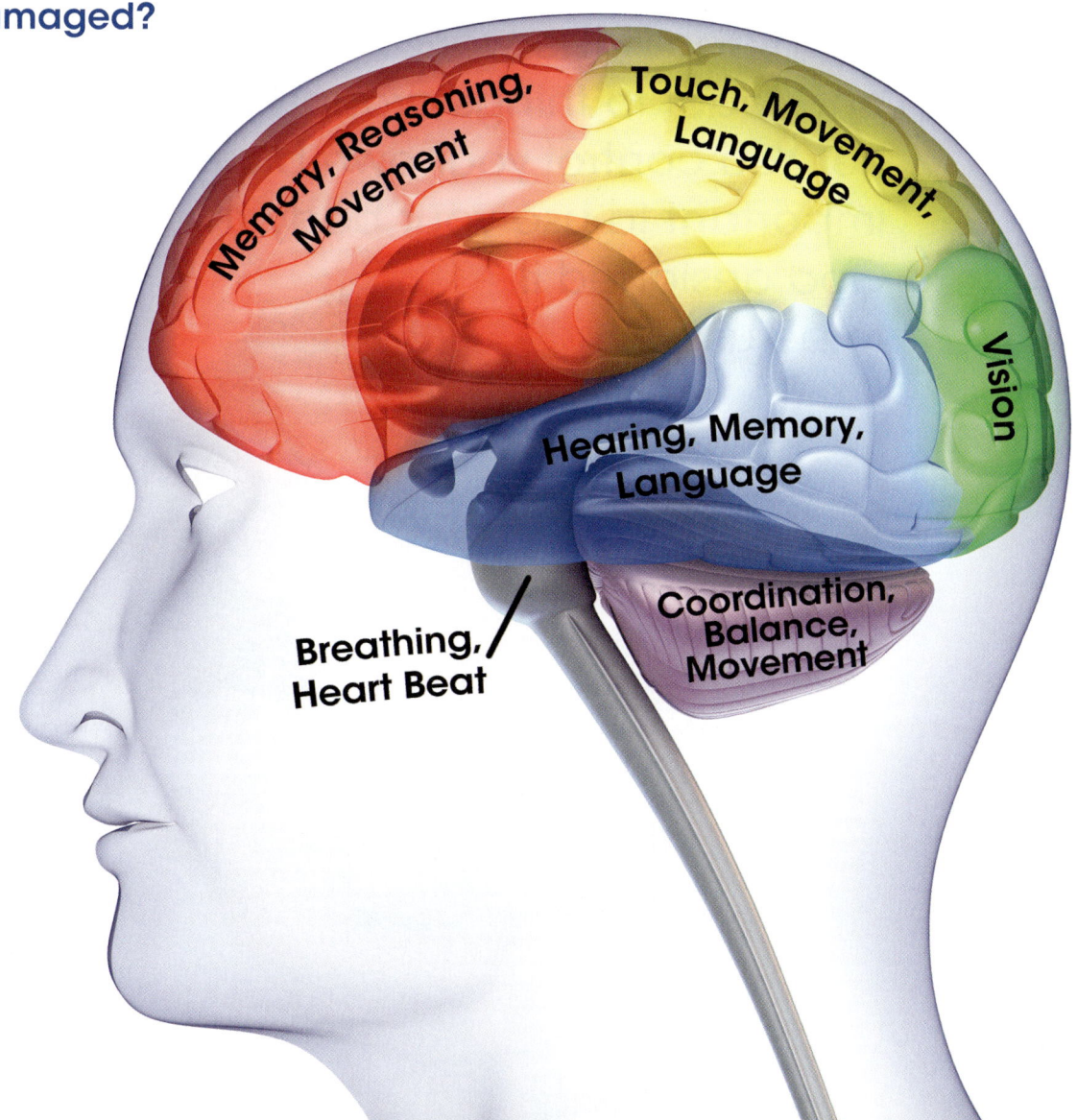

Think About It

Why must you wear goggles during some science labs?

Different sense organs allow you to notice things going on around you. Eyes let you *see* the beautiful world God created. Ears let you *hear* a song. With your tongue, you can *taste* fresh bread. With your nose you can *smell* flowers. You know something is smooth or rough when you *touch* it with your skin.

The nervous system is very complex. God designed it so each person can learn about the world, make decisions, and react to things around him or her. You control your own body. It is important to use your body the way God designed it to be used.

❓ **What senses are used in examining this flower?**

A Network of Nerves  Explain

Sense organs, such as your eyes and ears, gather data from all around you. Your brain figures out what the information means. Then your brain tells other body parts how to react.

Your brain is connected to every part of your body by fibers called nerves. **Nerves** carry messages between sense organs, other body parts, and the brain.

Nerves are long and have thin fingerlike tips called *nerve endings* that reach into different parts of the body. Nerve endings in the skin react to touch, and feel heat, cold, pain, and pressure. The nerves in your eyes are designed to receive information for sight. Nerve endings in the ears send signals about hearing and balance. Nerves in the nose react to smells. Taste buds on the tongue contain nerve endings that respond to four different tastes: sour, sweet, bitter, and salty.

Faith Connection

How do you use your sense organs to learn about God?

Check out your *Science Journal* for a Guided Inquiry that explores reflexes.

Discover

The **spinal cord** is a bundle of nerves. It runs from your brain down your spine in your back. It is protected by the bones in your back that make up your spine.

The spinal cord has an important job. Messages between your brain and most of your body travel through the spinal cord. It controls reflexes. A **reflex** is your body's response to something without you even thinking about it. When you touch something hot, you pull your hand away quickly. This is a reflex.

Explore-a-Lab
Guided Inquiry

 How do your reflexes help protect you?

Work with a partner. One person holds up a plastic sheet about 5 cm (2 in.) from the end of his or her nose. The partner tosses a cotton ball toward the other person's face. Watch carefully. Does your partner blink? Change roles and repeat the activity. How does this blinking reflex protect you?

Look at the diagram of the nervous system. See how complex it is. Even the most powerful computer cannot duplicate what a brain can do. God designed it so that you can play, learn, love, and live. God's design is so complex that scientists still do not understand everything about the brain!

Think About It

Why is it important that the spinal cord be protected?

The Nervous System

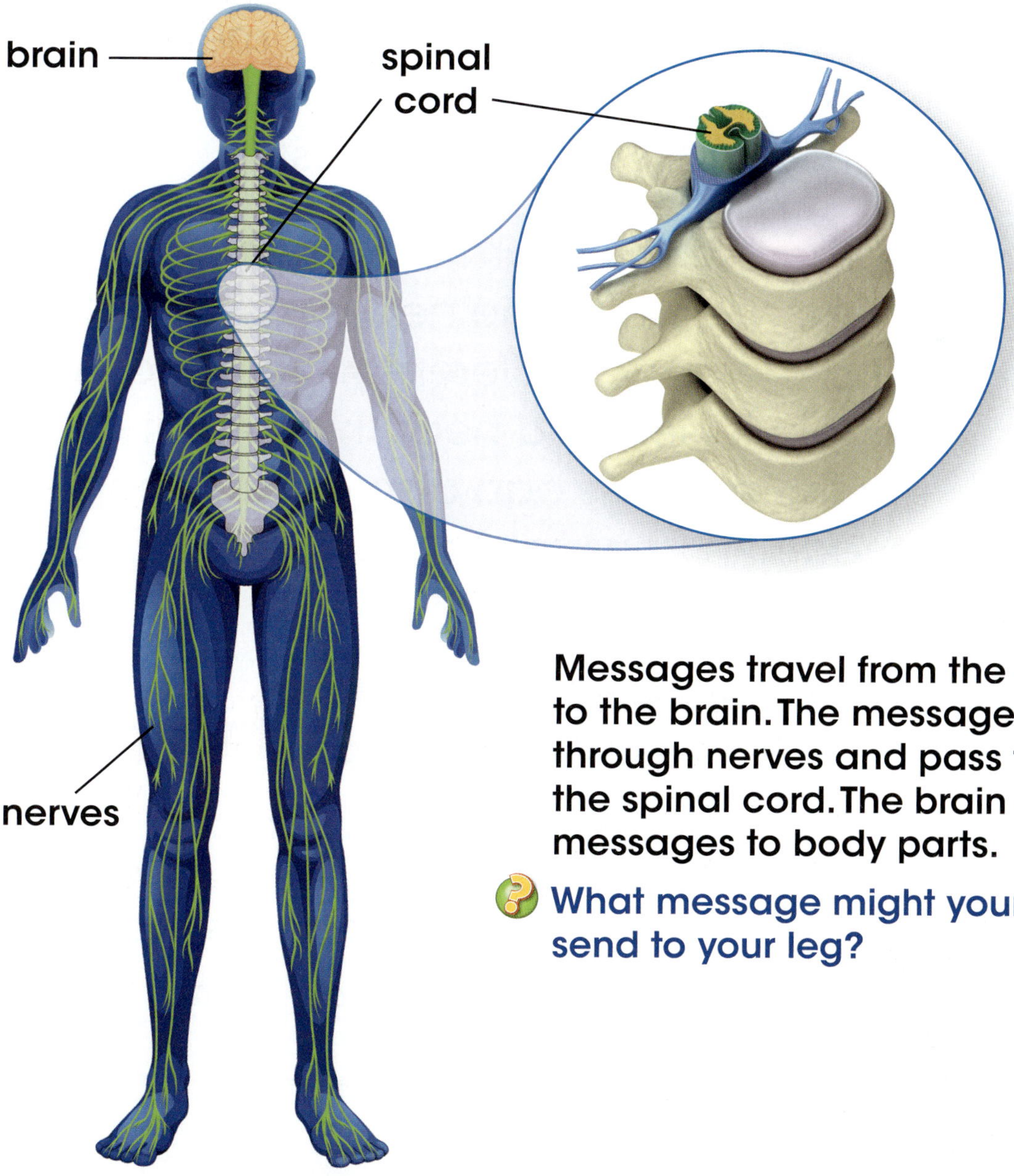

- brain
- spinal cord
- nerves

Messages travel from the body to the brain. The messages travel through nerves and pass through the spinal cord. The brain sends messages to body parts.

❓ What message might your brain send to your leg?

Injuries to Nerves _{Explain}

Think About It

Why is it important to wear a helmet on a bike and a seat belt in a car?

Some people have nervous system disorders. Some disorders make it hard for people to remember things or make people lose control of their bodies.

Injuries to the head or spine can cause damage to the nervous system. Severe injuries may not heal. If you hit your head, it may affect your memory, reflexes, speech, or balance. But this injury usually heals if you rest.

Drug use also harms the nervous system. It causes the nervous system to send messages differently. It can cause people to see and hear things that are not there. Drugs can also cause people to react in unusual ways.

Lesson Activity

Make a poster with the title "Don't Use Drugs." List the ways drugs harm the nervous system.

What can drugs do to the nervous system?

Make a Connection Extend

Almost all animals have a nervous system. Pick an animal such as a fish or a worm. Use books or the Internet to find out about its nervous system. Share what you learn with your classmates.

Lesson Review Assess/Reflect

Summary: How does your nervous system work? The nervous system is the body's control center. It is made up of the brain, nerves, and spinal cord. Nerves carry messages between the brain and the body.

1. **Graphic Organizer** Make a main idea and details chart about the nervous system.

2. **Vocabulary** What is a reflex action? Give an example.

3. **Test Prep** What part of the nervous system controls every part of the body?
   A. nerve   B. brain   C. eye   D. spinal cord

4. Why is the spinal cord's job important to the nervous system?

5. How do your sense organs and nervous system work together to control reactions to outside events?

Family Link With your family, list ways you use your nervous system every day. Discuss how this helps you know God and how He designed you.

Lesson 2

Vocabulary

communication
　　　p. 152

verbal
　communication
　　　p. 155

nonverbal
　communication
　　　p. 156

Find out what these words mean as you study this lesson.

Essential Question

How Do You Communicate?

Engage

Get Ready to Learn Is there a way to communicate without using your voice? People who use sign language use hand movements to talk with other people.

Try This! How can pictures communicate a message? Make a list of words or phrases. Draw pictures to communicate the message to your teammates. Take turns.

Record your work for this inquiry. Your teacher may also assign the related Guided Inquiry.

No Talking!
How can you communicate a health message without using words?

Your Group Needs
- health messages
- paper bag or other container

Step 1 Choose a slip of paper and read the message to yourself.

Step 2 Communicate the message to your team without using words. Stop when someone guesses your message.

Step 3 Switch roles. **Observe** the presenter's face and actions. Make guesses.

Step 4 Continue until everyone has a turn.

Create Explanations

1. How can you communicate a health message without using words?

2. How can you communicate with a person who speaks a different language? How about with someone who cannot speak at all?

151

Communication Explain

Communication is the sharing of ideas, thoughts, feelings, and information. Good communication also includes listening carefully to others. You may draw, write, talk, or use sign language to communicate. How do you communicate after a science activity? You may draw a picture about your observations. This helps others use what you learned.

Communication involves three parts:

1. A *sender* is the person who is sending a message.

2. A *receiver* is the person who gets the message.

3. The *response* is how the receiver reacts to the message.

🌀 **How do people use computers to communicate?**

Suppose someone is doing something that hurts you or someone else. That person may be a bully. You might find it hard to communicate about it to an adult. But if you do not speak up the hurtful activity might not stop.

Some adults do things that harm children. An adult may get mad and hit a child, or touch the child in a way that feels uncomfortable. Or the adult may ask a child to do something that is not safe or legal. This is called child abuse. Child abuse is never the child's fault. Tell an adult you trust if you or your friends think you are being or have been abused.

❓ **What are some ways to deal with a bully?**

Think About It

Why should you only call 9-1-1 if it is an emergency?

Do you know what an emergency is? It is any time a person's safety or property is in immediate danger. Emergencies include fires, crimes, or if someone is hurt badly. If there is an emergency, look for an adult for help. If you cannot find one, call 9-1-1. It is the number used *only* for emergencies.

Lesson Activity

Work in groups of 3-4 students. Discuss what you should do in an emergency such as an injury, a crime, or a fire. Select one of these emergencies and plan a skit in which one member of the group must call and talk with the 9-1-1 operator. Decide what information the operator will need to help handle the emergency. Include good communication skills in your presentation. Perform your skit for the class.

What information does the 9-1-1 operator need to know in order to help you?

A 9-1-1 operator sends police, firefighters, or medics to an emergency.

Forms of Communication [Explain]

When you use words, you are using **verbal communication**. The words can be spoken or written. You use verbal communication at home and at school. It is done on television, paper, and radio. It can be live or recorded. It is done through phones and computers. Verbal communication gives information and often provides entertainment.

Scripture Spotlight
Read **Proverbs 15:1**. What does the passage say about verbal communication?

❓ What message might this person be communicating?

Scripture Spotlight

Read **Matthew 7:20–21**. Why is it important to do what we say we are going to do?

When you give information without using words, you are using <mark>nonverbal communication</mark>. It includes the way you sit, move your hands and body, and how your face looks (happy or sad). People know you care if you smile and wave. If you frown, slouch, and look down, people might think you are not interested. Both verbal and nonverbal forms of communication may lead you to do or buy something, or think in a certain way.

A drawing can be a form of nonverbal communication when it expresses a message without using words. You might make a drawing to communicate what happened during a science project. Artists may use pictures to communicate feelings.

This street sign does not need words to communicate its message. Sometimes words are added to the pictures to tell a more complete story.

❓ Is this street sign a form of verbal or nonverbal communication?

Some nonverbal communication uses sound to send messages. A siren communicates that police, fire, or other emergency vehicles are coming. Whistles and horns may be warning signals, too.

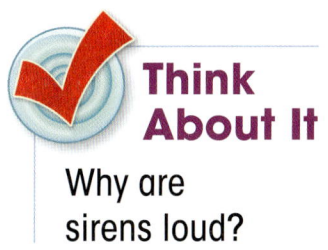

Think About It

Why are sirens loud?

❓ **What kinds of nonverbal communication do you see in this picture?**

Communicating about Health [Explain]

Many people study medicine. They help you stay healthy or get better when you are sick. Doctors, dentists, nurses, and parents care about your physical health. Do not be shy. They need to know what you are feeling. Be clear. Then they will know how to best help you get better.

Think About It

What could happen if you do not tell your doctor everything that you are feeling when you are sick or injured?

Scripture Spotlight

Read **Genesis 27**. Jacob lies to Isaac. Why does the Bible tell us not to lie?

Lesson Activity

Form a line. The first person whispers a message to the second person. Continue to the last person. That person repeats the message aloud. How did the message change?

 Why should an ill person speak directly with a health-care professional?

Communication with health-care professionals is important.

Make a Connection Extend

Use the Internet to search for paintings of people. Look at the faces and hands of each person in the painting. What forms of nonverbal communication are shown in the painting? Why do you think the people were shown in these ways?

Lesson Review Assess/Reflect

Summary: How do you communicate? Communication involves a sender, a receiver, and a response. Verbal communication uses words. Nonverbal communication uses pictures, sounds, or body motions.

1. **Graphic Organizer** Make a main idea and details chart about communication.

2. **Vocabulary** Why is a siren an example of nonverbal communication?

3. **Test Prep** Which is an example of verbal communication?
   A. a smile   B. a whistle   C. a symbol   D. a speech

4. You tell a doctor that you hurt all over. But only your throat hurts. What might happen?

5. How would you use verbal and nonverbal communication to help a friend who is being bullied?

Family Link Talk with your family about what to do in an emergency. Make a list of emergency phone numbers. Write down your family's emergency plan. Then practice a fire drill with your family.

Lesson 3

Vocabulary
personality p. 162
relationship p. 162
emotion p. 163
value p. 165

Find out what these words mean as you study this lesson.

Essential Question
What Is Mental Health? Engage

Get Ready to Learn How are you different from your mother? Do identical twins always look and act exactly the same? God made each of us special and unique. Each person looks, acts, feels, and thinks a different way.

Try This! What is your favorite thing about yourself? Make a drawing with the title *How I Am Special*. Show more in your drawing than how you appear on the outside. Include something to represent how you think or feel. Share and explain your drawing.

Structured Inquiry — Discover

Record your work for this inquiry. Your teacher may also assign the related Guided Inquiry.

What Do You Think?

How do your opinions compare to those of your classmates?

Your Group Needs
- paper and pencil

Step 1 Read the following statements. **Record** if you agree or disagree with each one.

1. Reading is more important than math.
2. Parents should require children to wash their hands at least three times per day.
3. Giving children an allowance for doing their chores teaches them responsible money habits.

Step 2 Make a bar graph to **display** the class **data**.

Create Explanations

1. How do your opinions compare to those of your classmates?
2. Why is it important to respect other people's opinions?

Body and Mind Explain

Faith Connection

How is your relationship with Jesus similar to the relationship you have with your parents or a close friend?

To be a healthy person, you must have a healthy body and mind. Mental health deals with how you think and what you know about yourself.

God created us in His image. But each of us is different. Your **personality** is made up of thoughts, feelings, and behaviors that are special to you. Your personality gives you character. It is one of the things that makes you interesting and different.

Good mental health helps you have positive relationships. A **relationship** is how you get along with another person. Many people have strong, healthy relationships with their close family members, neighbors, and friends. The most important relationship you have is with Jesus. A good relationship with Jesus helps your mind stay healthy.

You make your relationship with Jesus stronger by going to church, praying, and regularly studying and sharing Jesus' word.

Emotions

How do you feel right now? Are you happy? Sad? Angry? Jealous? Scared? Worried? Content? Hopeful? These are all emotions. **Emotions** are feelings or moods.

Your body reacts to emotions. If you worry often, your stomach might hurt. If you are looking forward to something, it may be hard to sleep.

Faith Connection

1 John 1:9 tells us that Jesus forgives our sins. How does knowing this affect your emotions?

Lesson Activity

Draw several pictures of people's faces on index cards. Your pictures should show basic emotions. Write the name of the emotion each picture stands for on the back of the card. Share your pictures with a partner. See if your partner can guess the emotion each card shows.

- **What body language and tone of voice would go with each face and emotion?**

Think About It

Why is talking to an adult about your feelings a good way to deal with your emotions?

Emotions are natural and may change often. It is important to learn how to deal with your emotions. If you are angry you may say hurtful things. You might get a stomachache if you get really upset and do not talk to others. You can talk to Jesus about your emotions in prayer. You can also talk to a trusted adult or write about your emotions in a journal.

As Christians, we rejoice and celebrate Jesus' love for us. When things make us sad, we should still be hopeful. That's because we look forward to heaven, where God will "wipe away all tears" **(Revelation 7:17).**

What emotions do you think the children in this photo are feeling?

Values Explain

Do you know what compassion, sharing, honesty, friendship, cooperation, respect, and responsibility have in common? They are values. **Values** are the ideas or beliefs a person tries to live by. You develop your values from your family, the Bible, friends, education, and your experiences. They show others the kind of person you are. Your values affect how you view the world and care for the things God created.

People who volunteer at a food bank show compassion. They are helping to care for people who are in need.

Lesson Activity

Choose five values from the list on this page. Tell why they are important. Discuss your list with other students.

❓ **Which values on your list do you think were also Jesus' values?**

Think About It

Are values and emotions the same thing? Explain.

165

What Should I Do? Explain

You make many decisions every day.

To make good decisions, think about and follow these steps:

1. *Define the problem.*
2. *Gather facts and information.*
3. *Make a list of your choices.*
4. *Consider the outcome.*
5. *Make the decision and act on it.*

Some decisions affect your relationships. Suppose you and your friends are using the swings on the playground. Another group of classmates wants to use the swings, too. You were there first, so you do not want to leave. You could get upset and be mean to the other group. You also could work together to find a solution.

An important decision may affect other people. It may have an effect that lasts for a long time. Suppose a friend says he is sorry for hurting you. If you choose to forgive him, you may become better friends.

Faith Connection

We make decisions based on the things we admire most. If we admire Jesus most in our lives, we will try to become like Him.

Think About It

What was a good decision you made recently? How did you decide what to do?

You can decide to work together with others. Teamwork can help you finish a project faster.

What can you do to work well within a group?

Good Decisions (Explain)

Scripture Spotlight

Read **Romans 12:2**. How does this text say we should make decisions?

Think About It

Sometimes you may feel very angry. What can you do to control that emotion?

Have you ever heard the saying "Think before you act"? You need to think about what might happen as a result of your decision.

Emotions can affect the decisions you make. If you make a decision when you are angry, you might make a poor choice.

Your values are the most important thing to consider when you make a decision. Sometimes, making the right decision is not easy. For example, Jesus was listening to teachers and asking questions at the temple when he was twelve years old. He chose to go home and honor His parents instead of staying at the temple. Before you make a decision, stop and ask "What would Jesus do?"

Millie needs to decide which snack to eat.

 How could her decision affect her body?

Make a Connection *Extend*

Make a list of five jobs that adults might have. Write one decision that each person must make. Tell what will happen because of each decision that is made.

Lesson Review *Assess/Reflect*

Summary: What is mental health? To be healthy, you must care for your body and mind. You do this by understanding emotions, having Christian values, and making good decisions.

1. **Graphic Organizer** Make a sequence graphic organizer to show what happens when you make good decisions.

2. **Vocabulary** How do your ==values== show who you are?

3. **Test Prep** What is the first step in making a good decision?
   - A. Compare the choices with your values and beliefs.
   - B. Make a list of your choices.
   - C. Define the problem.
   - D. Gather facts and information.

4. Why should you deal with your emotions?

5. Compassion is a value. How did Jesus show compassion?

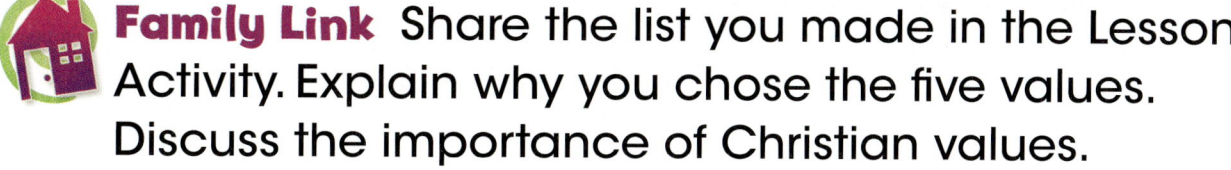

Family Link Share the list you made in the Lesson Activity. Explain why you chose the five values. Discuss the importance of Christian values.

People in Science

Extend

Get to Know Yourself

A healthy body takes more than a good diet and exercise. You also need a healthy mind. Your mind affects the way you feel about yourself. It also affects how you feel about people. A healthy mind finds good ways to handle thoughts and feelings.

Here is a list of things you can do to have a healthy mind.
- Be happy
- Laugh and have fun
- Work on problems
- Have goals
- Learn new things
- Balance work and play
- Build good relationships
- Build self-confidence

Fun Fact

Children laugh about 400 times each day. Adults laugh only about 15 times each day.

✓ Concept Check

1. What three things do you need to be healthy?
2. Why is having a healthy mind an important part of feeling good?

Careers in Science
Extend

Counselor

Counselors help people solve problems. They teach people new ways to think and act. Counselors share ideas about how to have a healthy mind.

A counselor might work with one person, a group of people, or families. Counselors do not tell people what to do. They help people make their own choices.

Some counselors work in schools. Counselors know how to listen to children. They help children find ways to deal with their problems.

Social Worker

Social workers help people live better. They can help a family find a home. They can help a sick person get better care.

School social workers help families work together. They help teachers and students. They talk about how to be a friend. They show people how to get along with each other.

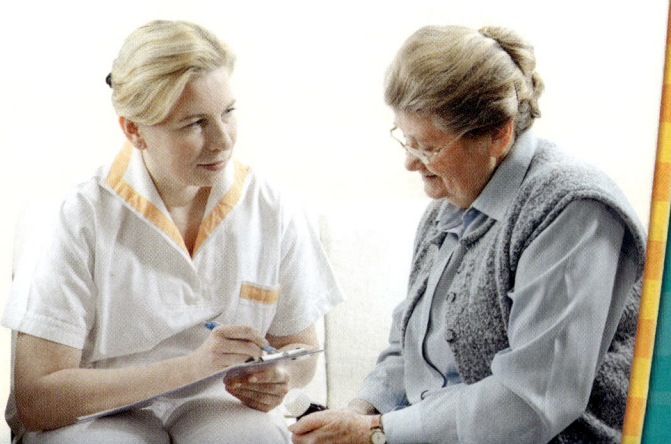

Concept Check

1. What kind of problem might a counselor help a student solve?
2. How are counselors and social workers alike and different?

Chapter 5

Keeping Your Body Safe and Healthy

Lesson 1
How Can You Avoid Germs? 174

Lesson 2
Why Is Hygiene Important? 184

Lesson 3
What Are Common Safety Hazards? 194

Scripture Spotlight

Health is a wonderful gift from God. God designed our bodies to be healthy. Sickness and disease were introduced when sin entered the world. Someday, God will rid the world of sickness and disease and it will be perfect again. Until that happens, you, with God's help, are responsible for your own health and safety. You will read the following passages in this chapter.

Luke 11:39 (p. 186)   2 Samuel 22:3 (p. 197)   Psalm 4:8 (p. 197)

The Big Idea

We have faith that Jesus will watch over us. In the Bible, Jesus has told us that we are to take care of our bodies. There are many things that we can do to keep our bodies healthy and safe.

❓ **What can you do to protect yourself from injury while riding a bicycle or skating?**

Lesson 1

Vocabulary

germ p. 176
symptom p. 176
doctor p. 177
checkup p. 178
vaccine p. 181
antibiotic p. 182

Find out what these words mean as you study this lesson.

Essential Question

How Can You Avoid Germs? Engage

Get Ready to Learn When was the last time you were sick? How did you feel? Did you have to stay in bed? Do you know what caused you to get sick? In this lesson, you will learn about things that make you sick. You will also learn what you can do to avoid getting ill.

Try This! How is this child preventing the spread of germs? Think about the last time you were sick. What was one thing you did to help prevent spreading germs? Draw and write about one way that helps you stay healthy. Make a class list of things that help you stay healthy.

Structured Inquiry
Discover

Record your work for this inquiry. Your teacher may also assign the related Guided Inquiry.

Stopping Germs
How do germs spread?

Your Group Needs
- paper with glitter

Step 1 Your teacher will hand out a sheet of paper with glitter. Pass it around to each of your classmates.

Step 2 Observe your hands. Look for glitter. **Record** your observations in the table on the *Science Journal* page.

Step 3 Communicate with a partner. Talk about how the glitter spread.

Step 4 Imagine that the glitter represents germs. Wash your hands, and repeat Step 2. **Observe** and **record** your observations.

Create Explanations

1. How do germs spread?
2. Why is it important to keep germs from spreading?
3. What are two ways you can slow the spread of germs?

Signs of Sickness _{Explain}

Think About It
What symptoms have you felt when you were sick?

A **germ** is something that can make you sick. Germs are very small and can only be seen with a microscope. They are everywhere. They can be in things that you touch, drink, or eat. They can get in your body through a cut or an animal bite. Touching, coughing, and sneezing help spread germs. You need to be careful about spreading germs when you are sick.

Germs can affect how you feel. You can tell you are sick because you have **symptoms**, or signs of being sick. Germs can cause different symptoms. Your head may hurt. You may feel sick to your stomach. You may have chills and feel cold, or you may feel hot and sweaty. You may even have an earache or a sore throat. Symptoms happen because your body is fighting the germs.

See the person in the photo checking the young girl? She is a doctor. A **doctor** is a person who treats sick people and helps them get well. Doctors work with nurses and other people to find out what is making someone sick.

? In what way is a doctor like a detective?

If you are sick, you may visit the doctor. The doctor may ask about your symptoms. Symptoms help the doctor figure out what germs you are fighting.

Sometimes you need to visit a doctor even if you don't have any symptoms. A **checkup** is a doctor's visit to help find out how healthy you are. A doctor can also check for signs of health problems during regular checkups.

This nurse is taking the boy's temperature. A fever is when your body is warmer than normal. It is a symptom of being sick.

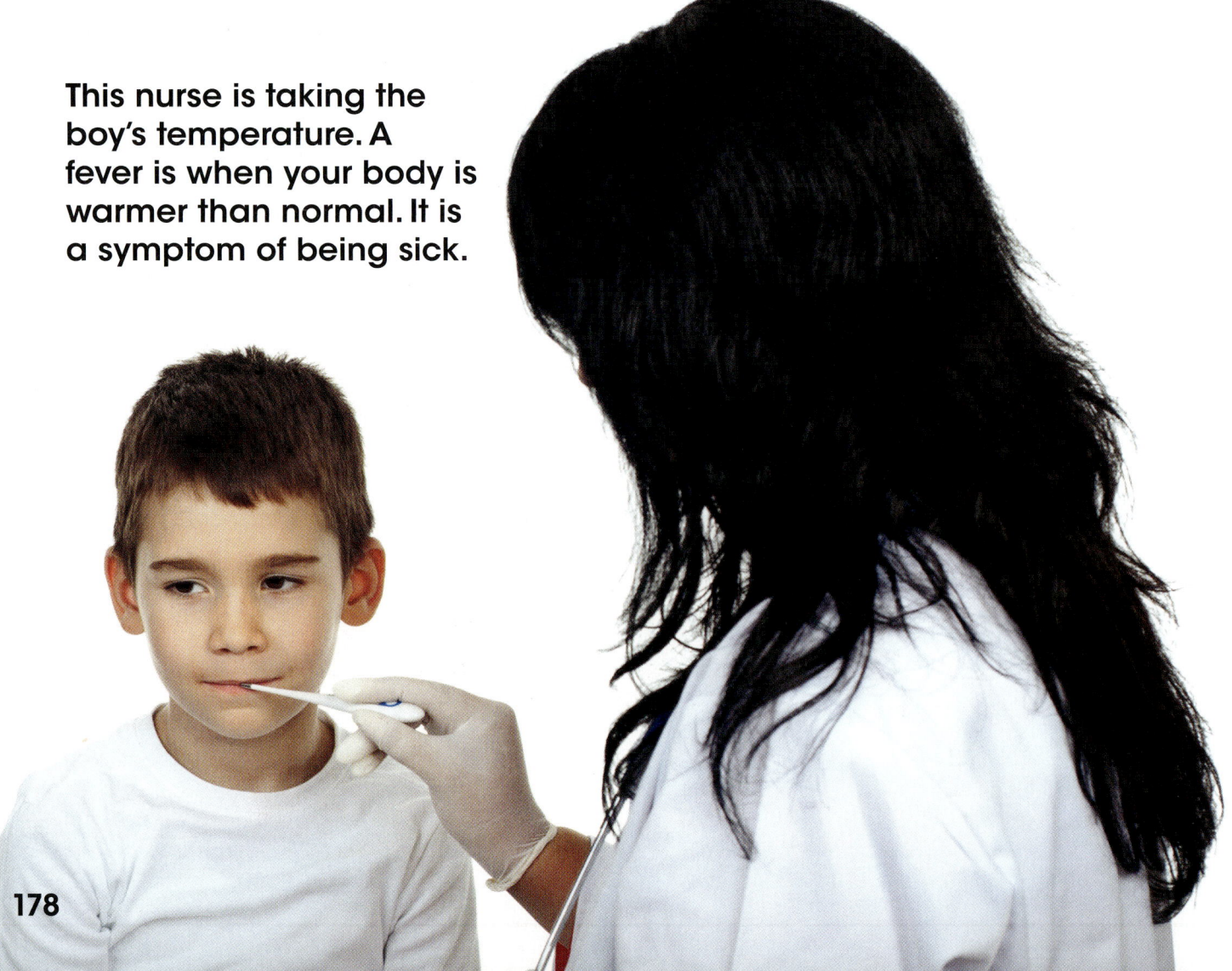

Germs All Around [Explain]

It is amazing how God cares for you. He created your body so that most germs have no effect on you. This is because God designed your body with an immune system. Your immune system works like an army to protect your body from invading germs. Your immune system destroys most germs before they can make you sick.

Germs can get on your hands when you touch things. They can get into your body through your nose, eyes, mouth, and blood. When they get inside your body, they can make you sick. Healthy habits help stop germs from spreading.

Explore-a-Lab
Structured Inquiry

How do you know that germs are all around?

Wait two days after completing the Structured Inquiry. Look for glitter in the classroom. List the places you found glitter. Record your observations in a chart. Explain why you did or did not find glitter.

Think About It

Why is it so easy to spread germs?

Germs can be on the floor or in the soil. Your shoes spread germs when you walk. Germs can get on a table if you put your backpack on it.

Foods also can have germs on them. Some foods, such as meat or eggs, need to be cooked properly to kill any germs. Some foods must be kept cold in a freezer or refrigerator to keep germs from growing.

Fruits and vegetables come from gardens or farms. They can have dirt and germs from the ground. It is important to wash fruits and vegetables before you eat them.

Healthy Habits

- Wash your hands with soap and water often.
- Always wash your hands before you eat.
- Cover your mouth when you cough or sneeze.
- Keep your table, desk, plates, and bed clean.

Covering your mouth will help you remain healthier.

Why is it better to cough into your arm than into your hands?

Fighting Germs Explain

Scientists look for ways to get rid of harmful germs. They have learned how to weaken some germs. Scientists use weakened or dead germs to make a vaccine. A **vaccine** teaches your immune system how to fight off some germs. Then your body can fight off the stronger germs, too.

Some vaccines are sprayed into your nose. Others are given as a shot. Vaccines have stopped the spread of many germs. Polio, measles, mumps, and chicken pox are germs that can be avoided with a vaccine.

Think About It

How do vaccines help you stay healthy?

Vaccines help your body prepare to fight off harmful viruses.

Think About It

Why should you not take antibiotics that are prescribed for someone else?

Scientists and doctors fight some germs with antibiotics (an•ty•by•AHT•iks). <mark>Antibiotics</mark> are medicines that kill some germs, but not all germs. For example, antibiotics can kill most germs that cause ear infections. If you need antibiotics for an illness, always exactly follow the doctor's directions on how to take them.

A pharmacist makes sure medicine is labeled correctly.

? Why is it important for medicines to be labeled correctly?

182

Make a Connection Extend

Make a health poster. Choose a tip that helps stop viruses, bacteria, and other germs from spreading. Draw a picture on your poster and put it up at school.

Lesson Review Assess/Reflect

Summary: How can you avoid germs? Germs are everywhere and can make you sick. A vaccine or antibiotics can help your body fight some germs. Avoid spreading germs. Develop habits that keep you healthy.

1. **Graphic Organizer** Show effects of not covering your mouth when you sneeze.

2. **Vocabulary** Name one symptom of an illness.

3. **Test Prep** What part of our bodies did God design to help fight germs?
   - **A.** vaccine
   - **B.** symptoms
   - **C.** antibiotics
   - **D.** immune system

4. Explain a habit that you have that helps you stay healthy and free from germs.

Family Link Ask your parents if you have had any vaccines. Are there any vaccines that you will need in the future? Make a list of diseases you have had vaccines for and those you will still need in the future.

Lesson 2

Vocabulary
hygiene	p. 186
enamel	p. 188
pulp	p. 188
dentist	p. 189
floss	p. 189
cavity	p. 189
grooming	p. 190
head lice	p. 191

Find out what these words mean as you study this lesson.

Essential Question

Why Is Hygiene Important?

Engage

Get Ready to Learn How is the girl in the picture taking care of her health? Why is it important to comb your hair, brush your teeth, and take baths regularly?

In this lesson, you will learn about a healthy lifestyle. You should spend time each day on personal care. You will prepare yourself for good health.

Try This! How do you take care of your health every day? Draw a series of pictures to show what you do. Draw the pictures in the order in which you do them during the day.

Structured Inquiry Discover

Record your work for this inquiry. Your teacher may also assign the related Guided Inquiry.

Hole in Your Mouth
What happens if a cavity is left untreated?

Your Group Needs
- apple
- sharp pencil or wooden skewer

Step 1 **Observe** the apple closely. **Record** your observations by drawing and coloring a picture of the apple.

Step 2 **Predict** what will happen if you make a hole in an apple and do not protect it.

Step 3 Use the sharp pencil or skewer to puncture the apple. **Observe**, draw, and color the apple with the puncture again.

Step 4 Leave the apple exposed for several days. Draw and color the apple each day.

Step 5 **Compare** all the pictures. **Record** your observations by writing a description of what happened to the cavity.

Create Explanations

1. What happens if a cavity is left untreated?

2. Why should you visit a dentist regularly and tell the dentist if you have any pain in your mouth?

Hygiene Hints Explain

God designed our bodies, and they are amazing. Taking care of your body is one way to honor God. It also helps you stay healthy.

There are many ways to care for your body. Eat healthy food. Exercise every day. Brush your teeth at least twice a day and remember to floss once a day. Wash your hands often. Take a bath or shower regularly.

Hygiene is keeping yourself and the things around you clean and healthy. You have learned that germs can make you sick. When you have good hygiene, you kill many germs.

Scripture Spotlight

How do you think someone could be clean on the outside but still dirty on the inside, like it says in **Luke 11:39**?

Washing your hands with soap and water is good hygiene.

What good hygiene habits do you have?

Hygiene is important. When you are clean, you help your body stay healthy. Start a hygiene habit. Here are some things to do.

- Take a bath or shower regularly.
- Wash your hair regularly.
- Wash your hands with soap and warm water after using the bathroom and before eating.
- Clean your fingernails regularly.
- Brush your teeth twice a day.

It is up to you to be responsible for your own grooming. Staying clean helps to stop germs from spreading.

Think About It

How does having good hygiene habits help you stay healthy?

Keeping your hair clean is part of good grooming.

Why is it important for you to be responsible for your own hygiene habits?

A Clean Mouth Explain

Keeping your teeth and gums clean is an important part of good hygiene. Your teeth were not ready to work when you were born. The first baby teeth appear at about six months of age. By age three, most people have their first set of baby teeth (20 teeth in all). Permanent teeth grow in a child's mouth and push out the baby teeth. This begins at the age of five or six. There are 32 teeth in a complete set of adult teeth.

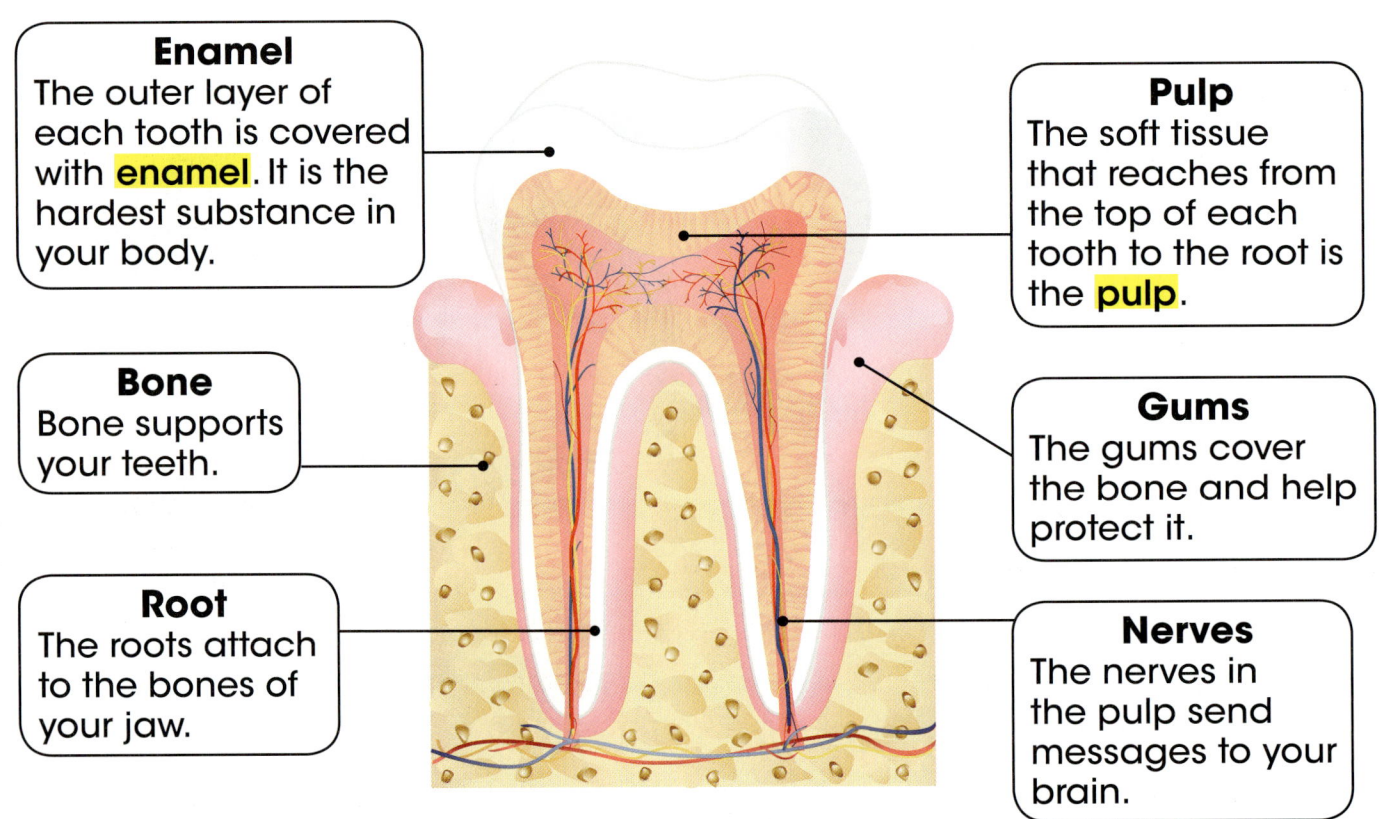

Enamel
The outer layer of each tooth is covered with <mark>enamel</mark>. It is the hardest substance in your body.

Bone
Bone supports your teeth.

Root
The roots attach to the bones of your jaw.

Pulp
The soft tissue that reaches from the top of each tooth to the root is the <mark>pulp</mark>.

Gums
The gums cover the bone and help protect it.

Nerves
The nerves in the pulp send messages to your brain.

A **dentist** is a person who takes care of people's teeth. A dentist or dental assistant can show you how to brush your teeth correctly.

Brush your teeth and tongue at least twice a day. It's important to brush your teeth for about two or three minutes.

The dentist or dental assistant can also show you how to use floss. **Floss** is a string used to clean between your teeth and gums. Floss your teeth at least once a day.

You floss and brush your teeth to prevent cavities. A **cavity** is a hole in a tooth. Germs eat tiny bits of food left on your teeth and make acid. This acid can form cavities in your teeth.

Think About It

If you floss every day, do you still need to brush your teeth daily? Why?

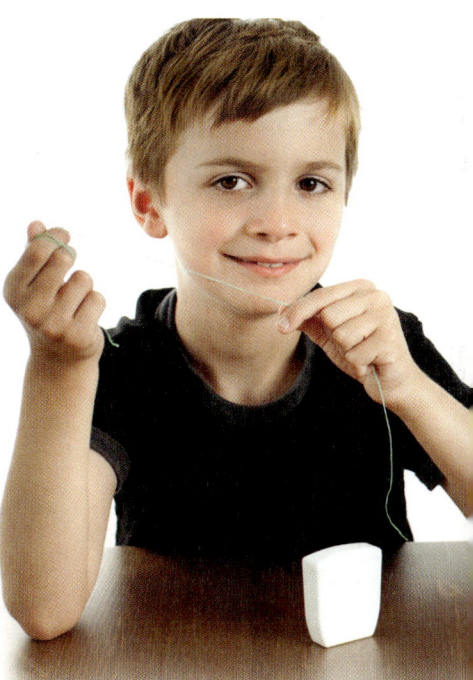

Flossing helps you clean between your teeth.

Explore-a-Lab
Structured Inquiry

How should you care for your teeth?

Use clay and candy corn to make a model of your teeth, tongue, and mouth. Draw a picture of your model. Label the parts. Use the model to show how to brush your teeth and floss them.

Good Grooming Explain

Think About It
How are hygiene and grooming alike and different?

Besides cleaning your body, you also want your hair clean, combed, and brushed, too. Clothes and shoes do not need to be fancy or new. They should just be clean.

Grooming is caring for your body and the way you look. Good grooming means that you have good hygiene. Your clothes and shoes should be as clean as possible. Your hair should be clean and cared for. Good grooming helps you stay healthy and look good.

You feel great with good grooming habits.

Head lice are tiny bugs that live in hair. They make your head itch. Even people with good hygiene may get head lice. They spread easily. But there are ways to prevent them and medicines and other ways to get rid of them. Here are some ways to prevent the spread of head lice:

- Do not use other people's combs or brushes.
- Do not share hats, scarves, or hair clips.

Keep Home Clean (Explain)

Think About It
What do you think are the best home cleaning chores for someone your age?

Do you want to know another way to stay healthy? Help keep your home clean. A clean home helps fight germs. That helps keep you and your family healthy.

Help by keeping the dishes clean. Sweep floors and dust furniture. Hang up your clothes. Even family pets need to be clean.

Maybe you have a cleaning chore or two. Many children have the important chore of keeping their room clean. Hang up clean clothes. Put dirty clothes together to be washed. Throw away trash and put away toys.

How is this girl helping to keep her home clean?

Make a Connection Extend

It's a good idea to hum a little song when you brush your teeth. This helps you brush your teeth for a few minutes. Write a silly song or poem to think about while you brush your teeth.

Lesson Review Assess/Reflect

Summary: Why is hygiene important? Hygiene helps prevent germs from spreading. Good hygiene includes bathing regularly, washing your hair, and brushing your teeth.

1. **Graphic Organizer** Use a Venn diagram to compare and contrast brushed and unbrushed teeth.

2. **Vocabulary** What good habits can keep a cavity from forming?

3. **Test Prep** Which of the following is a good health habit?
   - A. watching TV
   - B. taking a bath
   - C. eating candy
   - D. coloring a picture

4. What could happen without good hygiene habits?

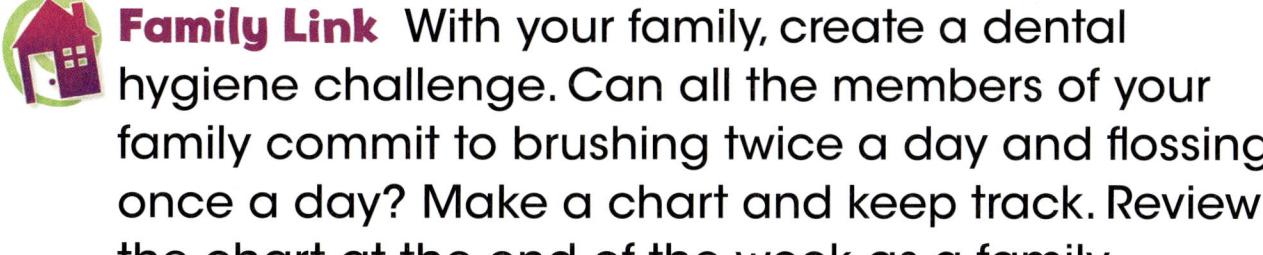 **Family Link** With your family, create a dental hygiene challenge. Can all the members of your family commit to brushing twice a day and flossing once a day? Make a chart and keep track. Review the chart at the end of the week as a family.

Lesson 3

Vocabulary
smoke detector p. 197
poison p. 198
first aid p. 200
crosswalk p. 202

Find out what these words mean as you study this lesson.

Essential Question

What Are Common Safety Hazards?

Engage

Get Ready to Learn When was the last time you wore a safety helmet? Do you know anyone who was wearing one during an accident? Why do you think it is important to wear a safety helmet? When should you wear one? In this lesson, you will learn about ways that you can stay away from danger and keep yourself safe.

Try This! What did you do at the last fire drill at school? Make a four-panel comic strip showing what you should do during a fire drill at school. Where are the best building exits? Show the comic strip to the class. Discuss fire safety.

Record your work for this inquiry. Your teacher may also assign the related Guided Inquiry.

Be Seen to Be Safe
What colors would be the safest when walking or riding a bike?

Your Group Needs
- crayons, including neon colors
- small strips of paper

Step 1 Color four strips of paper. You will **experiment** with light, dark, and neon colors.

Step 2 Predict which colors of paper you will be able to see in a dimly lit place.

Step 3 Ask your teacher to darken the room lights. **Observe** which color is easiest to see. **Record** your observations.

Step 4 Go outside with your class. **Observe** which colors can be seen from the farthest away. **Record** your observations in a chart.

Create Explanations

1. What colors would be the safest when walking or riding a bike?
2. What color are the safety vests construction workers wear? Why is that color used?

Safety Rules Explain

Think About It

How could a scientist test a seat belt?

Check out your *Science Journal* for a Guided Inquiry about seat belts. Discover

There are many rules created to keep you safe. You follow safety rules when you work on experiments. Some safety rules are laws. In many cities and towns a helmet must be worn when you ride your bike. A helmet protects your head if you fall or crash.

Laws about driving help keep people safe in cars and trucks. In many states and provinces, children need to sit in a safety seat or booster. Everyone in a car or truck needs to wear a seat belt. A seat belt is a harness in a car or truck. It holds you safely in place with two straps. One goes across your lap and the other goes across your chest.

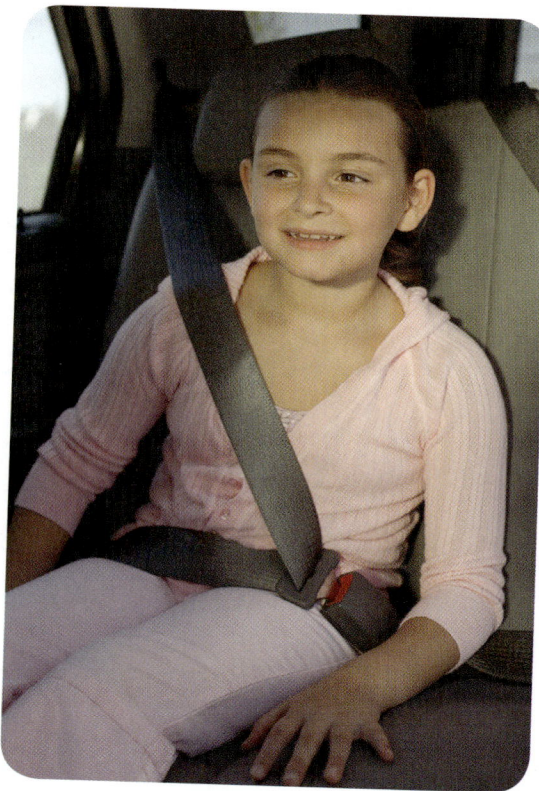

Always buckle up in a car.

Fire Safety

What would you do in case of a fire? Knowing what to do can help protect you and save lives. It is important to have early warning when a fire breaks out in a building.

A **smoke detector** is an alarm that sounds when it senses smoke. When a smoke detector goes off, it alerts people there is a fire.

Develop a fire safety plan with your family. It should include an escape route and meeting place. If you hear a smoke detector, get out quickly. In a fire, get down low to crawl to safety. If your hair or clothing catches on fire:

- STOP moving immediately.
- DROP and cover your face.
- ROLL to put out the flames.

Think About It

Why should each family have a fire escape plan?

Scripture Spotlight

Read **2 Samuel 22:3** and **Psalm 4:8**. Do you ask Jesus to keep you safe? Why do you think this is important?

An alarm sounds when a smoke detector senses smoke.

❓ Have you ever heard a smoke detector make a chirping sound once in a while? What do you think that means?

Leave Poisons Alone Explain

Scientists have invented many things. They come in liquids, pills, and other forms. Some kill harmful insects or weeds. Others help fight diseases. Many of them are dangerous to living things. A **poison** is a substance that causes injury, illness, or death. Stay safe around poisons. Stop when you see a strange container. Do not touch. Know these hazard symbols.

Stay Safe Symbols		
Symbol	**Dangers**	**Examples**
	The container may explode if punctured or heated.	Hair spray Spray paint
	This product will burn your skin, eyes, or throat.	Toilet bowl or oven cleaners
	This product will catch fire easily.	Gasoline or alcohol
	Eating, drinking, or smelling this product could cause death.	Furniture polish or windshield wiper fluid

Some poisons use other symbols to warn you to avoid them. One warning symbol is a face with a tongue sticking out, called Mr. Yuk™. Another warning symbol is a skull with two crossed bones. Not all poisons will have symbols. Do not touch, taste, drink, or eat anything without asking a parent or adult first.

If someone does get poisoned, call the Poison Control Center. They can tell you what to do. You can ask someone at home to post the phone number for the national or local poison control helpline.

Think About It

If things are poison, why are they made?

Mr. Yuk™

Why do you think Mr. Yuk™ looks this way?

This sign warns others that a poison has been placed on the lawn.

Get Help Fast   Explain

First aid is fast help for someone who is sick or hurt. Did you ever fall and get a cut? Someone probably cleaned the cut and put a bandage on it. Sometimes first aid helps a person until a medical person can help.

In case of an emergency, call 9-1-1. Fires, badly injured people, poisoning, or an intruder are examples of emergencies. When the operator answers your call:

- give your name and address
- stay calm and speak slowly
- describe the emergency
- explain who needs help
- answer any other questions

Sometimes first aid helps until a medical person arrives.

❓ **Why is it important to remain calm in an emergency?**

Lesson Activity

Discuss what to do in case of an emergency with your group. Then role-play to show what you would do. Use basic first aid as you role-play.

 What will you do if there is an emergency?

If someone near you gets hurt, you can help them if you know basic first aid. When treating someone who is injured, remain calm. This can help the injured person stay calm, too.

Think About It

Why is it important to know basic first aid?

Basic Rules of First Aid

- **Bruises**—Put ice or a cold cloth on right away.

- **Small cuts**—If you get cut, wash the cut with soap and water. Then press on the cut with a bandage or cloth to help stop the bleeding. When bleeding stops, cover with a bandage.

- **Burns**—Put cold water or ice on the burn immediately and keep it there until the pain stops, or a parent or medical person gives other instructions.

Street Smarts Explain

Think About It

What do you do to stay safe in a crosswalk?

To keep safe when you are walking or biking, use the crosswalk. A **crosswalk** is a marked place on a road so that people can get from one side to the other safely.

Cross streets at crosswalks but be alert. Look both ways before crossing. Do not run out into the street or play in the street. Obey lighted signals, if present, that tell you when it is safe to use a crosswalk. Ride your bike with the flow of traffic on streets without bike paths. Walk against the flow of traffic on streets without sidewalks. Wear brightly colored clothing when you walk along streets and crosswalks at night.

Cross a street at a crosswalk.

Why should you look both ways before crossing a street?

Make a Connection Extend

Draw an escape route you would follow to get out of your bedroom in the event of a fire. Then draw an escape route map from your classroom. Draw a safe meeting place on each map.

Lesson Review Assess/Reflect

Summary: What are common safety hazards? You are learning ways to stay safe. Wear a seat belt. Know about fire safety, poisons, handling emergencies, and first aid. Be alert and stay safe on streets, roadways, and in crosswalks.

1. **Graphic Organizer** Draw a sequence chart telling what you would do in an emergency.

2. **Vocabulary** What are three ways a poison can be harmful?

3. **Test Prep** Which is not safe?
   A. walking in a crosswalk
   B. chasing a ball into the street
   C. wear bright clothing at night
   D. looking both ways before crossing a street

4. Cara needs glue for a project. She sees a bottle with handwriting that says *glue* and nothing else is on the bottle. What is a safe decision she could make?

Family Link Make a first aid kit for your home. Include a poster that tells when to call 9-1-1 or the Poison Control Center and what to say.

People in Science

Extend

Get to Know
John Snow

John Snow was born in 1813. He went to school to become a doctor. When John was a doctor, many people got sick from cholera. Most doctors thought cholera came from germs in the air. John thought it came from germs in food and water.

For a long time, no one believed John Snow. Finally, he proved he was right. Today, we know that we need clean water and safe food to stay healthy.

Fun Fact

Almost all the water on Earth is in the oceans. Less than 1% of Earth's water can be used for drinking.

Concept Check

1. Why is it important to have clean water and safe food?
2. How can you make sure you are drinking water that is safe and healthy for you?

Careers in Science

Extend

Microbiologist

A microbiologist studies tiny living things. These living things are too small for us to see.

Microbiologists use microscopes to study cells. Cells make up every living thing. Some living things have only one cell. Others have many, many cells.

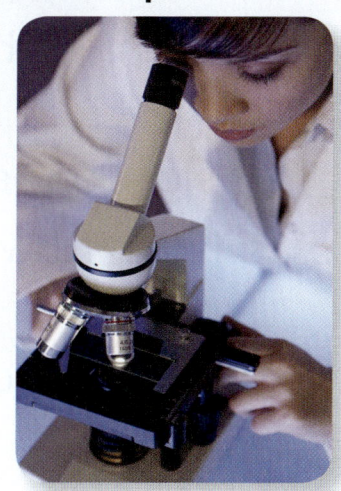

Some microbiologists study bacteria. Bacteria can cause illnesses. Microbiologists learn how to prevent and treat illnesses.

Dentist

A dentist is a doctor who takes care of teeth. Dentists make sure your teeth and gums are healthy. They also check to see if your teeth line up correctly.

A dentist studies X-rays of teeth. X-rays show how your teeth are developing in your jaw.

A dentist helps with emergencies. A dentist can help fix cracked or knocked out teeth.

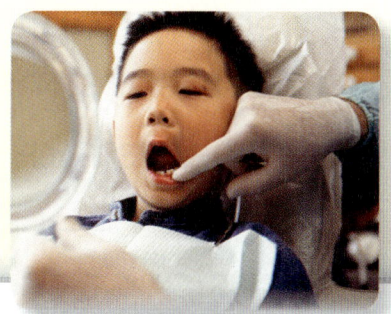

Concept Check

1. Why do microbiologists need microscopes?
2. How do dentists help us stay healthy?

Unit 2 Review — Assess/Reflect

Vocabulary

Use the words to complete the sentences.

nerves	vaccines	dentist	doctor
germs	head lice	floss	cavity
nutrient	crosswalk	symptom	checkup

1. Weakened or killed germs that teach the body to fight off certain illnesses are called _____.

2. A fever may be a _____, or sign, of being sick.

3. A person who goes to school to learn how to treat human illnesses is a _____.

4. Tiny living things that can make people sick are _____.

5. Tiny animals that live in hair are _____ _____.

6. A hole that germs make in a tooth is a _____.

7. A person who has trained to prevent and treat diseases of the mouth and teeth is a _____.

8. A visit to the doctor to check on health is a _____.

9. A healthy habit is to use _____ to clean out food and germs between teeth every day.

10. Long fibers that carry messages between body parts are called _____.

11. A substance that living things need to grow is a _____.

12. A marked path across a road that helps people get from one side to the other is a _____.

Describe What You See

13. What is shown? What does it tell you?

Use Science Practices

14. How do grains **compare** to fruits and vegetables?

Multiple Choice

15. Which is not listed on a food label?
 - **A.** ingredients
 - **B.** serving size
 - **C.** nutrients
 - **D.** color of the food

16. Which is not a part of the digestive system?
 - **A.** the spine
 - **B.** the esophagus
 - **C.** the intestines
 - **D.** the stomach

Short Answer

17. Why should every family have a fire escape plan?

18. How do nerve endings help you react to events in the outside world?

19. List two ways you can help your body digest food.

20. What things are important to remember about calling 9-1-1?

21. What should you do to help prevent cavities?

22. Why is it important to know the serving size of a food?

23. How can harmful germs get into your body?

24. Describe three ways to keep yourself safe and healthy.

Unit 3: Earth and Space Science

Chapter 6 210
Earth's Land, Air, and Water

Chapter 7 256
Weather and Seasons

Chapter 8 286
Space Science

Unit 3 Review ... 312

In this unit you will learn about things on Earth and things in space. Since Creation, Earth has changed in many ways. Some of these changes happened during the Genesis Flood. You will answer questions like these:

- How did the Flood change Earth?
- What causes the seasons?
- What things are in space?

Snow-covered mountains and hills can be a lot of fun! People ski and snowboard in winter.

Your teacher may assign an Open Inquiry lab and a Lifestyle Challenge activity. Use your *Science Journal* to record your work.

Chapter 6

Earth's Land, Air, and Water

Lesson 1
What Features Are on Earth's Surface? 212

Lesson 2
What Are Rocks and Minerals? ... 226

Lesson 3
How Does Earth's Surface Change? 236

Lesson 4
What Can We Learn from Fossils? 246

Scripture Spotlight

Evidence of God's planning and design of His Creation is everywhere, even in Earth itself. The Bible has many stories about Earth and its features. You will read the following passages.

Genesis 1:9–10 (p. 214)   Haggai 2:8 (p. 228)   Job 40:15 (p. 250)
Genesis 7:17–23 (p. 214) Revelation 21:18–21 (p. 233)
Job 38:8–11 (p. 220)   Acts 16:26 (p. 241)

The Big Idea

God made many landforms when He created Earth. The landforms on Earth's surface have changed over time and continue to change today. Some of these changes occur slowly, while others happen quickly.

❓ **What could be causing these rocks to change?**

Lesson 1

Vocabulary
landform p. 214
mountain p. 216
plain p. 217
canyon p. 219
ocean p. 220
lake p. 224

Find out what these words mean as you study this lesson.

Essential Question
What Features Are on Earth's Surface? Engage

The bottom of the Grand Canyon is 1.6 km (1 mile) from its surface.

Get Ready to Learn In your state or province, what are the natural features of Earth's surface? Some places have deep canyons where waters have cut away layers of rock. Mountains, like Mt. Robson in the Canadian Rockies, soar high above us. And the Great Plains in central North America are flat and level.

Try This! How is the land near your home shaped? Is it flat? Are there hills? Draw a picture. Add a sentence describing the land where you live.

Structured Inquiry

Discover

Record your work for this inquiry. Your teacher may also assign the related Guided Inquiry.

Land on a Map

What kind of landforms are found near where you live?

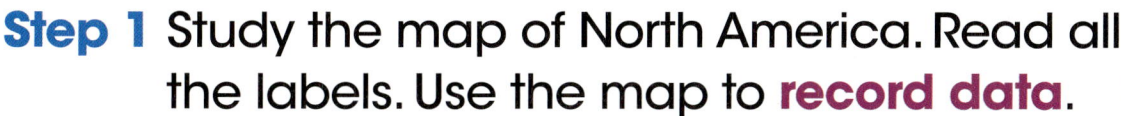

Your Group Needs
- map from your *Science Journal*
- colored pencils

Step 1 Study the map of North America. Read all the labels. Use the map to **record data**.

Step 2 Draw a star to show where you live.

Step 3 Find different types of land and water on the map. Color each type of land and water a different color:

oceans—dark blue   lakes—light blue
mountains—brown   plains—green
canyons and hills—yellow

Step 4 Fill in the key on your map.

Create Explanations

1. What kind of landforms are found near where you live?

2. How might the weather be different if you live near mountains rather than near the ocean?

Landforms Explain

Scripture Spotlight

Read **Genesis 1:9–10**. It tells us that on the third day of Creation, God created dry land. We believe many landforms were created by God in the beginning, while other forms occurred during and after the Flood. **Genesis 7:17–23** tells the story of Noah and the effects of the Flood.

During the third day of Creation, God separated the land from the waters. Many of Earth's surface features became visible at this time. You can see the shape of the land where you live. The land in other places has different shapes. That's because the surface of Earth is made of many landforms.

Landforms are the different natural shapes, or features, on Earth's surface. Mountains, plains, canyons, and islands are some of the landforms on Earth. Landforms may cover huge areas or be as small as a hill.

Explore-a-Lab

Guided Inquiry

 How do model landforms compare with real landforms?

Make models of several landforms inside a plastic shoebox. Use materials such as clay, rocks, sand, and water. Label the landforms.

214

We do not know what Earth looked like at the time of Creation. Landforms were probably changed a lot by the Flood described in **Genesis 7**. Can you see evidence of the Genesis Flood in the landforms around you?

Seven-tenths of Earth's surface is covered by water. Many terms are used for Earth's water features. They include streams, rivers, ponds, lakes, seas, and oceans. A stream can be a small body of water, or a general term for flowing water. Rivers are large streams flowing across land. They move water to and from larger bodies of water. Lakes or ponds are still bodies of water surrounded by land. Lakes may contain freshwater or saltwater. Seas are large bodies of saltwater, partly surrounded by land. They are connected to the largest bodies of saltwater on Earth—the oceans.

This landform is a natural arch. It was carved by wind and water.

Mountains Explain

Think About It
Some mountains have flat tops. What could have caused them to become flat?

The tallest landforms are mountains. A **mountain** is much higher than the land around it. Mountains are usually found in a group called a mountain range, such as the Rocky Mountains in North America. There are many mountain ranges on Earth's surface.

Most mountains have steep sides. Some have pointy tops. Others have rounded tops. The top of a mountain is a *peak*. The low area between two mountains is called a *valley* or a *pass*.

How might travelers use the low areas between these mountain peaks?

Plains

Mountains may be hard to climb. It is easier to walk across a plain. A **plain** is a large, flat area of land. Plains may be covered with grasses or forests.

Some plains are found in the middle of the United States. These grassy areas were once home to large herds of bison. Today, farmers grow crops and graze cattle on the plains.

Plains are also found along coasts. These low lands have sandy soil and swamps.

The Great Plains are between the Rocky Mountains and the Mississippi River.

Other land features have flat tops. They include plateaus, mesas, and some buttes. These features are common in the Southwest.

A plateau is the largest of these landforms. It is a raised, flat landscape with at least one steep side.

A mesa is a medium-sized, flat landform with steep sides. *Mesa* means "table" in Spanish, and these landforms are elevated with a flat top like a table. Outside the United States, these are called "tablelands."

A butte is the smallest of these land features. Buttes are what is left of what was once a mesa. The rest of it has been eroded away.

mesa

plateau

butte

Canyons Explain

A **canyon** is a long, narrow valley with steep sides. Canyons are found all over the world. There are canyons at the bottom of the ocean. There are even canyons on other planets!

Canyons vary in how deep, wide, and long they are. Many canyons have rivers running through them. Some canyons form slowly. Other canyons are carved much more quickly.

Think About It

What could cause a canyon at the bottom of the ocean?

Math in Science

Colca Canyon in Peru is 70 kilometers (km) (44 miles) (mi) long. The Grand Canyon in Arizona is 446 km (277 mi) long. Write <, >, or = to make the sentences true.

446 km (277 mi) __?__ 70 km (44 mi).

70 km (44 mi) __?__ 446 km (277 mi).

Grand Canyon

Rushing waters during and after the Genesis Flood formed the Grand Canyon. Today, the Colorado River continues to carve into the land in this deep canyon.

Oceans Explain

Scripture Spotlight

Read **Job 38:8–11**. God tells Job that He created Earth and seas.

Much of Earth is covered in water. **Oceans** are very large, deep bodies of saltwater. Seas are smaller than oceans. A sea can be part of an ocean, like the Caribbean Sea. A sea can be surrounded by land, like the Dead Sea and the Sea of Galilee.

The *coast* is where an ocean or a sea meets the land. Some coasts have beaches and sand dunes. Others have rocky cliffs.

All the oceans and seas are connected and make one huge body of water. This is called the world ocean. Scientists divide this one body of water into five oceans.

Earth's Oceans
Pacific
Atlantic
Indian
Arctic
Southern

What makes oceans salty? Rain dissolves many salts and minerals in rocks and soil when it flows over the land. Rivers and streams carry them into the ocean where they mix with seawater. When the water evaporates it leaves the salts and minerals behind. The ocean water is salty because of all the minerals and salts it contains.

Underwater Ocean Landforms Explain

Think About It

Where did most of the salt in the oceans come from?

Many different landforms are found on the bottom of the ocean. There are mountains, canyons, plains, and volcanoes.

The longest mountain range on Earth is found on the ocean floor. It is called the *mid-ocean ridge.* Parts of this ridge are found in all of the oceans on Earth.

Earthquakes and volcanic eruptions are common along the ridge. Iceland is also part of this ridge.

volcanic island

mid-ocean ridges

The ocean bottom has its own special land features.

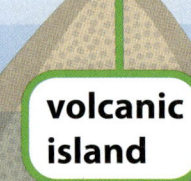 How do landforms at the bottom of the ocean compare with landforms on the surface?

The deepest ocean canyon is called the *Mariana Trench.* It is found in the Pacific Ocean. It is the lowest point on Earth.

Flat areas in deep parts of the ocean are called *abyssal plains.* These plains have a smooth, level surface. They are so deep that little light reaches them. The water here is near freezing.

Other underwater features include mountain peaks called *seamounts,* flat-topped mountains, island chains, and extinct volcanoes.

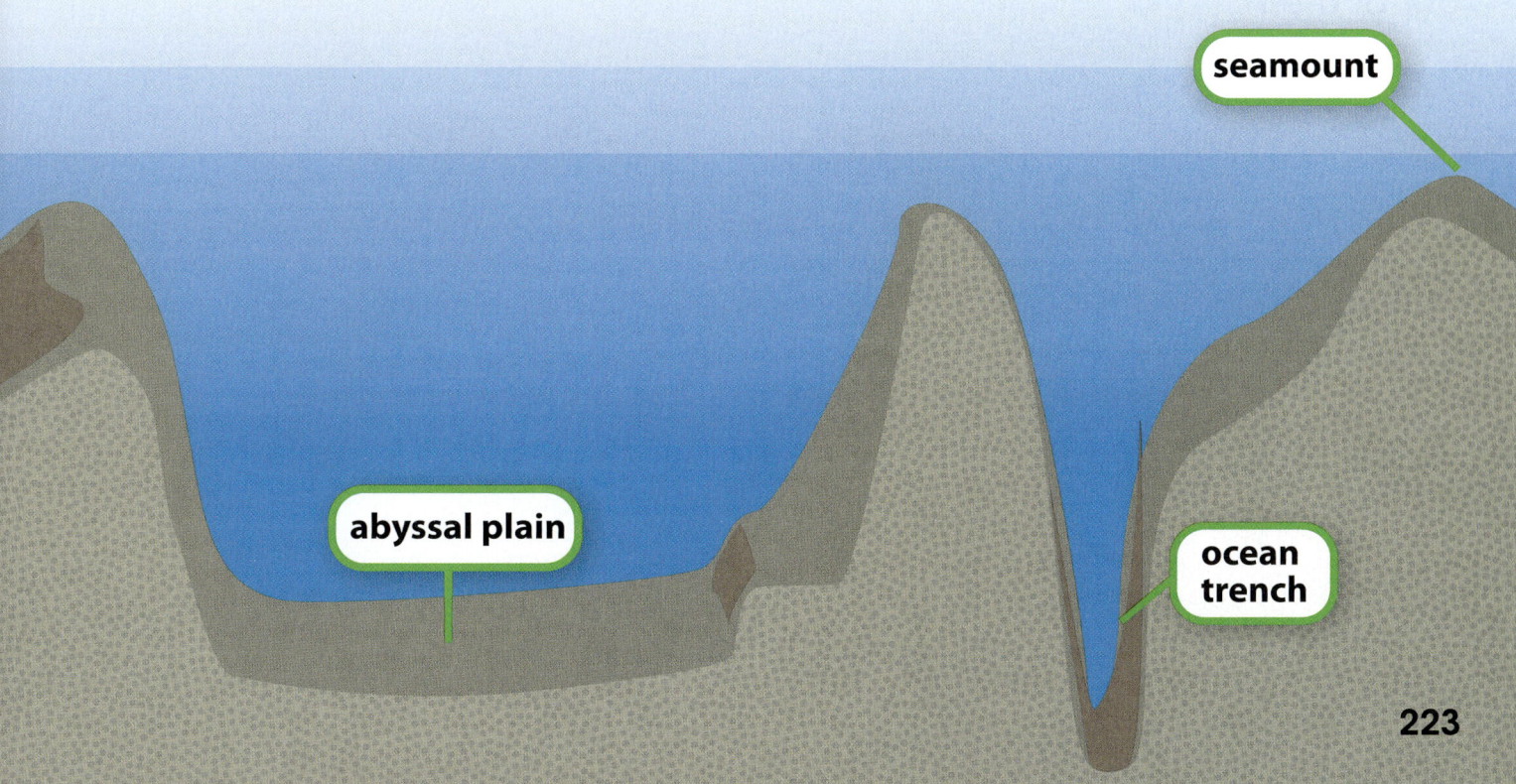

Lakes Explain

Think About It

How is a lake different from an ocean?

A <mark>lake</mark> is a large body of water that has land all around it. The water in a lake does not flow much.

Most lakes have freshwater, but some can be salty, like the Great Salt Lake in Utah. Lakes are habitats for fish and wildlife. Many lakes are deep. In deep lakes, the bottom is cold. The deeper the water is, the less sunlight can reach the lake bottom.

There are thousands of lakes on Earth. Lakes can change. They may dry up or fill up with materials washed in by rivers.

All lakes are surrounded by land, and many have streams that flow in and out of them.

Make a Connection Extend

Use the Internet or other reference sources to gather information about a named landform. On a sheet of paper, draw a picture of the landform. Then write at least three facts that were not in the lesson.

Lesson Review Assess/Reflect

Summary: What features are on Earth's surface?
Earth's surface is made of many kinds of landforms. Landforms have different natural shapes. Earth's surface includes mountains, plains, canyons, and plateaus. Water features include oceans, rivers, streams, and lakes.

1. **Graphic Organizer** Tell what you learned about landforms. Make a chart to show a main idea and details.

2. **Vocabulary** How is a canyon different from a valley?

3. **Test Prep** Which landform is large and flat?
   A. mountain   B. plain   C. canyon   D. valley

4. Why do you think Earth is sometimes called the "blue planet"?

Family Link Talk to family members about landforms in and around your community. Decide which place with special landforms that you would like to visit and research it together.

Lesson 2

Vocabulary

mineral p. 228
rock p. 229
sand p. 231

Find out what these words mean as you study this lesson.

? Essential Question

What Are Rocks and Minerals? Engage

Get Ready to Learn How are rocks and minerals different? What are some rocks you can name? What are some minerals you can name? God created rocks and other natural materials. Rocks are found in many sizes, shapes, and colors. They might feel rough or smooth. They can be hard or soft.

Try This! How do different kinds of rocks compare? Observe several rocks with a hand lens. Look for speckles or small colored particles in the rocks. Record your observations.

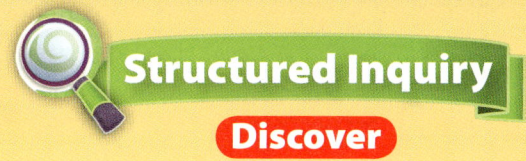

Record your work for this inquiry. Your teacher may also assign the related Guided Inquiry.

Sorting Sand

How do differences in sand grains provide clues to where they came from?

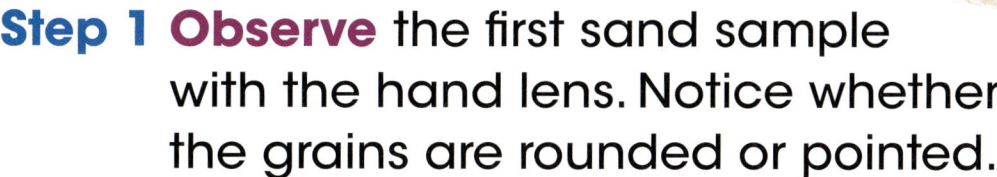

Your Group Needs
- hand lens
- toothpicks
- sand from different locations

Step 1 Observe the first sand sample with the hand lens. Notice whether the grains are rounded or pointed.

Step 2 Sort the grains of sand into groups by color and then by size and shape.

Step 3 Complete the chart to **communicate** your results.

Step 4 Repeat Steps 1–3 with each sand sample. Be sure to record where each sand sample came from in the chart.

Create Explanations

1. How do differences in sand grains provide clues to where they came from?
2. How were all your sand samples alike? How were they different?

Minerals and Rocks Explain

Scripture Spotlight

Read **Haggai 2:8**. What two minerals are mentioned? Who owns those minerals?

Quartz is one of the most common natural solids on Earth. Sand is mostly made from tiny grains of quartz. Glass is also made from quartz. A diamond is so hard that it can cut glass. So what do quartz and diamonds have in common? They are both minerals. A **mineral** is a natural solid that is the same all the way through. Minerals are not made from living things.

You can identify minerals by their properties. You already know that one property is hardness. Turquoise and gold are minerals. You can identify them by their colors. So, color is a property of minerals, too.

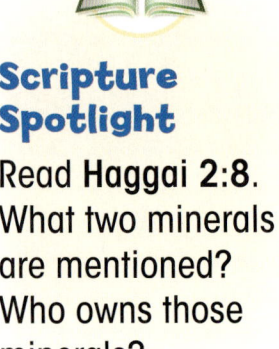

There are many kinds of minerals.

What do minerals have to do with rocks? A **rock** is a natural solid made from minerals. Like minerals, rocks are nonliving objects.

Rocks are found all over Earth because Earth is made of layers of rock. There is melted rock inside Earth. Some rocks form when the melted rock cools. Other rocks form from small pieces of rock that are stuck together. Rocks can also be changed by heat and pressure.

Think About It

Why would there be no rocks if there were no minerals?

Math in Science

Carlos has a rock collection. Tina gave him two more rocks. One has a mass of 8 grams. The other rock has a mass of 6 grams. The total mass of the collection is 37 grams. What was the original mass of Carlos' collection?

Granite is a type of rock. Granite contains mainly quartz and feldspar, mixed with other minerals. You can see some of the minerals that make it up.

feldspar

mica

quartz

hornblende

Different Kinds of Rocks Explain

One way rocks are classified is based on how they form.

Igneous rocks form when melted rock cools and becomes hard. *Igneous* means "from fire." These rocks are often found near volcanoes. Basalt, granite, and obsidian are examples.

Types of Igneous Rock		
Basalt		Basalt is the most common igneous rock. It forms when lava from volcanoes cools very quickly.
Granite		Granite is very strong and durable. Granite forms when melted rock found underground cools very slowly.
Obsidian		Obsidian rock is often called volcanic glass. It is formed when lava cools very rapidly.

Sedimentary rocks form when bits of broken rock, soil, and shells are pressed together. **Sand** is a loose mixture of pieces of broken rock and other solid material.

❓ What clue do you see that this piece of sandstone is a sedimentary rock?

Types of Sedimentary Rocks		
Sandstone		Sandstone is composed mainly of sand mixed with particles of minerals and fragments of rock.
Limestone		Limestone is mainly made up of the mineral calcite. It often forms in shallow, calm waters.
Shale		Shale is a fine, layered rock that is formed from the pressing together of clay and other small particles, or silt or mud.

Explore-a-Lab
Structured Inquiry

❓ **What can you observe about a rock by using your sense of touch?**

Close your eyes and select a rock. Notice how it feels and choose five words to describe it. Does the rock look the way you thought it would?

Think About It

Why do scientists believe metamorphic rocks form deep inside Earth?

Metamorphic rocks form when heat and pressure change older rock into another kind of rock.

Metamorphic rocks form deep inside Earth, when buried rocks are squeezed and folded. This kind of change often occurs during mountain building. The minerals in these rocks sometimes separate into bands that you can see. They may have swirling patterns caused by the pressure or by melting.

Marble

Limestone

🔍 Compare this piece of marble with the sedimentary rock it comes from. How are they alike? How are they different?

Using Minerals and Rocks Explain

You use minerals every day. Minerals are found in the chips that run video games and computers. They are also found in microwave ovens and satellites.

There are even minerals in your toothpaste if it has fluorite! Colorful and rare minerals are used for rings, watches, and other jewelry.

Scripture Spotlight

Read **Revelation 21:18–21**. It describes a vision of what the New Jerusalem will look like. How are rocks and minerals used?

Think About It

Look around your classroom or home. Name two uses for rocks or minerals that are not described in the text.

Rocks are used for buildings, statues, and roads. People use rocks to decorate their yards and for artwork.

An *ore* is a rock used to obtain minerals or metals. Mines are dug to obtain ores. Most metals come from these rocks. For example, we obtain aluminum from a rock called bauxite (BAWKS•eyt). Metals are used in cars, airplanes, and pots and pans.

Bauxite

People carve statues out of some kinds of rock. This statue is made of marble.

Make a Connection Extend

Write a paragraph that compares and contrasts how rocks were used in the past with how they are used today.

Lesson Review Assess/Reflect

Summary: What are rocks and minerals? Minerals are natural solids and are the same all the way through. Rocks are made from minerals. Rocks can be classified into three groups based on how they form. Rocks and minerals have a variety of uses.

1. **Graphic Organizer** Make a chart to tell what you learned about minerals and rocks.

2. **Vocabulary** How are rocks and minerals alike?

3. **Test Prep** Which sentence best describes how sedimentary rocks form?
    A. Melted rock cools and becomes hard.
    B. Bits of rock, soil, and shells are pressed together in layers.
    C. Older rocks are changed by heat and pressure.
    D. Rocks break apart and are sorted by size.

4. How would your life be different without rocks or minerals?

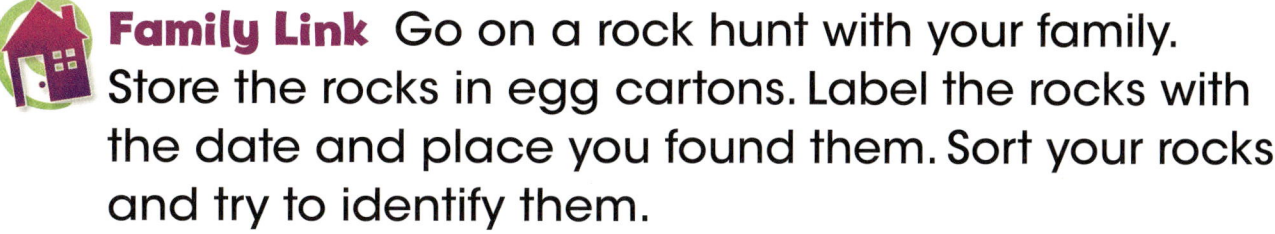 **Family Link** Go on a rock hunt with your family. Store the rocks in egg cartons. Label the rocks with the date and place you found them. Sort your rocks and try to identify them.

Lesson 3

Vocabulary
weathering p. 238
erosion p. 238
earthquake p. 241
volcano p. 244

Find out what these words mean as you study this lesson.

Essential Question

How Does Earth's Surface Change?

Engage

Get Ready to Learn What causes changes in Earth's surface? Earthquakes cause cracks to form. Flowing water wears away layers of rock. Wind moves sand and bits of dirt to other places.

Try This! How does the size of an object affect how far the wind moves it? Using powder, sand, and pebbles, blow on each material with a straw using the same strength. Which substance travels the farthest?

Structured Inquiry — Discover

Record your work for this inquiry. Your teacher may also assign the related Guided Inquiry.

Water Changes Land
How does water change the shape of the land?

Your Group Needs
- soil
- wood blocks
- large plastic shoebox
- watering can and water

Step 1 Make a soil "mountain" in one half of a plastic shoebox. Place a block under the end that has the soil.

Step 2 Slowly pour the water over the soil.

Step 3 **Observe** what happened to the soil. **Observe** the color of the water.

Step 4 Draw a picture to show what happened. **Communicate** your results with other groups.

Create Explanations

1. How does water change the shape of the land?
2. What would happen if the soil was held together by plants, such as grass?

Erosion Explain

Wind, water, and ice break large rocks into smaller pieces. This breaking up of rock is **weathering**. Smaller pieces of rock are easier to move. The movement of rocks and soil is **erosion**. Wind and flowing water are the two main causes of erosion.

Water moves soil and the other products of weathering when it flows over land. The faster water flows, the more material it can carry. When it stops flowing, water builds up landforms because it drops the material it carries.

The water in this river is wearing away the river's bank.

? Why does the water turn brown?

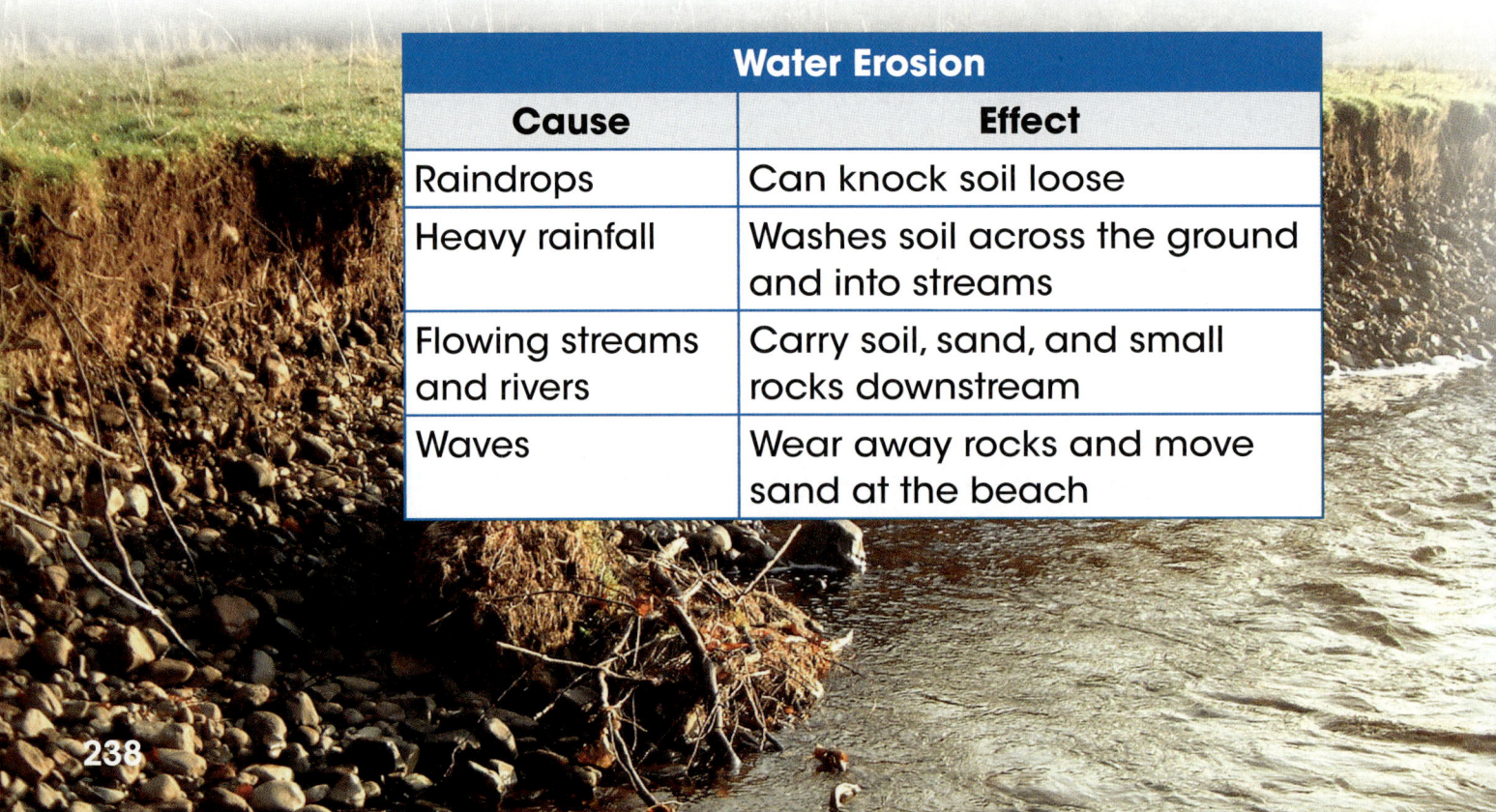

Water Erosion	
Cause	**Effect**
Raindrops	Can knock soil loose
Heavy rainfall	Washes soil across the ground and into streams
Flowing streams and rivers	Carry soil, sand, and small rocks downstream
Waves	Wear away rocks and move sand at the beach

During the Genesis Flood, Earth was covered with water. All that water must have caused many changes, so the world looked very different when Noah and his family left the ark. New valleys, canyons, mountains, and other landforms must have been formed.

We see layers of rock, mountains, canyons, and other evidence today that may have been formed during the Flood. Rocks made out of sediment are found all over the world and commonly appear to have formed underwater. People who don't believe the Bible explain sedimentary rocks by saying they formed over millions of years. Try to find some sedimentary rock layers and look at them yourself. Do the layers look as if they were eroded by wind and water over a long period of time? Did animals dig up the layers before they turned into stone? What do you think? Did they form over millions of years, or could they have been formed as the result of the Genesis Flood?

Faith Connection

In Genesis, the story of Noah's Flood is recorded. Many landforms we see today provide evidence of this Flood.

Check out your *Science Journal* for a Structured Inquiry to see how the Genesis Flood affected land.

Discover

Think About It

How does erosion change Earth's surface?

Water is not the only thing that erodes land. Wind and gravity also cause erosion. Wind erosion happens when wind picks up sand and soil. Sand dunes are landforms made by wind erosion. Places with low rainfall and strong wind every day have more wind erosion.

Gravity is the force that keeps things on the ground. It also causes erosion. Gravity pulls soil and rocks down mountains and hills. When large amounts of rock and dirt slide down quickly, it is a *landslide.*

Math in Science

In January, there were 21 landslides. There were 14 in February, 17 in March, and 12 in April. Make a bar graph to display this data. Write two sentences about the data. Why do you think the numbers are higher in January and March?

This small landslide covered part of a road. Large landslides can be dangerous, covering entire towns.

Earthquakes Explain

Have you ever felt the ground shake under you? An **earthquake** is the movement of Earth's surface.

Earth has three main layers: the crust, the mantle, and the core. The *core* is at Earth's center. The *mantle* is the middle layer. The *crust* is the outside layer, at or near Earth's surface. It is made of huge plates of rock that move. Sometimes the plates stick, and energy builds up. When the energy releases, the plates of rock slip past each other. This can cause an earthquake.

Scripture Spotlight

Read **Acts 16:26**. What effects did the earthquake have?

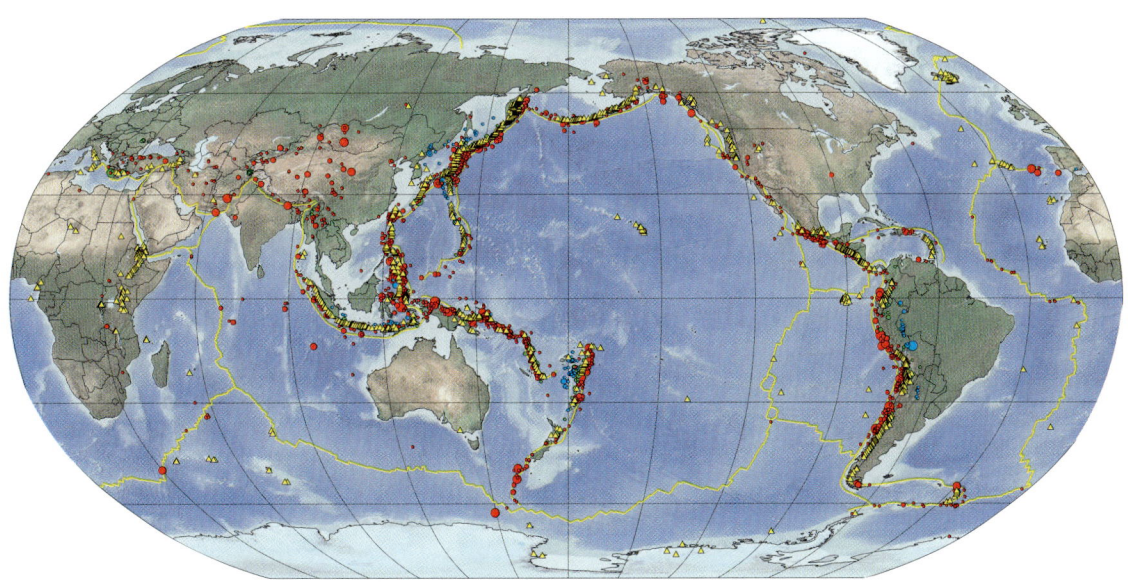

This map shows where there have been strong earthquakes.

Can you tell from this map where there are plates moving past each other?

Strong earthquakes can damage buildings.

Millions of earthquakes happen each year. Many are too small to notice. Strong earthquakes can change Earth's surface. They can make the ground uneven and can cause cracks, called *fissures*, to form. Earthquakes may also lead to floods, landslides, fires, and other natural disasters.

In 1812, a powerful earthquake made parts of the Mississippi River run backward for a short time. Islands in the river disappeared. It created new waterfalls and several large lakes.

When the huge rock plates of Earth's crust push into each other, they may crinkle, or be pushed up, forming mountains. In all of these ways, earthquakes have the power to change the surface of Earth.

Think About It

What happens when there is an earthquake underwater?

Explore-a-Lab

Structured Inquiry

? **How can you model the movements that cause earthquakes?**

Gather two small books. Put the books together by overlapping the pages so that the first page of one book overlaps the first page of the other book. Continue to do this until you have about 30 overlapping pages. Now try to pull the books apart. Is this easy to do? It takes a lot of energy to pull the books apart. How does this model how much energy is needed to make the huge rock plates slide past each other?

Volcanoes Explain

Think About It

What are the effects of volcanoes?

A **volcano** is an opening in Earth's surface from which gas, volcanic ash, and melted rock called *lava* erupt. When volcanoes erupt, hot gas shoots clouds of ash into the air. They may also shoot rocks and lava into the air. Lava from eruptions flows down volcanoes, forming new rocks. These materials build up to form the cones of volcanic mountains. During eruptions, ash and lava may kill plants and animals, but afterward they form fertile land for plants to grow on.

Lava is coming out of this volcano.

❓ What will the lava become when it cools?

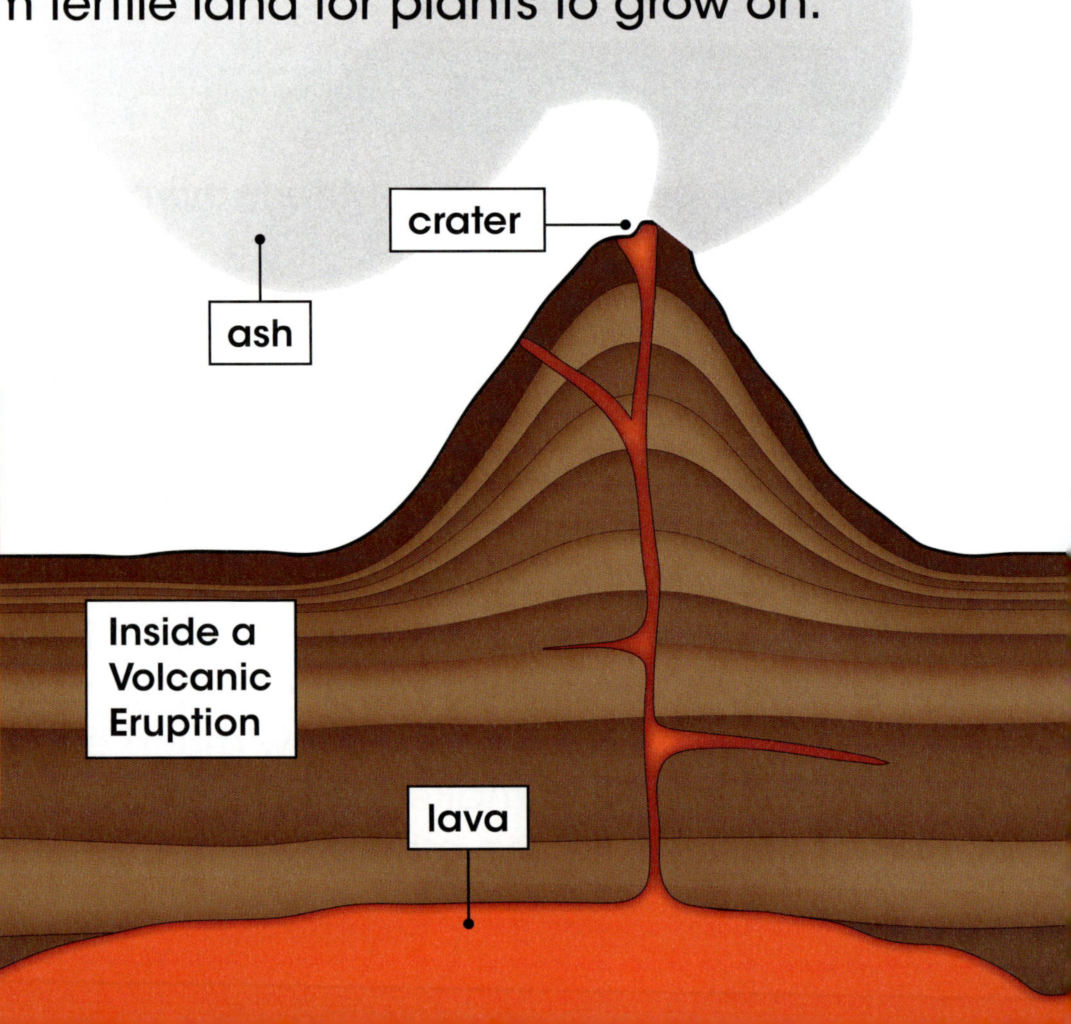

ash

crater

Inside a Volcanic Eruption

lava

Make a Connection **Extend**

Gather information about a real volcano. Then make a model of your volcano. Share the model volcano with your classmates.

Lesson Review **Assess/Reflect**

Summary: How does Earth's surface change? Landforms change. The Flood created many of the landforms on Earth today. Weathering, erosion, earthquakes, and volcanoes change landforms in many ways.

1. **Graphic Organizer** Make a main idea and details chart to tell about changes to Earth's surface.

2. **Vocabulary** What are some differences between an <mark>earthquake</mark> and a <mark>volcano</mark>?

3. **Test Prep** Which item is an effect of water erosion?
   A. More fertile land can be created.
   B. Mountains can be formed.
   C. Rocks can be washed away and sand moved at the beach.
   D. The crust may slip suddenly.

4. What is an example of erosion where you live? What is causing the erosion?

5. How could the Flood have affected landforms?

Family Link Talk with your family about what to do during and after a natural disaster. Make a family plan.

245

Lesson 4

Vocabulary

fossil　　p. 248
dinosaur　p. 250
extinct　　p. 252

Find out what these words mean as you study this lesson.

Essential Question

What Can We Learn from Fossils?

Engage

Get Ready to Learn What questions do scientists ask about fossils? Where do they look for fossils? What can scientists learn from fossils? A scientist uses a brush to clean soil from a rock. She uncovers a shape in the rock. It looks like part of an animal. What part is it? What did it belong to? How did it live?

Try This! What would you do if you found a fossil? What would be your first question? Get a fossil or picture of a fossil from your teacher. Look at it carefully. How do you know that it is a fossil and not just a rock? Draw what you think the organism looked like when it was alive.

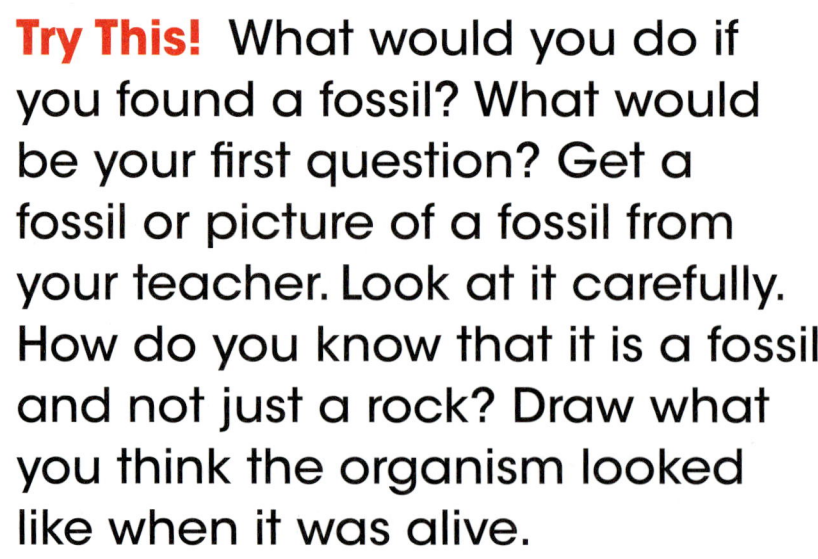

Structured Inquiry — Discover

Record your work for this inquiry. Your teacher may also assign the related Guided Inquiry.

Tracking Clues

What can you learn about an object from the tracks it makes?

Your Group Needs
- flour
- black paper
- three wind-up toys or three model cars

Step 1 Spread a thin layer of flour on a sheet of black paper.

Step 2 Use wind-up toys or model cars to make tracks in the flour. **Observe** and draw the tracks made by each object.

Step 3 **Investigate** another group's tracks. What can you **infer** about the objects that made the tracks?

Step 4 Ask the group if you were correct.

Create Explanations

1. What can you learn about an object from the tracks it makes?

2. Are there different ways of interpreting the clues? Explain.

3. What other objects could you use to make tracks so you could study them more easily?

Fossils Explain

Scientists want to learn about life on Earth long ago, so they dig for fossils. A **fossil** is what is left from a living thing that died long ago.

Most fossils are found in layers of rocks. Most form after a plant or an animal dies and is covered rapidly with dirt and sand. Layers of dirt and sand turn to rock over many years. No one knows for sure how fossils got where they are found. All scientists who study fossils try to explain what they find. Many scientists who are Christians do this too, but they use what the Bible says along with the facts they find.

? What kind of animal do you think made this fossil?

Not all Christian scientists agree about how or why things happened. But they do know that scientific ideas change all the time and God's Word never changes. These scientists do not let the current limits of science understanding affect their belief in the Bible.

Many Christians believe that most fossils and layers of rock were formed by the Flood. The Bible says that the Flood killed all land animals that were not on the ark. It probably also killed many sea animals, plants, and other living things. These organisms buried by mud during the Flood could be the fossils we find today.

Animal fossils include bones, teeth, feathers, and shells. These may be replaced by stone. Marks left by animals, such as tracks, are another kind of fossil. Plant fossils include leaves, twigs, and flowers.

Think About It

How are all fossils alike?

This fern fossil was found in West Virginia. It looks like it was made from a fern similar to a golden tree fern found in New Zealand.

Dinosaurs Explain

Scripture Spotlight

Read **Job 40:15**. What do you think it describes?

Dinosaurs were reptiles that are now extinct. Most dinosaurs were normal-sized creatures and huge ones were the exception, just as elephants and giraffes are exceptional today. Dinosaurs appear to have been mostly vegetarian and are not the largest creatures known to exist. Scientists learn about dinosaurs from fossils. Fossils tell scientists dinosaurs' lengths and the shape of their teeth. Scientists infer the dinosaurs' weights, how they moved, and what they ate. Their colors are only a guess. As scientists gather evidence, their views of dinosaurs change.

Explore-a-Lab — Guided Inquiry

How do the sizes of some dinosaurs compare?

The length of an iguanodon was about 9 m (30 ft). The length of a velociraptor was about 3 m (10 ft). A compsognathus was a meter or less in length. With a partner, decide how to measure these lengths and display them side by side.

Name	Speed and Number of Legs They Walked On	Teeth and Food	Unusual Features
Apatosaurus	slow; 4 legs	peg-like; plants	was one of the largest dinosaurs
Spinosaurus	fast; 2 legs	sharp; meat	had a sail-like fin on its back
Triceratops	slow; 4 legs	teeth for cutting and grinding on sides and back; plants	had 3 horns and a bony plate on its head
Velociraptor	fast; 2 legs	sharp; meat	had deadly claws and fast-moving legs
Stegosaurus	slow; 4 legs	small teeth with bumps; plants	had spikes on its tail and plates on its back
Carnotaurus	slow; 2 legs	sharp; meat	had two bull-like horns near its eyes

Check out your *Science Journal* for a Structured Inquiry to find out more about dinosaurs and how we use fossils to learn about past life.
Discover

Think About It

How are the teeth of meat-eaters different from the teeth of plant-eaters?

The End of Dinosaurs Explain

Groups of animals and plants that have all died are **extinct**. They are gone forever. Dinosaurs are extinct. Many other animals and plants became extinct at the same time dinosaurs died out. No one is sure what caused so many organisms to become extinct. Some scientists think a meteorite, or rock from space, hit Earth. Others think a huge volcano erupted. Some believe these events happened at the same time!

Genesis 7 tells about violent events during the Flood. Could these events have caused the extinction of the dinosaurs? Many Christians believe the Flood produced many fossils, including dinosaurs, that we find today. Christian scientists use the clues given in the Bible to interpret what they learn from fossils.

Faith Connection

Many Christians believe that fossil evidence that scientists find supports the story of the Flood found in the Bible. They believe the Bible is true and that this evidence shows that Earth is not as old as many believe.

Think About It

Why is no one sure what caused dinosaurs to become extinct?

The Genesis Flood may explain why dinosaurs are extinct.

Make a Connection Extend

Design five dinosaur trading cards. Draw and color pictures of dinosaurs on the front side, along with their names. On the back write four facts about the dinosaurs. Trade with classmates and learn about their dinosaurs, too.

Lesson Review Assess/Reflect

Summary: What can we learn from fossils? Fossils are evidence of things that lived long ago. Some fossils are found in rock layers. Scientists use them to learn what Earth was once like.

1. **Graphic Organizer** Make an idea web. Tell what we can learn from fossils.

2. **Vocabulary** What is an ==extinct== animal?

3. **Test Prep** Which is the first step in a fossil being formed?
   A. The layers change to rock.
   B. The animal dies.
   C. A scientist finds its bones.
   D. A scientist brushes off soil.

4. What can scientists learn by studying fossils?

5. What clues does the Bible give us about the formation of fossils?

 **Family Link** Go on a city fossil hunt. Look for fossils in the rocks used to build public buildings. Draw pictures or take photos.

Careers in Science
Extend

Paleontologist

A paleontologist studies fossils. A fossil is evidence of a living thing from long ago.

Paleontologists use shovels, brushes, and drills to gather rocks that contain fossils. They carefully chip away at the rock to expose fossils.

By studying fossils, paleontologists can learn about what Earth was like a long time ago.

Geologist

Geologists also study rocks. They study Earth and everything about it. They learn about how Earth formed and how Earth is changing.

Geologists also study fossil fuels. Oil, coal, and natural gas are fossil fuels.

Geologists learn about Earth to help people. They work to predict events such as landslides and volcanic eruptions. This can help keep people safe.

Concept Check

1. Why do paleontologists need shovels, brushes, and drills to do their work?
2. How are the jobs of geologists and paleontologists the same? How are they different?

Science and Technology

Extend

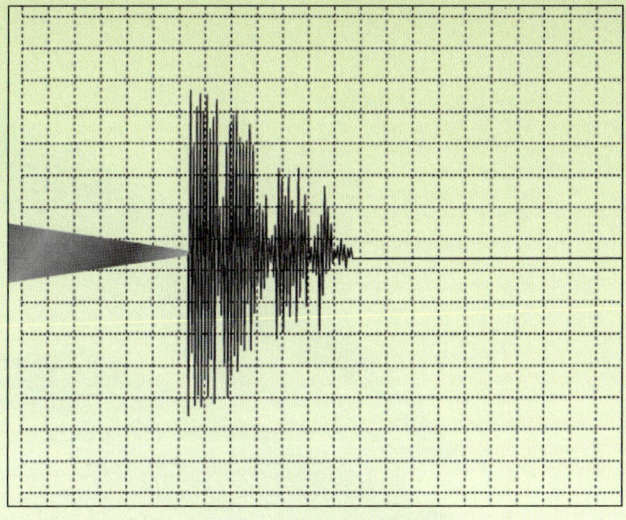

Seismograph

A seismograph is a tool that records the strength of earthquakes. It records the movement of Earth during an earthquake.

It draws lines on paper to show how much Earth shakes. Longer lines show more shaking. Shorter lines show less shaking. These measurements help scientists learn about earthquakes.

Weather Balloon

Almost 900 weather balloons are released two times every day. The balloons are filled with gas that makes them rise in the air.

Each balloon carries scientific tools. The tools record weather information such as the temperature. They send the information back to scientists. The scientists use the data to forecast the weather.

 **Concept Check**

1. Why would scientists put a seismograph in a stone building?
2. Why do you think it is important to release all the weather balloons at the same time?

Chapter 7
Weather and Seasons

Lesson 1
How Is the Weather Predicted? ..258

Lesson 2
What Is the Water Cycle? 268

Lesson 3
What Causes the Seasons? 276

Scripture Spotlight

God created Earth as a perfect home for people. We can only imagine the perfect weather in God's perfect world. The Bible describes many weather events, such as the Flood and storms. You will read the following Bible passages in this chapter.

Job 38:33–35 (p. 262)   Ecclesiastes 1:7 (p. 273)
Psalm 63:1 (p. 270)

The Big Idea

The weather in our world is always changing. But God does not change. He helps us appreciate each season.

❓ During which season does it rain the most?

Lesson 1

Vocabulary

anemometer p. 263

weather map p. 263

weather satellite p. 265

thunderstorm p. 266

tornado p. 266

hurricane p. 266

Find out what these words mean as you study this lesson.

? Essential Question

How Is the Weather Predicted?　Engage

Get Ready to Learn Which words tell about the weather where you live today? Is it rainy and cool? Maybe it is sunny and warm. Is the wind blowing, or is it calm outside? Each of these words describes the weather.

Scientists who study weather are *meteorologists*. They forecast, or predict, what the weather will be like.

Try This! What information can you find out from a weather map? Look in a newspaper or on the Internet for a weather map. Observe the map. Describe what you see. What are some of the predictions that the meteorologist made?

Structured Inquiry Discover

Record your work for this inquiry. Your teacher may also assign the related Guided Inquiry.

Weather Watch

How does the weather where you live change or stay the same?

Your Group Needs
- pencil and paper
- thermometer, rain gauge, meterstick, barometer, anemometer, or wind vane

Step 1 Gather data about the weather for three days. **Observe** cloud cover and wind. **Measure** the temperature and any rain or snow. Use all the weather tools your teacher has.

Step 2 Make a chart to **record data**. Draw or write what you observe every day.

Step 3 Compare your observations with those of a classmate. How are they the same or different?

Create Explanations

1. How does the weather where you live change or stay the same?
2. How do you think the weather where you live will change in three months?

259

Weather Reports Explain

Have you ever listened to a weather report? It tells about wind, clouds, and temperature. These are parts of *weather*, or the conditions of the air around you. The weather may change a lot in just a few hours. In some places, the weather does not change much at all.

The weather is nice. The skies are clear. It is sunny and warm. There is a gentle breeze.

When you go outside, you know if the air is warm or cold. You can feel the air temperature. Sunshine warms Earth's surface and air temperature rises during the day. The Sun warms the daytime air. Then the Sun sets in the evening. The air temperature usually goes down.

Think About It

How does the Sun affect weather?

If you walk outside and your hair gets blown, you know it's a windy day. Wind is moving air. It pushes things. A breeze moves things gently. Other winds are so strong that they may cause trees to snap. Winds bring weather changes, sometimes including storms.

Scripture Spotlight

Read **Job 38:33–35**. It explains that God has dominion over Earth. Weather follows God's natural laws. People cannot control the weather.

Suppose the day starts with clear skies. Then clouds start to form. The sky changes to partly cloudy. Later it becomes mostly cloudy.

Clouds are made of very small drops of water or ice. If the drops get too heavy, they will fall. They fall as rain when it is warm. It may snow if the air temperature is below 0 °C (32 °F).

What can you tell about the weather in this photograph?

Weather Tools Explain

Meteorologists use tools to measure weather. A thermometer shows the temperature. An **anemometer** measures the wind's speed. A wind vane shows the wind's direction. A rain gauge tells how much rain fell. A barometer measures changes in air pressure.

A **weather map** shows weather information for a large area. It shows how warm or cold the air is. It shows where it's raining and where it's sunny. Weather maps are always changing because the weather is constantly changing.

Check out your *Science Journal* for a Guided Inquiry about weather maps. Discover

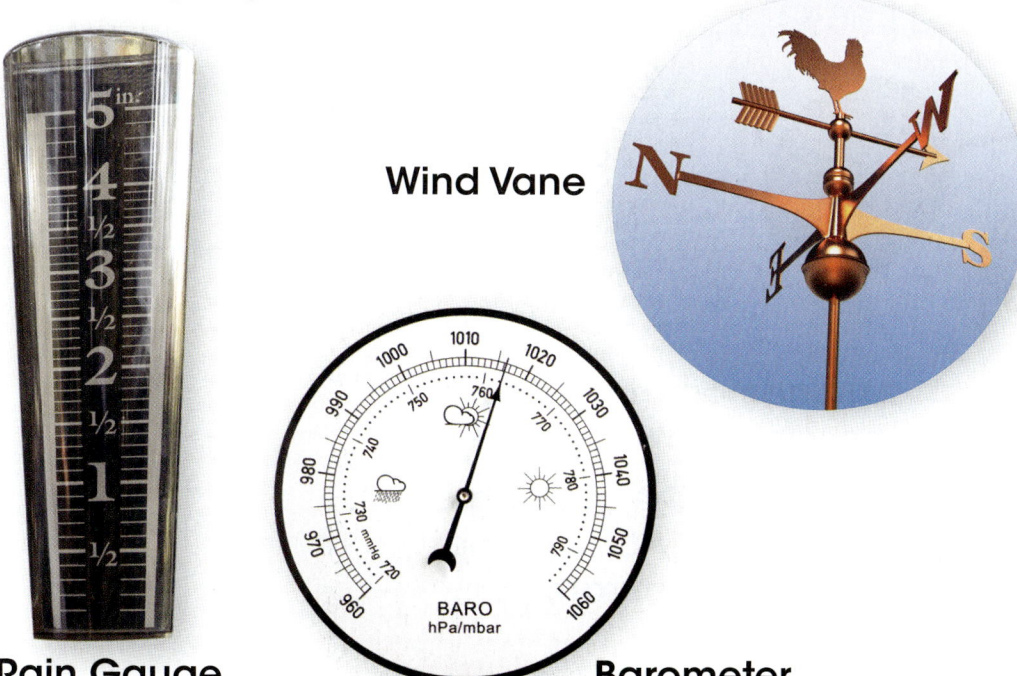

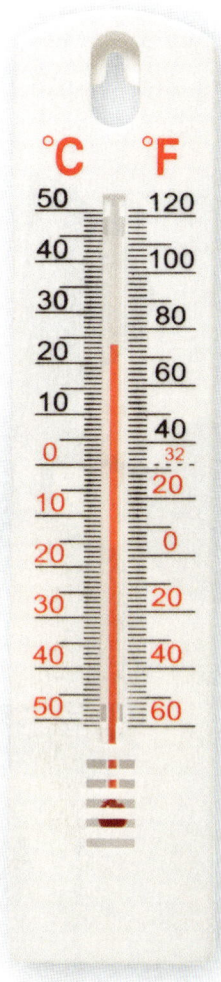

Rain Gauge   **Wind Vane**   **Barometer**   **Thermometer**

263

Think About It

Suppose a meteorologist was unable to use radar to forecast a severe storm. What might happen to people in the area of the storm?

Have you ever seen a weather report that uses radar? Radar measures the direction, speed, and amount of snow or rain that is falling. It helps weather forecasters find and track storms. Radar is used to warn people about storms.

Math in Science

Look at the three wind speeds below. Put them in the correct row in the table.

Wind Speeds: 3 km/hr (2 mi/hr), 10 km/hr (6 mi/hr), 30 km/hr (18 mi/hr)

Anemometer Data	
How fast the anemometer is spinning	Wind speed (km/hr)
Very fast	
Fast	
Slow	

An anemometer spins when the wind blows.

Why might the reading of an anemometer placed next to a tree be inaccurate?

A *satellite* is an object in space that orbits around a larger body, such as a planet or star. ==Weather satellites== are human-made objects that travel around Earth. Their instruments give weather forecasters information they can use to predict weather.

Think About It

How do weather maps show storms?

Explore-a-Lab
Structured Inquiry

? What do you think the weather is like in your state or province?

Observe the map. It has labels that tell about wind and storm conditions. Information found on weather maps comes from ground observations, radar, or satellites.

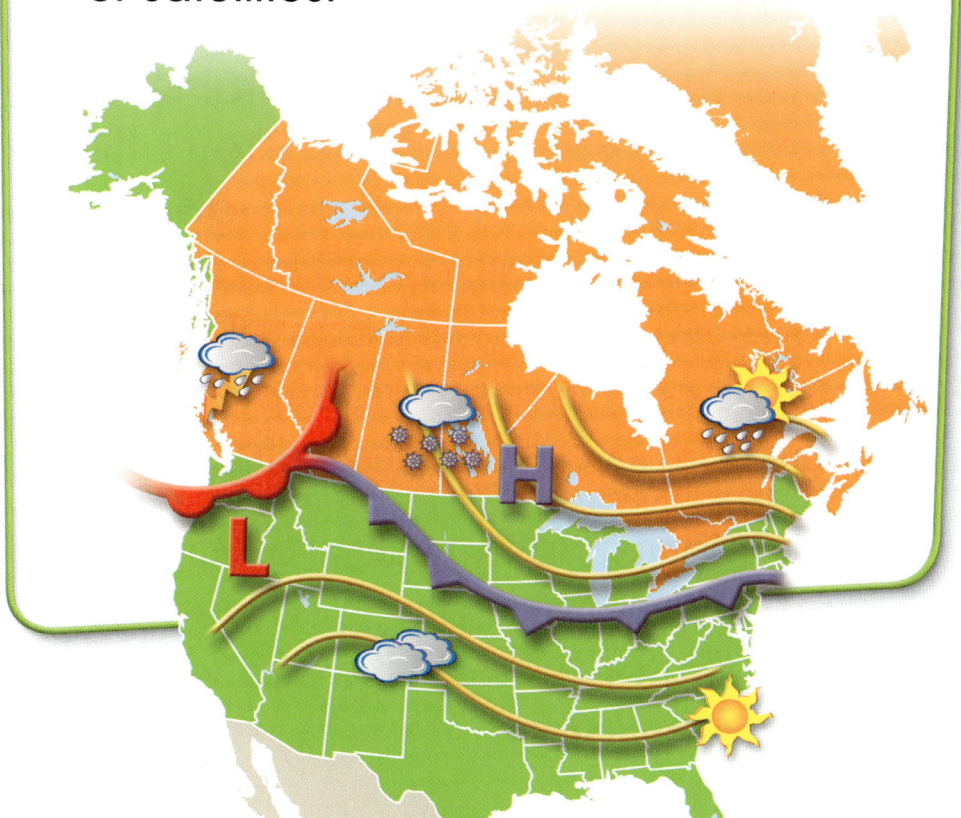

Weather Danger Explain

Thunderstorm

Tornado

Hurricane

Weather can be frightening. It is always best to respect storms and follow the warnings about being safe.

A **thunderstorm** has heavy rains, lightning, and thunder. Lightning may strike objects. Heavy rain may cause floods. Thunderstorms develop from clouds that grow very tall.

A powerful windstorm that may form within a thunderstorm is a **tornado**. It forms a funnel shape because its winds spin faster and faster. The strong winds lift even very heavy objects.

Hurricanes are huge powerful storms that form over warm waters. They often cover large areas and bring high, swirling winds, floods, and tornadoes to inland areas as well as coastal areas. Hurricanes can cause widespread damage to the areas they affect.

Meteorologists use radar to track storms. They give warnings so people can find shelter or leave areas where storms may happen.

Think About It
How are thunderstorms and hurricanes alike?

Make a Connection Extend

Choose one of the storms described in the lesson. Use library or Internet sources to gather information about how to stay safe during that storm. Make a poster to show others what to do.

Lesson Review Assess/Reflect

Summary: How is the weather predicted? Temperature, wind, and sky conditions are common weather features. Anemometers, rain gauges, thermometers, radar, and satellites are weather prediction tools. Weather maps show what current weather is like. Thunderstorms, tornadoes, and hurricanes are powerful storms.

1. **Graphic Organizer** Make a chart. Show details you learned about types of weather.

2. **Vocabulary** How is a tornado different from a hurricane?

3. **Test Prep** Which tool would a meteorologist use to measure wind speed?
   - A. thermometer
   - B. anemometer
   - C. wind vane
   - D. satellite

4. How do radar and satellites help meteorologists?

Family Link Talk to family members about storms that have occurred in and around your community. Write sentences to describe one of these storms. Share them with classmates.

Lesson 2

Vocabulary

water vapor   p. 270
evaporate   p. 270
condense   p. 271
water cycle   p. 272
precipitation   p. 273
hail   p. 274

Find out what these words mean as you study this lesson.

Essential Question

What Is the Water Cycle? Engage

Get Ready to Learn Why is water important to you? How have you used water today? Without water, you would not be able to live. Other animals and plants need water, too. Think about rain and snow. What do you think water has to do with our weather?

Water has three forms—liquid, solid, and gas. It changes form when heat is added or taken away.

Try This! Why does water form on the outside of a glass filled with water? Put ice cubes inside a glass. Fill the glass with water and stir. Is the glass leaking? Talk with a partner about why the water formed on the glass. Talk about where the water came from.

268

Structured Inquiry — Discover

Record your work for this inquiry. Your teacher may also assign the related Guided Inquiry.

How Clouds Form

How can a model help you explain how clouds form?

Your Group Needs
- two glass jars
- warm water and cold water
- clear plastic wrap
- two rubber bands
- four ice cubes

Step 1 Fill one jar halfway with warm water. Fill the other jar halfway with cold water.

Step 2 Cover the opening of each jar with clear plastic wrap. Put a rubber band around the plastic wrap to hold it in place. The jars will **model** what happens in the air.

Step 3 Place two ice cubes on the plastic wrap on each jar.

Step 4 **Observe** what happens for five minutes. **Record** your observations.

Create Explanations

1. How can a model help you explain how clouds form?

2. What happened when the plastic wrap and ice were put on the jars?

Water Changes Explain

Scripture Spotlight

Read **Psalm 63:1**. Compare the land described to the photograph on this page.

If you could look down at Earth from space, it would look blue. That is because water covers much of Earth. Oceans, rivers, and lakes hold water. But you might be surprised to know that air holds water, too. You cannot see it because it is in the form of a gas. Water in the form of a gas is **water vapor**.

Have you ever left a bucket of water outside? It lasts until the Sun's energy changes the water from a liquid to a gas. Some of the liquid water will **evaporate**, or change into water vapor. Most liquids change into gas form when heated.

You cannot see water vapor. But it is in the air.

This puddle is evaporating. Some of the liquid water is turning into water vapor.

270

Explore-a-Lab
Structured Inquiry

 What causes water to evaporate?

Fill two flat shallow pans with the same amount of water. Place one pan in the shade. Place the other pan in the sunshine. Which pan evaporated faster? Why do you think this happened?

Remember when you filled a glass with water and ice? The air around the glass was cooler than the room's air. Cool air cannot hold as much water vapor as warm air. So some of the water vapor comes out of the air. The water vapor turns into liquid, or **condenses**. When water vapor is cooled, it condenses into a liquid.

Faith Connection

Water always follows God's natural laws. God's natural laws enabled scientists to learn how, when, and why water changes form.

Think About It

How is evaporation different from condensation?

This man is exhaling on a cold day. You can "see his breath." The cloud is made of water vapor from his lungs that is condensing into tiny droplets that you can see in the cold air.

271

The Water Cycle Explain

Faith Connection

God cares for us and knew we would need freshwater. He designed the water cycle so there would always be freshwater for people, plants, and animals on land to use.

Did you know that water is used over and over again? The water you use every day is thousands of years old! That means water is recycled. The moving of water from Earth's surface into the air and back again is the **water cycle**. Water in the water cycle must obey God's natural laws.

The Water Cycle

Study the diagram.

❓ What provides energy for the water cycle?

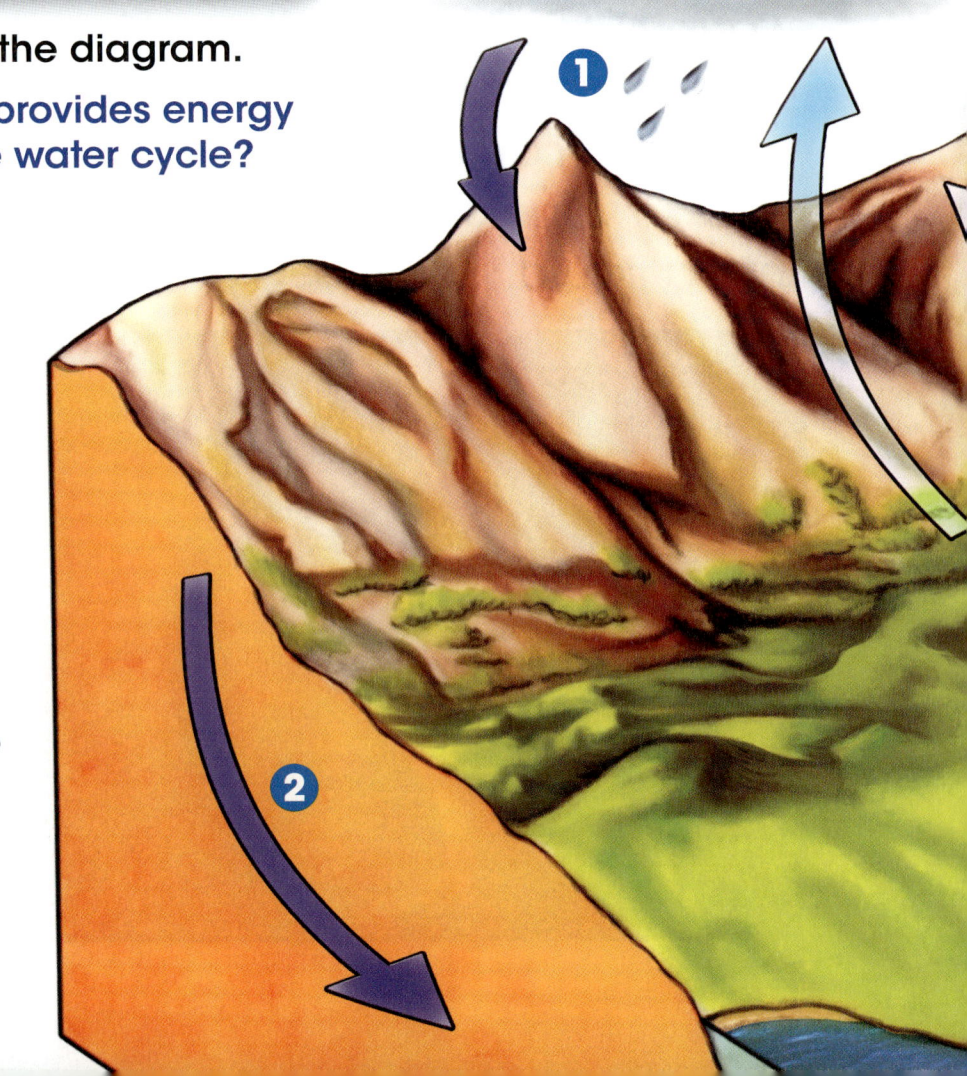

❶ Water drops and ice crystals in clouds become larger. Precipitation falls from the clouds.

❷ Precipitation falls to the ground and into bodies of water. Some soaks into the soil. It is used by plants and animals.

272

The water cycle needs energy from the Sun. The energy causes water on Earth's surface to evaporate. The water vapor condenses and then falls as precipitation. **Precipitation** is water that falls to Earth as rain, snow, sleet, or hail. Water moves over land, to streams, lakes, and rivers, and into oceans. The cycle continues.

Scripture Spotlight

Read **Ecclesiastes 1:7**. How does it relate to the water cycle?

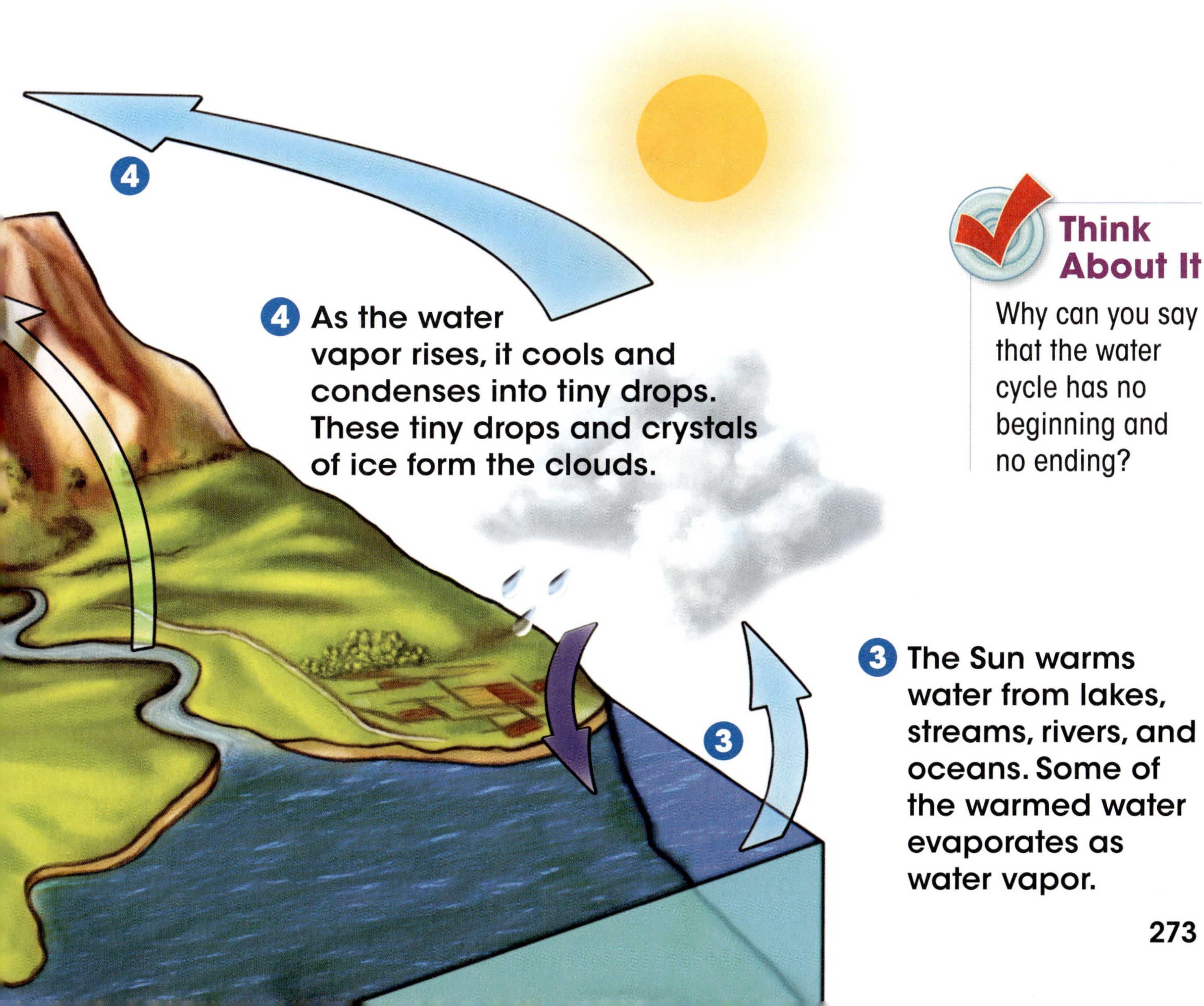

④ **As the water vapor rises, it cools and condenses into tiny drops. These tiny drops and crystals of ice form the clouds.**

Think About It

Why can you say that the water cycle has no beginning and no ending?

③ **The Sun warms water from lakes, streams, rivers, and oceans. Some of the warmed water evaporates as water vapor.**

Types of Precipitation Explain

Think About It

How are rain and snow alike and different?

All precipitation is water that falls from the sky. Rain is liquid water. Too much rain may cause flooding.

Snow is made of tiny ice crystals. It falls from clouds when the air is cold. Heavy snow with high winds is a blizzard.

snowflake

Hail may damage houses and cars.

A drop of rain could freeze as it falls and form ice. *Sleet* is precipitation that is tiny pellets of ice. **Hail** is precipitation that falls as large pellets of ice. Hail forms when a pellet of ice grows in size as it is blown around inside a cloud. One of the largest hailstones found was nearly the size of a soccer ball!

 **Math in Science**

Over two years, it rained 240 cm (94 in.) in Arkansas. It rained 210 cm (82.7 in.) in Maryland. How many more centimeters did it rain in Arkansas than Maryland? Use mental math.

Make a Connection Extend

Think about something you like to do when it rains or snows. Draw a picture of yourself doing it. Then write sentences describing what you like to do.

Lesson Review Assess/Reflect

Summary: What is the water cycle? The moving of water from Earth's surface into the air and back again is the water cycle. Water changes into different forms.

1. **Graphic Organizer** Use a circle graphic organizer to show how water moves through Earth's land, air, and water. Start with water in the ocean. Label each process the water goes through until it returns.

2. **Vocabulary** What is hail?

3. **Test Prep** Which is an example of water evaporating?
   A. a wet towel on a towel rack dries out
   B. a glass with droplets on the outside
   C. "seeing someone's breath"
   D. a window that fogs up

4. What would happen if precipitation did not evaporate?

5. How does God provide fresh water for living things?

Family Link With a family member, find how much water your family uses in an average day. Discuss with your family whether you should use more or less water each day, and why.

Lesson 3

Vocabulary

equator   p. 278
pole   p. 278
autumn   p. 279
orbit   p. 280

Find out what these words mean as you study this lesson.

Essential Question

What Causes the Seasons? Engage

Get Ready to Learn What are the four seasons? How do you know what season it is? How do living things act during each season?

In many places, the seasons bring temperature changes. What activities can you do when the weather becomes cooler in places like Michigan and Canada? What could you do in a place like Florida during a much warmer winter season?

Try This! How are the seasons different? Fold a sheet of paper into four sections. Draw a picture of yourself in each section showing some of the activities you do during each season. Share your pictures. Talk about what makes each season different.

Length of Days

How does the amount of daylight in winter compare to the amount of daylight in summer?

Your Group Needs
- pencil and paper

Step 1 Study the data below for Chicago.

Date	Sunrise	Sunset
March 20	7:00 A.M.	7:00 P.M.
June 21	5:15 A.M.	8:30 P.M.
September 23	6:45 A.M.	6:45 P.M.
December 22	7:15 A.M.	4:30 P.M.

Step 2 Use numbers to count the number of daylight hours for each of the four dates.

Step 3 Display the data in a bar graph.

Create Explanations

1. How does the amount of daylight in winter compare to the amount of daylight in summer?

2. Twice a year, the Sun shines directly on the equator. On which dates do you think this occurs? Why?

Four Seasons Explain

Think About It

If it is autumn in Earth's southern half, what season is it in Earth's northern half?

The **equator** is an imaginary line that runs around the middle of Earth. It divides Earth into a northern half and a southern half. The seasons are opposite in the two halves of Earth. When it is summer north of the equator, it is winter south of the equator. When it is winter north of the equator, it is summer south of the equator.

Another imaginary line, Earth's axis, goes through the North Pole and the South Pole. These **poles** are the two opposite points on the "top" and "bottom" of Earth. The axis is tilted.

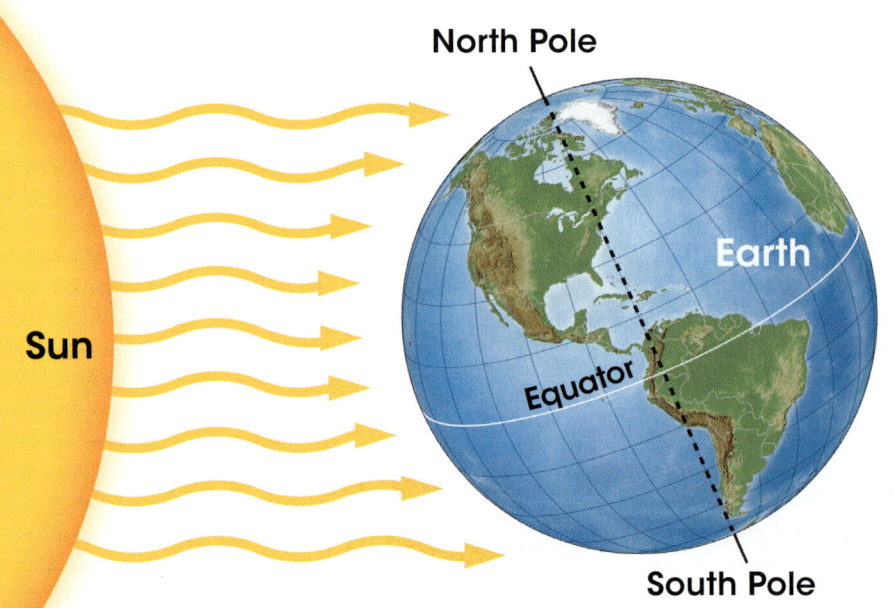

Earth's northern half is pointed toward the Sun. It is summer in North America.

At the same time, Earth's southern half is pointed away from the Sun. It is winter in South America.

In the northern half of Earth, summer has more daylight hours than winter. Spring and autumn have about the same number of daylight hours. **Autumn**, or fall, is the season after summer and before winter. Spring comes after winter and before summer.

Faith Connection

God made the Sun, the Moon, and the stars. They help people keep track of days, years, and the seasons.

Season in Earth's Northern Half	Daylight Hours	Where the Sun Shines More Directly
winter	less than 12	on the southern half
spring	about 12	equally on the northern and southern halves
summer	more than 12	on the northern half
autumn	about 12	equally on the northern and southern halves

Summer

Winter

The Sun's path changes a little each day. In winter the Sun is lower in the sky.

The Cause of Seasons [Explain]

Earth is shaped like a large ball. The Sun's rays hit Earth's round surface in different ways. Places that get direct rays have warmer temperatures. Places that get slanted rays have cooler temperatures.

Earth travels around the Sun one time every year. An orbit is the path an object takes as it moves around another object. As Earth travels around the Sun in its orbit, the seasons change. This is because Earth is tilted on its axis.

Explore-a-Lab
Directed Inquiry

 How does the sunlight hitting Earth change as Earth moves?

Look at the diagram of Earth's seasons. Use a ball to represent Earth and a flashlight for the Sun. Make a model that is similar to the diagram.

Earth's Seasons

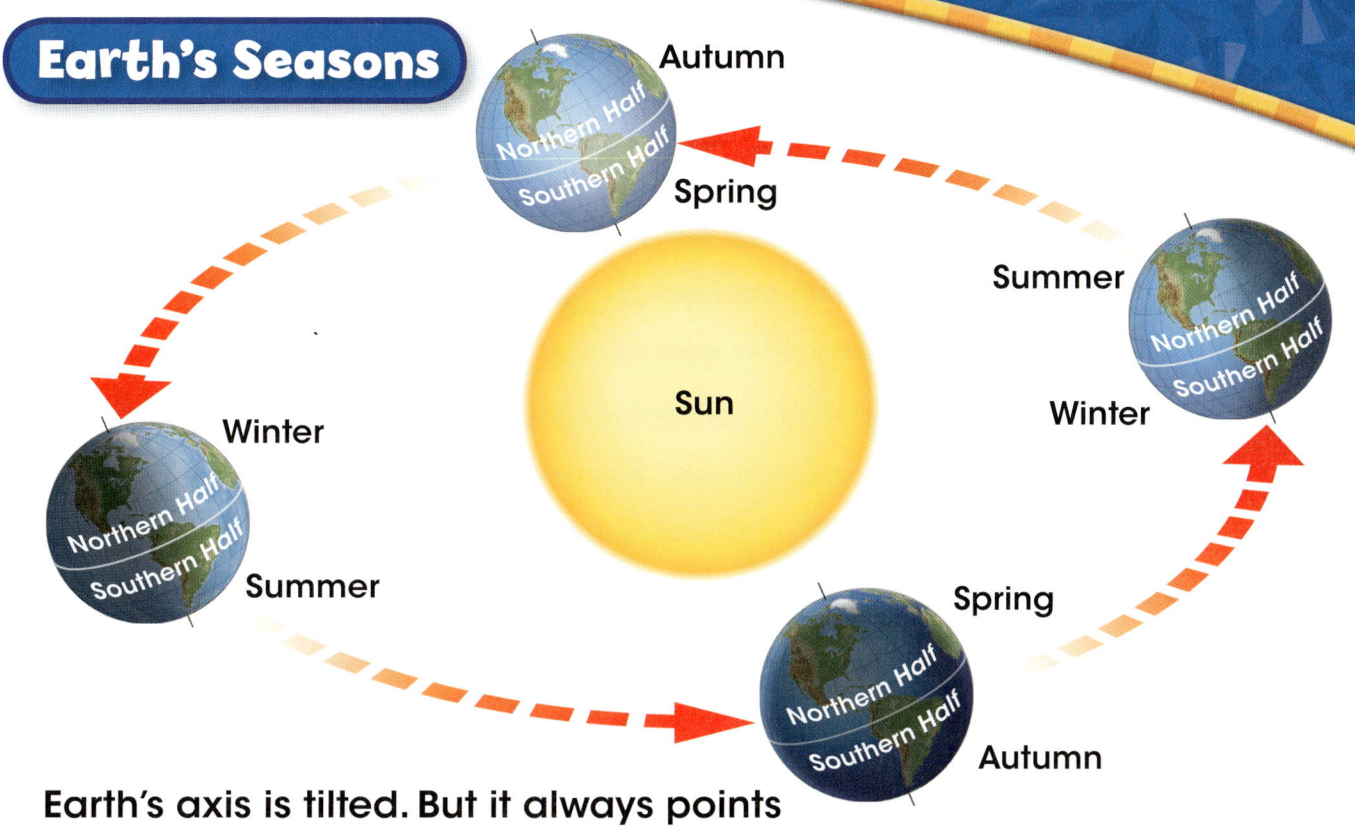

Earth's axis is tilted. But it always points in the same direction. This causes the seasons as Earth travels around the Sun.

Part of the year, the North Pole tilts in the Sun's direction. Earth's northern half gets direct sunlight, so it is summer. The South Pole tilts away from the Sun. The sunlight on the southern half is not direct. It is winter there.

In spring and autumn, neither pole is tilted in the Sun's direction. The northern and southern halves get the same amount of light. Days and nights are close to the same length. It is spring in one part and autumn in the other.

Think About It

What does Earth's orbit have to do with the seasons?

Seasons Affect Living Things Explain

Think About It

How do you know spring is a season for growth?

Winter

Spring

Summer

Autumn

During winter, you may wear warm clothing. Some animals leave their homes and go south to stay safe from the cold. Plants do not grow much. Many tree branches are bare.

When spring comes, many animals give birth. Flowers begin to bloom, and leaves grow. You no longer wear heavy clothing.

With summer, leaves turn green. Fruits and vegetables ripen. Many animals do much of their feeding and try to keep cool from the hot Sun.

During autumn, deciduous leaves change color and fall off trees. You might wear a jacket. Animals gather and store food for winter, and some migrate.

 **Math in Science**

In spring, Maria bought seeds for her garden that cost $6.99 and $11.20. How much did Maria spend?

Make a Connection Extend

Write about each season. Describe the temperature, how sunlight strikes Earth, and the length of the day. Describe your favorite activity in each season.

Lesson Review Assess/Reflect

Summary: What causes the seasons? As Earth orbits, the seasons change. Different parts of Earth get different amounts of sunlight at different times of the year.

1. **Graphic Organizer** Make a chart. Compare and contrast: the direction of Earth's axis, the temperature, and the length of day for each season in the northern half of Earth.

2. **Vocabulary** Where is the equator?

3. **Test Prep** Why does Earth have seasons?
   A. The Sun orbits Earth.
   B. Earth is closer to the Sun sometimes.
   C. Earth's axis is tilted.
   D. The Sun shines equally on all parts of Earth.

4. Why is it winter in the northern half of Earth when it is summer in the southern half of Earth?

5. Describe how seasonal changes affect living things.

Family Link Choose a season. Gather information about how living things change during the season and why. Make a booklet with your findings.

Careers in Science
Extend

Oceanographer

Oceanographers study how the ocean works. They also study living things in the ocean. They want to know how the ocean and living things work together.

Oceanographers study how the ocean affects Earth's climate and weather. They want to know how the ocean stores and releases heat. They study the tides and currents. They even study how light and sound travel through water.

Geophysicist

Geophysicists study Earth. They also study other planets and moons. Geophysicists study Earth's crust as well as the inside of Earth. They study Earth's ocean, too.

Geophysicists study Earth's atmosphere and weather patterns. They look at how the ocean affects Earth's climate.

Geophysicists help measure and map Earth. They also help find resources like oil, iron, and copper.

✓ Concept Check

1. What kinds of things do oceanographers study?
2. How could geophysicists be helpful when building a dam?

Science and Technology
Extend

Wind Turbines

Wind is a form of energy. Wind can be used to make other kinds of energy, like electricity.

Wind turbines change the wind energy into electricity. A wind turbine is a tall post that has blades at the top. A group of wind turbines is called a wind farm.

Wind turbines are installed in windy places. They can be installed on land or in the ocean. When wind blows, it pushes the blades of the wind turbine. The blades turn and generate electricity.

Aquarius Undersea Lab

Aquarius is an undersea lab. It is located in the Florida Keys. It sits on the ocean floor about 60 feet down.

Scientists use *Aquarius* to study the coral reef. They study how climate changes affect plants and animals. They study how pollution affects plants and animals, too.

Concept Check
1. Why are wind turbines a good way to make electricity?
2. Why is *Aquarius'* undersea study of coral reefs important?

285

Chapter 8

Space Science

Lesson 1
What Makes Up Our
Solar System? 288

Lesson 2
What Is the Universe? 298

Lesson 3
How Do We Explore Space? 304

Scripture Spotlight

We are familiar with our home—Earth. God's Creation includes many more objects in space. His Creation is larger than we could ever explore. You will read the following passages in this chapter.

Genesis 1:14–18 (p. 292)   Amos 5:8 (p. 301)

The Big Idea

Earth—the home God created for us—is just one small part of His Universe.

❓ What are the people in the photo doing?

287

Lesson 1

Vocabulary

star	p. 291
Sun	p. 291
planet	p. 292
Earth	p. 292
moon	p. 293
revolve	p. 293
Solar System	p. 293

Find out what these words mean as you study this lesson.

Essential Question

What Makes Up Our Solar System?

Engage

Get Ready to Learn Why do you think Earth is called the blue planet? Look at the picture of Earth. What colors do you see?

Try This! What colors do you see in the Moon picture? See how many similarities and differences you can list between Earth and the Moon.

Structured Inquiry — Discover

Record your work for this inquiry. Your teacher may also assign the related Guided Inquiry.

Orbit Me
How does the movement of Earth and the Moon compare?

Your Group Needs
- a tennis ball
- a basketball
- a golf ball

Step 1 Communicate with your group members. Decide which ball should represent the Sun, Earth, and the Moon.

Step 2 Use models to show how Earth orbits the Sun. Have one member hold the Sun and stand still. Another member will hold Earth and walk around the Sun.

Step 3 Show how the Moon moves. Earth should keep doing Step 2. Another group member should hold the Moon and walk around Earth.

Create Explanations

1. How does the movement of Earth and the Moon compare?

2. Which ball did not move in this model? What did it represent?

The Sun Explain

When you think of stars, do you think of daytime or nighttime? On a clear night away from city lights you might see many twinkling stars in the sky. Did you know that you also see a star during the daytime?

🔎 What objects can you see in the night sky?

Nighttime

Daytime

Never look directly at the Sun! Looking at the Sun even for a second can damage your eyes.

A **star** is a huge ball of hot gases. The **Sun** is the closest star to Earth. The Sun looks much larger than the other stars because it is closer to Earth. God created the Sun, the other stars, and the Moon to give us light both during the day and at night.

We could not live without the Sun. We need the heat and light that the Sun gives off. Plants use light from the Sun to make food.

How are daytime and nighttime different?

Think About It

How does the Sun help provide food for people?

291

Our Solar System Explain

Scripture Spotlight
Read **Genesis 1:14–18**. Why did God create the Sun, the other stars, and the Moon?

We live on a planet called Earth. A **planet** is a large ball of rock or gas that travels around a star. **Earth** is the third planet from the Sun.

Genesis 1 tells us that God made Earth to be a home for people. He put it in just the right place in space to provide living things what they need to thrive. If Earth had been nearer to the Sun, it would be too hot. If Earth had been farther away from the Sun, it would be too cold for living things.

There are eight planets that revolve around the Sun.

Some planets have moons. A **moon** is a large object that revolves around a planet. To **revolve** means to move around another object. The path that the objects take as they revolve around other objects is referred to as an *orbit*.

We live on a planet that is grouped with other planets in space. All these planets revolve around the Sun. This group of planets is part of the Solar System. The **Solar System** includes the Sun and everything that orbits the Sun, including the planets and the moons that orbit these planets.

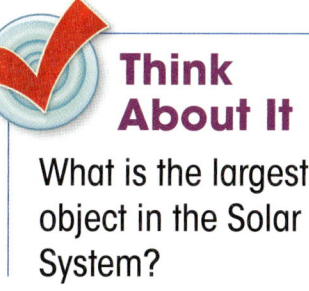

Think About It

What is the largest object in the Solar System?

Saturn   Uranus   Neptune

293

Each Planet Is Different Explain

Think About It

What are some ways in which the planets are different?

Some planets have many moons and others have no moons. Mercury and Venus have no moons. Mars has two moons. Jupiter, Saturn, Uranus, and Neptune each have many moons.

Earth has one moon. The Moon revolves around Earth. At the same time, Earth revolves around the Sun. It takes about 28 days for the Moon to revolve around Earth.

This shows how Earth moves around the Sun. It also shows how the Moon moves around Earth.

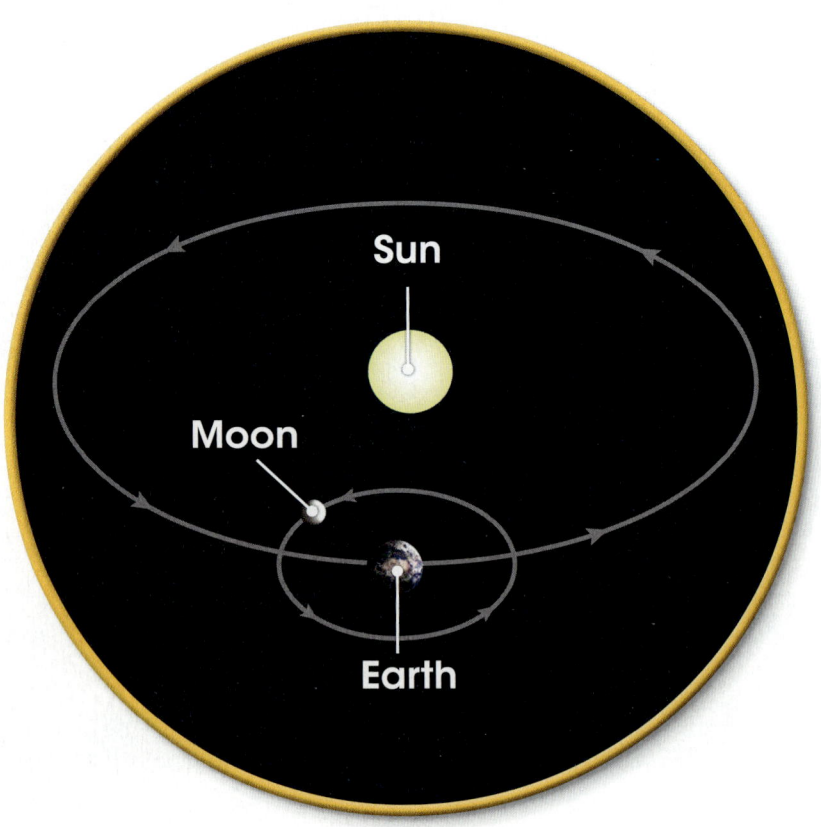

Many planets have rings around them. The gas giant planets Jupiter, Saturn, Uranus, and Neptune all have rings. The rings are small rocks and dust that revolve around the planet.

Some planets are very hot and some are very cold. God made sure Earth was just right for us to live on. Earth is in what scientists call the Goldilocks zone. Earth's temperature is just right for life.

Think About It

How did God make sure Earth was not too cold?

Math in Science

The farther a planet is from the Sun, the longer it takes to revolve around the Sun. It takes Earth about 365 days to revolve around the Sun. It takes Venus about 225 days. How many more days does it take Earth to revolve around the Sun than Venus?

Saturn is the sixth planet from the Sun. It has large rings made of ice and dust.

Comparing Planets Explain

The chart below shows some ways the planets in our Solar System differ.

Planet	Size	Moons	Rings	Temperature
Mercury	small	none	no	very hot
Venus	small	none	no	very hot
Earth	small	one	no	just right
Mars	small	two	no	cold
Jupiter	giant	many	yes	very cold
Saturn	giant	many	yes	very cold
Uranus	giant	many	yes	very cold
Neptune	giant	many	yes	very cold

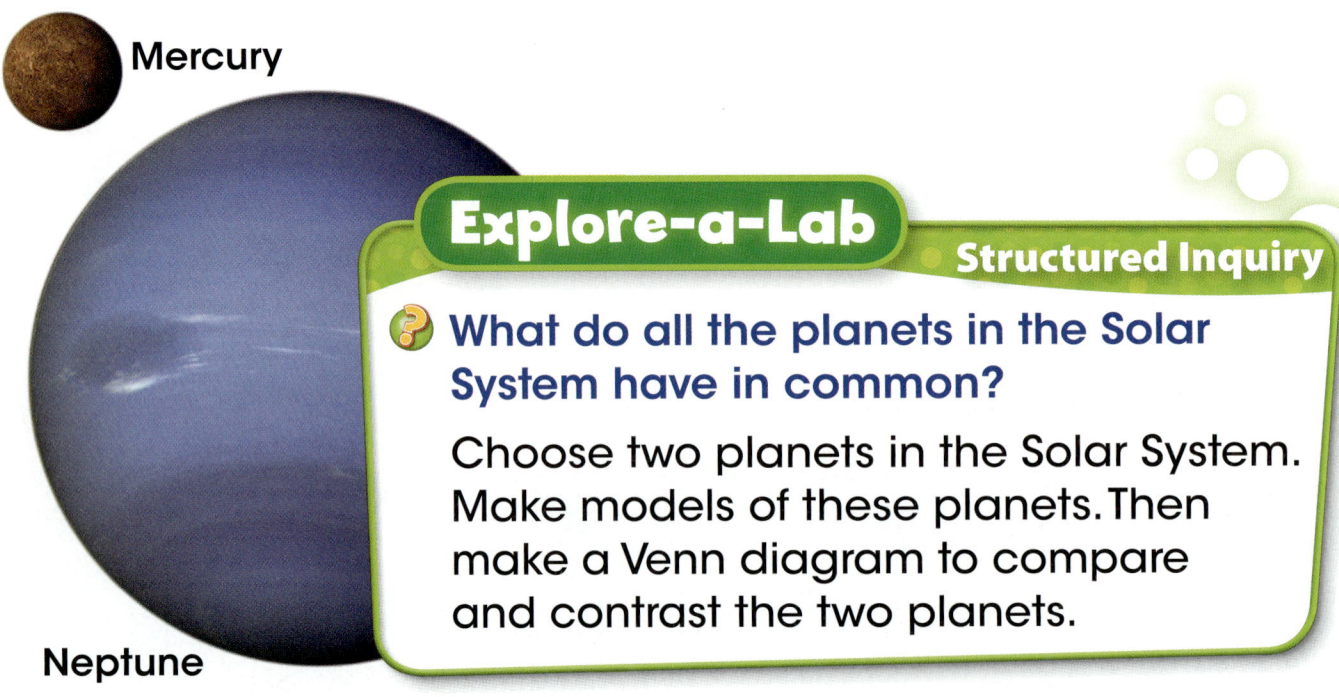

Mercury

Neptune

Explore-a-Lab
Structured Inquiry

What do all the planets in the Solar System have in common?

Choose two planets in the Solar System. Make models of these planets. Then make a Venn diagram to compare and contrast the two planets.

Make a Connection Extend

A compound word is made of two or more words. Use the word *sun* and list five compound words. Look in a dictionary if you need help.

Lesson Review Assess/Reflect

Summary: What makes up our Solar System? Earth, the seven other planets, and their moons all revolve around the Sun.

1. **Graphic Organizer** Make a Venn diagram. Compare and contrast Earth and the Moon.

2. **Vocabulary** How could you tell if an object is a planet or a moon?

3. **Test Prep** What does Earth revolve around?
   A. the Moon
   B. another planet
   C. the Solar System
   D. the Sun

4. Why do other stars look smaller than the Sun?

5. What does the Bible say is the purpose of the Sun and the Moon?

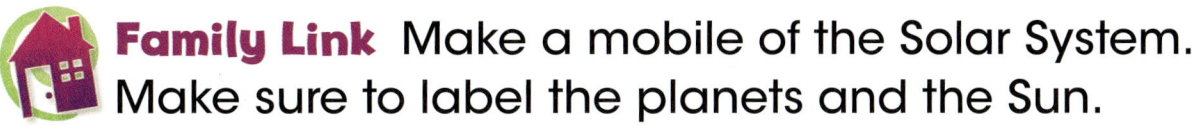

Family Link Make a mobile of the Solar System. Make sure to label the planets and the Sun.

Lesson 2

Vocabulary
galaxy p. 300
constellation p. 301
Universe p. 302

Find out what these words mean as you study this lesson.

? Essential Question

What Is the Universe? Engage

Get Ready to Learn What do you see when you look at the sky at night? Stars can light up the night sky. Some stars are larger and brighter than others. Some groups of stars look like objects or patterns we recognize. What are some star patterns you know?

Try This! Have you ever wondered why stars in the sky look so small? Have a partner hold a big ball in front of his or her body. Stand three meters (about nine feet) away. Hold a meterstick near your face. Measure how big the ball looks. Have your partner move three meters (about nine feet) farther away. Measure how big the ball looks now. Talk about what seemed to happen to the ball.

Structured Inquiry
Discover

Record your work for this inquiry. Your teacher may also assign the related Guided Inquiry.

Make a Constellation
How are constellations recognized?

SAFETY: Remember to be careful with sharp objects.

Your Group Needs
- empty cereal box
- black sheet of construction paper
- tape
- flashlight
- sharp pencil

Step 1 Get information about the pattern of a constellation.

Step 2 Draw the constellation on the black paper. Tape it on the front or back of the cereal box to **make a model.**

Step 3 Have your teacher help you. Use the pencil to punch the constellation through the cereal box.

Step 4 Place the flashlight in the cereal box. Turn on the flashlight. Turn off the lights in the room. Make a drawing to **record** the constellation you **observe**.

Create Explanations

1. How are constellations recognized?
2. What did turning off the lights model?

299

Galaxies Explain

Think About It

Scientists estimate the Milky Way galaxy contains about 200 billion stars. How many solar systems do you think there are?

A **galaxy** is a very large group of stars, planets, their moons, asteroids, comets, dust, and gases. Our Solar System is part of the Milky Way galaxy. God created many billions of galaxies.

This image shows the Milky Way galaxy from above as seen from the Hubble Telescope. You will learn more about telescopes in Lesson 3.

Explore-a-Lab

Structured Inquiry

❓ **How is your galaxy model similar to the picture of the galaxy on this page?**

Make your own model of a galaxy. Flatten a white coffee filter. Use watercolors to design a galaxy on the coffee filter. When you are finished, hang your coffee filter up to dry. Once dry, cut your galaxy out and paste it on black paper.

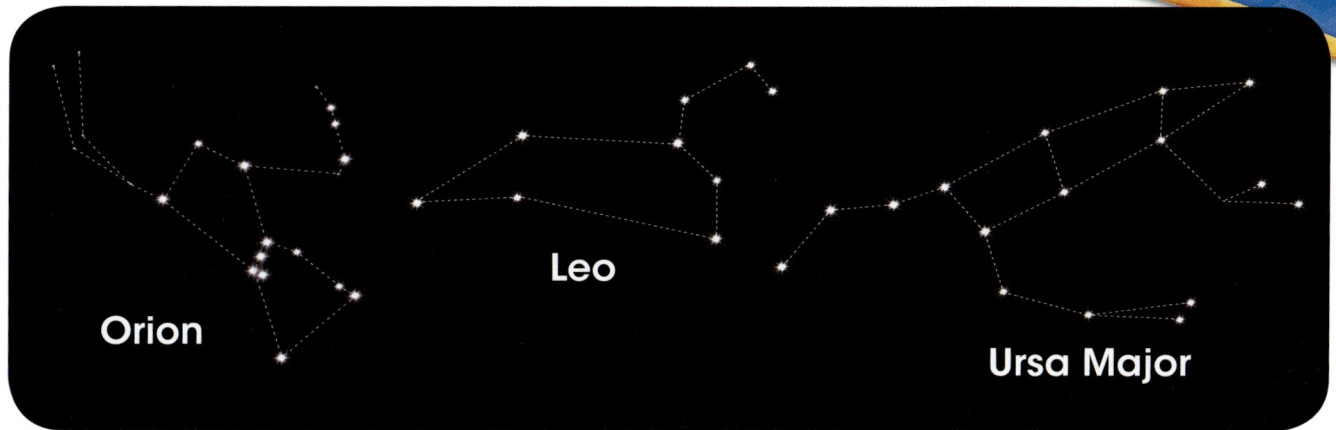

Constellations

Have you ever looked at the stars in the sky on a clear night away from city lights? Did you try to use the stars to make an object or pattern? A pattern of stars is called a **constellation**. Some constellations you might know are Orion (the Hunter), Leo (the Lion), and Ursa Major (the Big Bear).

Check out your *Science Journal* for a Guided Inquiry that explores more constellations.
Discover

Math in Science

Make up and draw a constellation. It should have at least seven stars and be made of at least two geometric shapes. Write the names of the shapes in your constellation.

Scripture Spotlight

Read **Amos 5:8**. What objects does it mention God created?

The Universe Explain

Think About It

What words would you use to describe the Universe?

What is in the Universe? The **Universe** is everything that exists. It includes all the galaxies, stars, solar systems, planets, and their moons.

There appears to be much empty space in the Universe. It is very large. Most things in the Universe are so far away that they are difficult for scientists to study.

God is the Creator of the Universe. He created everything in it. God's power keeps everything in the Universe moving, from the biggest galaxy to the smallest insect. Only He can know and understand everything that happens in the Universe.

These large columns of dust are part of a nebula, one small part of the Universe. God created our world by the "Word" of His mouth. We don't know the details of His Creation of the Universe, but we have faith that He did it.

Make a Connection Extend

Research a famous astronomer. Make a trading card about the person. Include a picture on the front of the card and facts about the astronomer on the back of the card. Share your cards with a partner.

Lesson Review Assess/Reflect

Summary: What is the Universe? God created the Universe. The Universe includes all things that exist, including many galaxies. Earth is part of the Milky Way galaxy.

1. **Graphic Organizer** Use *Universe* as the main idea. Make a web showing at least five things that are part of the Universe.

2. **Vocabulary** What makes up a galaxy?

3. **Test Prep** What objects make up the constellations we see from Earth?
   A. dust   B. planets   C. gases   D. stars

4. Where did the Universe come from?

5. Why do the stars we see look so small?

Family Link Look at pictures of constellations on the Internet or in a book on stars. Find out some objects and animals the constellations were named for. Draw and label a picture of your family's favorite constellation.

Lesson 3

Vocabulary

astronomer p. 306
telescope p. 306
space probe p. 307
rocket p. 308
astronaut p. 308

Find out what these words mean as you study this lesson.

? Essential Question

How Do We Explore Space? Engage

Get Ready to Learn What things would you like to see in space? What would you use to see them? Scientists use telescopes to take pictures. The image on this page was taken by the Hubble remote-controlled telescope in space!

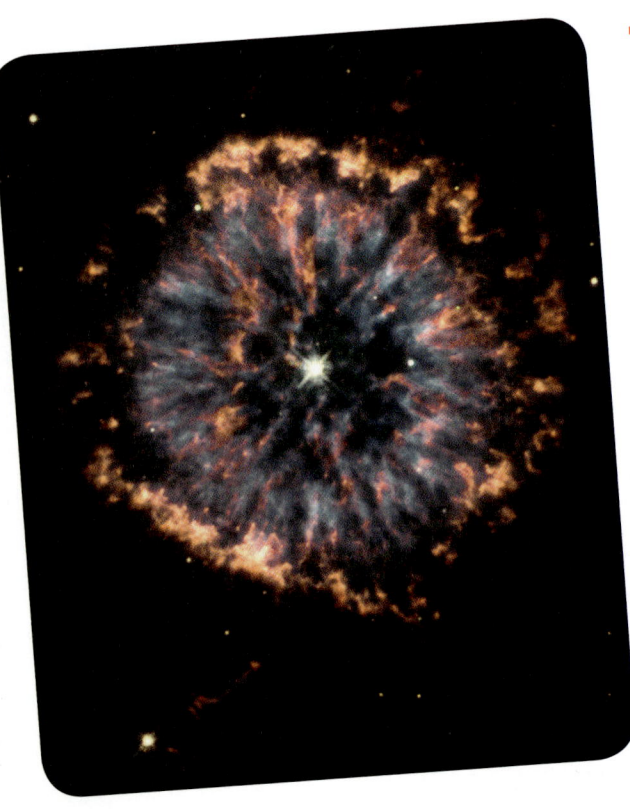

Try This! Have you ever thought about traveling in space? Design a bedroom for your spacecraft. What things woud you need? What things might you want to bring with you? List your "wants" and your "needs" for your space bedroom. Share your design with the class.

Structured Inquiry Discover

Record your work for this inquiry. Your teacher may also assign the related Guided Inquiry.

Far, Far Away
Why is it difficult to see constellation models from far away?

Your Group Needs
- black paper
- star stickers
- meterstick

Step 1 Place the stickers on the black paper to make up your own constellation.

Step 2 Your teacher will attach the constellation models to a classroom wall while you are not looking.

Step 3 Line up in the back of the room. Walk slowly toward the front of the room. Stop when you can tell which constellation is yours.

Step 4 **Measure** and **record** the distance between you and your constellation.

Create Explanations

1. Why is it difficult to see constellation models from far away?

2. Suppose you could not get closer to the constellations. How could you observe them from the back of the room?

Studying the Universe Explain

A person who studies stars, planets, and other things in space is called an **astronomer**. Have you ever looked at the sky on a clear night away from city lights? You probably saw many stars. You may have even seen another planet! To get a better look, you can use a telescope. A **telescope** is an instrument used to see objects far away. It magnifies objects so you see them better. Some telescopes are small and used at home. Others are large and used in special buildings called *observatories*.

Lesson Activity

Look at two images of Mars. Which one is how you see Mars with your eyes alone? Which one was taken using a telescope? Compare the two images.

❓ What can scientists learn from these images?

Another way to study the Universe is by using space probes. A **space probe** is a spacecraft that collects and sends information back to Earth from space. Space probes can go places that humans cannot go. We can learn a lot from the information a space probe sends us. Space probes have been sent to most planets in our Solar System.

Think About It

Why can you use a telescope at your home but not a space probe?

Workers are getting this space probe ready to launch.

Why do you think the workers are wearing white suits and covers on their heads?

Traveling in Space [Explain]

Traveling into space also helps us understand the Universe. People, dogs, and even monkeys have all gone into space. They were taken in spacecraft powered by rockets. A **rocket** uses burning fuel to push the spacecraft into space.

Have you ever thought of traveling in space? People who go into space or have trained to go into space in a spacecraft are called **astronauts**. When astronauts leave their spacecraft, they have to wear special suits in order to survive.

Think About It

What might happen to astronauts if they got too far away from the spacecraft?

When astronauts are in space outside of a spacecraft, it is called a spacewalk.

Why do you think astronauts might need to spacewalk?

Math in Science

The first person to walk in space was Alexi Leonov. He spacewalked for about ten minutes. About how many seconds did he spacewalk?

Make a Connection Extend

Astronauts complete many tasks while wearing special clothing. Write your name on a sheet of paper. Then write your name wearing a mitten. What does this tell you?

Lesson Review Assess/Reflect

Summary: How do we explore space? There are many ways to study the Universe. Telescopes, space probes, and rockets all help us explore space.

1. **Graphic Organizer** Make a Venn diagram. Compare and contrast telescopes and space probes.

2. **Vocabulary** How do scientists use rockets to study space?

3. **Test Prep** What has helped us learn most about other planets?
    - A. telescopes
    - B. space probes
    - C. astronauts
    - D. rockets

4. What does an astronomer study?

5. Why do you think most large telescopes are on mountains away from cities?

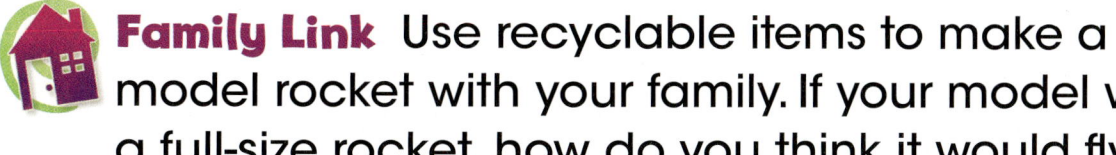

Family Link Use recyclable items to make a model rocket with your family. If your model was a full-size rocket, how do you think it would fly?

People in Science

Extend

Get to Know
Mickey Kutzner, Ph.D.

Mickey Kutzner is a physicist. He studies how particles within atoms interact with one another. His research can be used in astronomy (the study of the stars and space) or in X-rays. He believes, like David, that "the heavens declare the glory of God; the skies proclaim the work of His hands" **(Psalm 19:1)**.

Dr. Kutzner believes the Universe must be the Creation of a great and mighty God. Such a large system of stars and planets could not have formed by chance. As scientists like Dr. Kutzner discover and learn new things, they find more evidence of God's work.

Called to Serve
Dr. Kutzner believes that science shows God exists through the wonder of our world.

Concept Check
1. Where do you see evidence of God's work?
2. How does science support God as the Creator?

Careers in Science

Extend

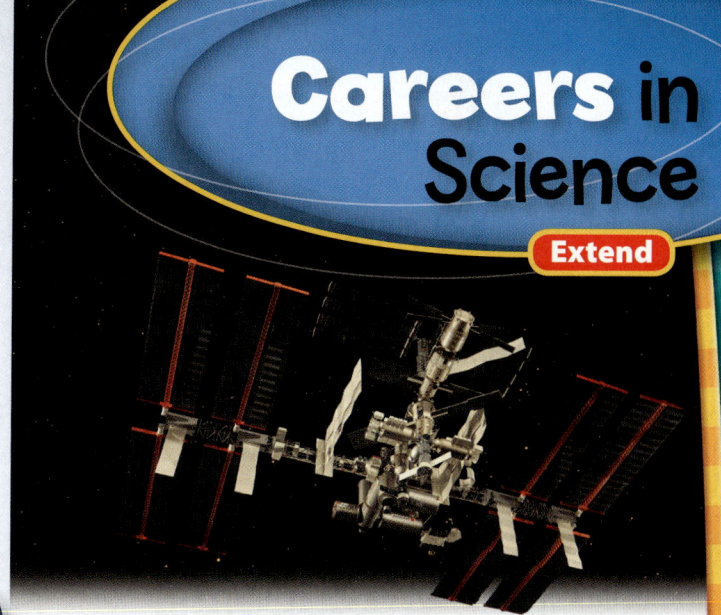

Astronomer

Astronomers study outer space. They study the stars, moons, planets, and energy in space. Astronomers want to know what these things are made of. They study how things in the Universe move. They study how things in space relate to each other.

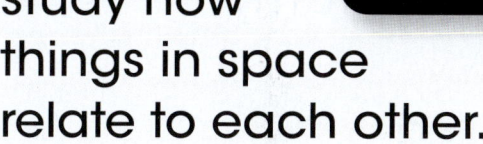

Astronomers look at pictures taken with telescopes. They spend a lot of time studying the pictures. Astronomers need a lot of patience. It can take years of hard work to find the answers to some of their questions.

Aerospace Engineer

Aerospace engineers make machines that travel through the air and in space. Some make airplanes. Some make spaceships or space stations. Others make satellites and missiles.

Aerospace engineers are good at math. They like to build things. Some want to know about space. Others want to find better ways of air travel closer to Earth.

 **Concept Check**

1. Why is the work astronomers do important to us on Earth?
2. How can aerospace engineers help astronomers and astronauts?

Unit 3 Review — Assess/Reflect

Vocabulary

Use the words below to complete the sentences.

revolve	plain	astronauts
canyon	tornado	astronomers
fossil	evaporate	precipitation

1. Rain, hail, and snow are three forms of _____.
2. Evidence of a living thing that died long ago is a(n) _____.
3. A deep, narrow valley with steep sides is a(n) _____.
4. People who travel in space are called _____.
5. People who study things in space are _____.
6. A large, flat area of Earth's surface is a(n) _____.
7. To move around an object is to _____.
8. When liquids _____, they change into a gas.
9. A powerful windstorm that forms a funnel shape and lifts almost anything in its way is a(n) _____.

Describe What You See

10. Name this landform. Describe it and tell how it was formed.

312

Use Science Practices

11. How do scientists **observe** objects in space?

Multiple Choice

12. Which of the following is not a property of minerals?
- **A.** color
- **B.** width
- **C.** smoothness
- **D.** hardness

13. Which of the following are extinct?
- **A.** dinosaurs
- **B.** giraffes
- **C.** bluebirds
- **D.** tigers

14. Which body of water is largest?
- **A.** lake
- **B.** river
- **C.** ocean
- **D.** stream

Short Answer

15. Tell one way you have used rocks recently.

16. How can earthquakes change Earth?

17. Explain how erosion causes changes to Earth's surface.

18. What does the water cycle need to work?

19. Why does the Sun look larger than the other stars?

20. What does the Bible tell us about God's Creation of the Universe?

21. What does the Flood in Genesis help us understand about our planet?

22. How do a moon and a planet differ?

Unit 4
Physical Science

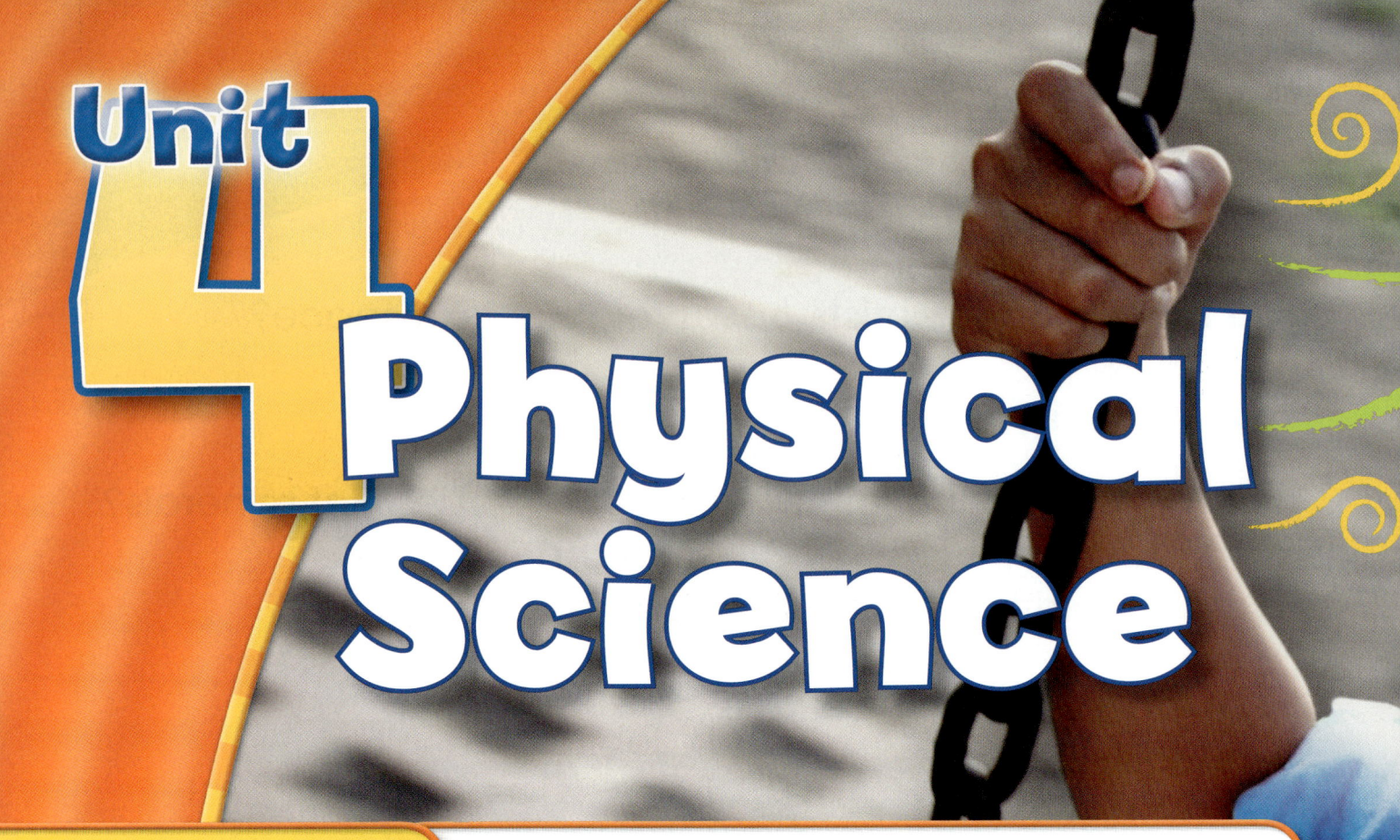

Chapter 9 316
Properties of Matter

Chapter 10 348
Energy and Machines

Unit 4 Review ... 392

The Bible tells us God "made the heavens and the earth." (Exodus 20:11) You are about to learn what the things around you are made of. Remember that God made everything. He keeps the world in order.

- What is everything around you made of?
- Where do you get the energy you need to work and play?
- How do simple tools help you work and play?
- What forms of energy do you use to worship God?

Wooosh! This boy is using energy to swing through the air.

Your teacher may assign an Open Inquiry lab and a Lifestyle Challenge activity. Use your *Science Journal* to record your work.

Chapter 9

Properties of Matter

Lesson 1
What Is Matter? 318

Lesson 2
What Are Solids, Liquids, and Gases? 328

Lesson 3
How Does Matter Change? 338

Scripture Spotlight

God is everywhere! You can connect your faith to what you are learning about matter. You will read the following passages in this chapter.

Colossians 1:16 (p. 320)
Hosea 6:4 (p. 336)
Leviticus 24:2 (p. 342)

The Big Idea

Everything you can touch is made of matter. God created all matter. Different kinds of matter have different properties.

❓ How can you use your senses to identify different kinds of matter?

Lesson 1

Vocabulary

matter   p. 320
atom   p. 320
property   p. 321
mass   p. 322
volume   p. 323

Find out what these words mean as you study this lesson.

? Essential Question
What Is Matter? *Engage*

Get Ready to Learn How are wet paint and paper different? Wet paint is runny and colorful. Paper is flat and can be folded. You can tell what an object is made of by observing it.

Try This! How can you tell what is inside a closed box? Do not peek! Use your other senses. Shake and listen. Then smell.

Structured Inquiry Discover

Record your work for this inquiry. Your teacher may also assign the related Guided Inquiry.

Sorting It Out
How can objects be sorted into groups?

Your Group Needs
- bag of objects
- index cards
- marker

Step 1 Observe the objects in the bag. How are they alike and different?

Step 2 Sort the objects into two or more groups. Each group should have at least two objects, and all the objects in a group should have one thing in common.

Step 3 Use a marker and an index card to label each group.

Step 4 Compare your groups to the groups that other students made. Talk about how your groups could be different.

Create Explanations

1. How can objects be sorted into groups?
2. What should scientists do if they do not agree with each other?

Matter and Mass Explain

Scripture Spotlight

Colossians 1:16 says that God is the Creator of all things, in Heaven and on Earth.

Your body is made out of something. So are all the objects around you. **Matter** is anything that takes up space. A sheet of paper is made of matter. So is a glass of water and the air you breathe. All matter is made of tiny parts that are too small to see. The tiny parts are called **atoms**.

If matter did not exist, you would not exist. By speaking, God made all matter during Creation. When God made matter, He made many different kinds. God created just the right kinds of matter to make you and everything around you.

You can describe matter by how it looks, feels, smells, and tastes. These are properties of matter. A **property** is a quality you can use to describe something. Color is a property. Shape and size are also properties.

Most objects are made of more than one kind of matter. Water, sugar, and starch are kinds of matter found in vegetables.

❓ What properties do these vegetables have?

One property of matter that you can measure is mass. **Mass** is how much matter is in an object. You use a balance to measure mass. Scientists measure mass in units called grams. A nickel has a mass of about five grams.

Some objects have a large mass. They are hard to move. Objects with less mass are easier to move. Steel and plastic are both types of matter. A small steel ball has more mass than a small plastic ball. That is because the steel ball contains more matter.

Think About It

How can you tell if one object has more mass than another?

Matter Takes Up Space Explain

Volume is another property. **Volume** is how much space something takes up. Small objects have a small volume. Large objects have a large volume.

A measuring cup can be used to measure the volume of a liquid or a powder. You can use milliliters to measure liquid volume. About 20 drops of water is equal to one milliliter.

Explore-a-Lab
Structured Inquiry

How can you measure the mass and volume of a water bottle?

Use a balance to find the mass of an empty bottle. Then use a measuring cup to figure out how much water the bottle could hold.

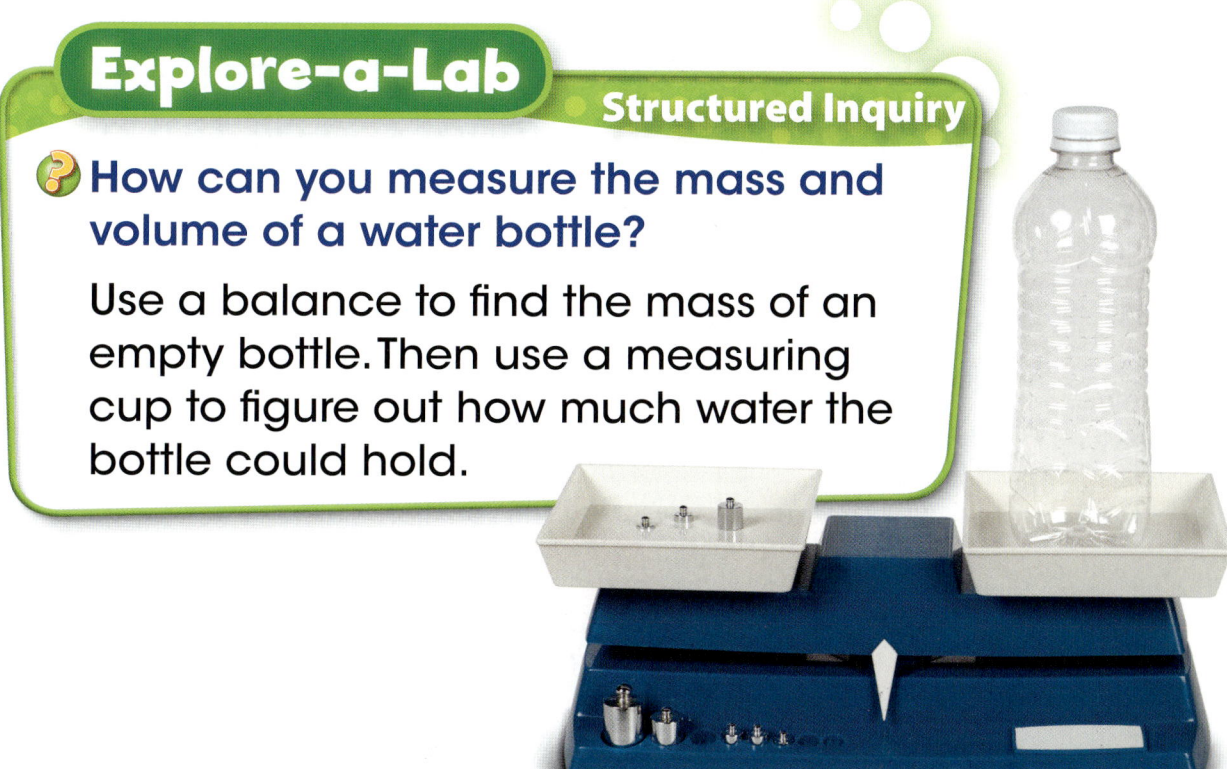

Faith Connection

Why can't God's love be measured with a measuring cup or a balance?

Think About It

How are mass and volume different? How are they alike?

All matter has mass and takes up space. A bell is made of matter. It has mass and takes up space. You can hear the sound a bell makes, but sound is not matter. Sound does not have mass or take up space.

There are some kinds of matter you cannot see. You cannot see air, but air is matter. The air in a balloon takes up space. The mass of a balloon filled with air is greater than the mass of an empty balloon. The extra mass is from the air in the balloon.

More Properties of Matter Explain

There are many other properties of matter. How something feels is called *texture.* Sandpaper has a rough texture. Ice has a smooth texture.

You can use your nose to smell matter. Some objects have a strong odor. Odor is how something smells. Flowers and candy have a nice odor. You might not like the odor of an onion. Odors are gases given off by objects.

Think About It

Think about all the properties of cardboard. What are five ways you could describe a cardboard box?

The gas released when you cut an onion is what makes you cry.

What are some other things that have a strong odor?

Some objects sink in water. Other objects float. A solid plastic ball will float. A solid metal ball will sink. Whether or not an object sinks or floats depends on the kind of matter it is made out of. It also depends on the amount of space an object takes up.

Explore-a-Lab
Guided Inquiry

How can you make something that sinks float?

Roll a piece of clay into a ball. Put it into a bowl of water. Watch it sink. Then take the clay out of the water. Use a paper towel to dry it off. Next, change the piece of clay in some way to make it float. Keep trying until the clay floats. Dry the clay each time you take it out of the water.

A tennis ball floats in the water.
What other objects float in water?

Make a Connection Extend

Think about people who direct traffic. How would you design a vest to help keep them safer? What properties should the vest have?

Lesson Review Assess/Reflect

Summary: What is matter? The things around you are made of matter. Matter has mass and takes up space. Different kinds of matter have different properties.

1. **Graphic Organizer** Make a chart about the properties of matter. List all the properties you learned about.

2. **Vocabulary** How do you know if something is made of matter?

3. **Test Prep** Which property tells you how large or small a ball is?
   A. odor   B. color   C. volume   D. texture

4. Describe an object that has a small volume and a large mass. Then describe an object that has a large volume and a small mass.

5. How was matter created?

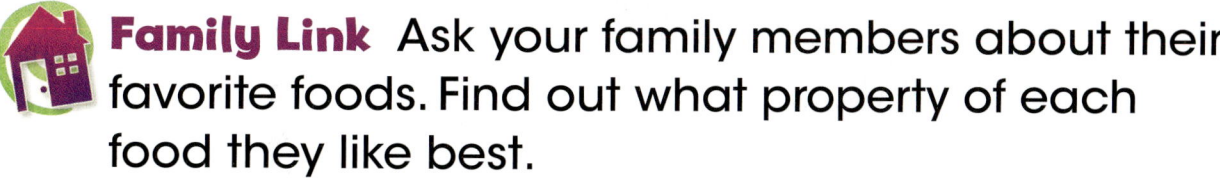
Family Link Ask your family members about their favorite foods. Find out what property of each food they like best.

327

Lesson 2

Vocabulary

solid   p. 330
liquid   p. 333
gas   p. 334
melt   p. 336
freeze   p. 336

Find out what these words mean as you study this lesson.

? Essential Question

What Are Solids, Liquids, and Gases? *Engage*

Get Ready to Learn What can you do with water? You pour it and drink it. You take a bath in it and swim in it. You can splash it and spill it. You can even add soap and make bubbles.

Try This! Have you ever blown bubbles? See who can make the biggest bubble. What do you think is inside a bubble?

Structured Inquiry — Discover

Record your work for this inquiry. Your teacher may also assign the related Guided Inquiry.

Forms of Matter
What affects how fast an ice cube changes?

 **SAFETY:** Wear safety goggles. Do not touch the hot lamp.

Your Group Needs
- lamp
- two small bowls
- two ice cubes

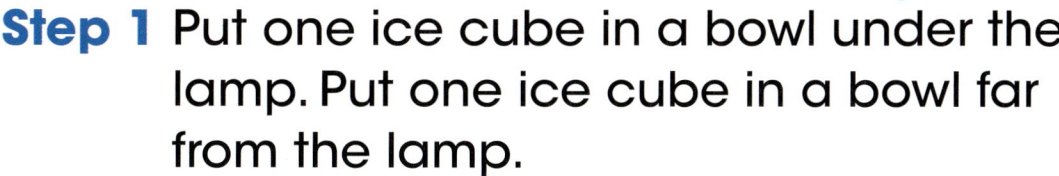

Step 1 Put one ice cube in a bowl under the lamp. Put one ice cube in a bowl far from the lamp.

Step 2 Turn on the lamp. **Predict** what will happen to each ice cube.

Step 3 Observe the matter in each bowl. **Record** what happens as time passes.

Step 4 Compare the solid ice and the liquid water. Try to change the shape of the ice. What happens?

Create Explanations

1. What affects how fast an ice cube changes?
2. How is an ice cube different from liquid water?

Solid as a Rock (Explain)

You learned that all matter has mass and takes up space. No two samples of matter can occupy the same space. Matter exists in different forms. You will learn about solids, liquids, and gases. God's natural laws determine what each form of matter is like.

A **solid** is a form of matter that has its own shape. You can see and feel the shape of a solid.

Some solids can be bent, broken, torn, or molded. This changes the shape of the solid.

How are these solids different?

Think about some of the things you use at school. You sit at a desk. You write with a pencil or pen. You read books. These are all solids.

Solids can have different textures. Some solids are smooth. Some are rough. Solids are many different colors, sizes, and shapes.

Faith Connection

A rock is a solid. Why do you think that some people call Jesus their Rock?

These rocks are solid objects, but they have some different properties.

How are the properties of the rocks different?

Think About It

How are a balance and a ruler alike? How are they different?

You can measure how long, tall, or wide a solid is. You need a meterstick or a ruler. Many rulers have a different unit on each side. One side has centimeters. The other has inches. Scientists use centimeters instead of inches.

Math in Science

Look at the ruler below. How much longer is the pencil than the eraser?

How to Measure Length

1. Pick five solid objects.
2. Place each object you want to measure next to the ruler.
3. Line up one end of the object with the 0-cm (0-in.) mark.
4. Read the number on the ruler that is closest to the other end of the object.

Liquids Explain

Liquids are another form of matter. A **liquid** does not have its own shape. It takes the shape of its container. Think about water in a bottle. The water takes the shape of the bottle. If you pour the water into a glass, then the water takes the shape of the glass.

Think of some examples of liquids. Maybe you like to drink orange juice. Maybe you put maple syrup on your pancakes. Some soaps used to wash hands are liquids.

Think About It

How is a liquid different from a solid?

You can pour a liquid. It goes from one container to another. Its shape changes.

Gases Explain

Think About It

Besides blowing up a balloon, what is one way you could show that a gas takes up space?

Gases are another form of matter. A **gas** is a kind of matter that always fills its container. It does not have its own shape. Air is made up of gases. You cannot see air, but it takes up space and has mass.

Imagine that you are blowing up a balloon. Air fills the space in the balloon. The more air that is inside a balloon, the bigger the balloon gets. The mass of the balloon filled with air is greater than the mass of the empty balloon.

Changes in Form

Matter can change from one form to another. For example, liquids can turn into gases and solids. A change in form can happen when matter gets warmer or colder.

Explore-a-Lab
Structured Inquiry

Do all solids melt at the same rate?

Set a metal pie plate on top of a bowl filled with very warm water. On one half of the plate, put a piece of chocolate bar. On the other half of the plate, put a piece of butter the same size as the piece of chocolate. Observe both solids to see if one melts faster than the other.

Think About It

How are melting and freezing different?

What happens if an ice cube gets too warm? It will **melt**, or change from a solid to a liquid. The ice cube turns into a puddle of liquid water. Almost any solid will melt if it gets hot enough.

Liquid water can turn back into ice if it gets cold. The water will **freeze**, or turn from a liquid to a solid. Liquid water can also turn into a gas if it gets hot.

Scripture Spotlight

Read **Hosea 6:4**. Dew is made of tiny drops of water. What change in form would cause dew to disappear?

? **What happened to this fruit pop?**

Make a Connection Extend

Get a cup of water and a straw. Slowly blow air through the straw into the water. Watch the shape of the air in the water. What shape does a gas have in a liquid?

Lesson Review Assess/Reflect

Summary: What are solids, liquids, and gases? You learned about three forms of matter. Solids have their own shape. Liquids take the shape of their container. Gases spread out to fill their container.

1. **Graphic Organizer** Make a chart about solids, liquids, and gases. Show how they are alike and different.

2. **Vocabulary** The butter in a pan is not melting. What can you do to make it melt?

3. **Test Prep** Which of these is a liquid?
   A. air   B. honey   C. paper   D. carrot

4. A solid has its own shape. What is a way you might change the shape of a solid?

5. How do God's natural laws apply to gases?

Family Link Use a ruler to measure different kinds of solid matter in your house. Make a chart showing your results. Which objects were the shortest? Which were the longest?

Lesson 3

Vocabulary

physical change p. 340

chemical change p. 343

Find out what these words mean as you study this lesson.

Essential Question
How Does Matter Change? Engage

Get Ready to Learn Have you ever cut a loaf of bread? Cutting is one way to change matter.

Try This! What is another way you can change matter? Observe a piece of bread before and after it is toasted. Draw pictures showing how the bread changed.

Structured Inquiry — Discover

Record your work for this inquiry. Your teacher may also assign the related Guided Inquiry.

Ways Matter Can Change

What are some ways matter can change?

Your Group Needs
- paper
- scissors
- seltzer tablet
- clear cup half-filled with water

Step 1 Use scissors to cut paper into different shapes. **Observe** how the paper changes.

Step 2 Place the tablet in a cup with water. What happens to the tablet? Describe the changes.

Step 3 **Compare** how the matter changed. Which matter is still the same? Which changed into different kinds of matter?

Create Explanations

1. What are some ways matter can change?

2. How was the change to the tablet different from the change to the paper?

3. Which was a physical change? Which was a chemical change?

Physical Change Explain

You know that God made all matter. He also made the natural laws that control matter. Matter follows God's natural laws when it changes.

You can change the size and shape of matter. This is a physical change. A **physical change** does not change the kind of matter. Cutting is an example of a physical change. You can cut a loaf of bread into pieces. The size and shape of the bread change. The kind of matter does not change. It is still bread.

Think about other ways that you change matter. You can bend a straw to put in a drink. You can tear lettuce. You can chop cucumbers and tomatoes.

❓ Why is bending a straw a physical change?

You can mix kinds of matter, too. A salad is one kind of mixture. It has different vegetables in it. The matter in a mixture does not change. You can separate the vegetables back out again.

Think About It

How do you know that mixing matter is a physical change?

 **Math in Science**

Julia cuts a cucumber into 12 pieces. Scott eats 3 of the pieces. How many pieces of cucumber does Julia have left?

What examples of physical changes can you see in this picture?

Scripture Spotlight

Read **Leviticus 24:2**. What change is described? Why is it a physical change?

Check out your *Science Journal* for a Structured Inquiry that explores how to make freshwater from saltwater.

Discover

You can make mixtures with liquids, too. Saltwater is a mixture of water and salt. You cannot see the salt. But if you taste the water, it will taste salty. The salt has not changed. These are all physical changes.

Explore-a-Lab
Structured Inquiry

How can you tell if salt is mixed with water?

Add two or three spoonfuls of salt to a cup of water and stir with a spoon. Look at the water. You cannot see the salt you mixed in. Pour a small amount of the mixture onto a small plastic plate. Put the plate in a warm place. Let it sit overnight so the water will change to a gas. Look at the plate the next day. Describe what you see. Explain what has happened.

Chemical Change **Explain**

Wood burns in a fire. The wood turns into charcoal, ashes, hot gases, and smoke. These are new kinds of matter. The matter cannot change back to wood. A change that makes a new kind of matter is a **chemical change**.

A cookie cannot change back to dough.

Think About It

Why is cooking a chemical change?

Imagine you are making cookies. The dough bakes in the oven. The color, shape, and taste of the dough change. It can never go back to being dough. Cooking is a chemical change.

Explore-a-Lab

Structured Inquiry

Is the change that happens to a penny a physical or chemical change? Why?

Put a penny in a cup. Sprinkle salt over the penny. Pour enough vinegar into the cup to cover the penny. Soak the penny for ten minutes. Take the penny out and put it on a paper towel. Leave it to dry overnight. Observe it the next day.

Make a Connection Extend

Use chemical changes to write secret messages. Dip a cotton swab in lemon juice. Write a message on a sheet of white paper. When the paper dries, your writing will disappear. Give it to a friend. Have your friend dip a paintbrush in purple grape juice and paint the sheet of paper. Your message will reappear.

Lesson Review Assess/Reflect

Summary: How does matter change? Matter changes in many ways. The kind of matter does not change in a physical change. Sometimes matter changes from one kind to another. These are chemical changes.

1. **Graphic Organizer** Choose a physical change. Tell what happens. Use a cause-and-effect chart.

2. **Vocabulary** Give one example of a **chemical change**.

3. **Test Prep** What changes when you cut bread?
   - A. color
   - B. shape
   - C. taste
   - D. kind of matter

4. How is burning paper different from cutting it?

5. What kind of change is a mixture? How do you know?

Family Link Rusting and rotting are chemical changes. Walk around your home with your family. Look for examples of chemical changes. List kinds of matter that are likely to rust or rot.

People in Science

Extend

Get to Know
Sir Isaac Newton

Sir Isaac Newton was born in England in 1642. He is one of the greatest scientists of all time.

Newton showed that white light has all the colors of the rainbow. He also made the first telescope that used mirrors. It was stronger than other telescopes. It showed objects as they really were. Today's telescopes still use Newton's model.

Newton also explored gravity. He showed that gravity keeps the planets in space. It is also why the oceans have tides.

Newton used the Bible and nature to study the Universe and answer his questions.

Called to Serve
Newton believed his work was to understand the truth of God through his work as a scientist.

Concept Check

1. In what ways does Newton's work help scientists today?
2. How does your faith help you study science?

Careers in Science

Materials Scientist

Materials scientists study materials. Some materials are found in nature. Wood comes from trees. Other materials are made by humans, such as paint.

Materials scientists study what materials are made of and how they work. They find out what materials to use to make things. They study how materials can be changed into new products. They look for and develop new materials. They also look for new ways to use old materials.

Organic Chemist

Organic chemists study things that contain carbon. Carbon is a part of all living things. Carbon is found in rubber, plastics, medicines, and soaps.

Organic chemists help make safe cleaning products. They help make shampoo that works better. They also help make natural bug sprays.

Concept Check
1. Do you think a material that can fix itself is a good idea? Explain.
2. How do organic chemists help make our lives better?

Chapter 10

Energy and Machines

Lesson 1
What Is Energy?........................350

Lesson 2
What Is Thermal Energy?............360

Lesson 3
What Are Sound and Light?.......370

Lesson 4
What Are Simple Machines?......380

Scripture Spotlight

God can be seen in all things. He created the world and the laws that energy and matter must follow.

You will read the following passages in this chapter.

Genesis 1:1–5 (p. 355)   Psalm 119:105 (p. 372)
Revelation 16:8–9 (p. 368)   John 8:12 (p. 376)

The Big Idea

Energy comes in many forms. All energy obeys God's natural laws. You can see and hear some energy. This violinist is using energy as he plays the violin.

❓ **What form of energy is made when the bow is pulled across the violin's strings?**

Lesson 1

Vocabulary
energy   p. 352
light   p. 355
sound   p. 355
battery   p. 358

Find out what these words mean as you study this lesson.

Essential Question

What Is Energy? Engage

Get Ready to Learn Why are you able to kick a ball, climb a hill, and run fast? Sometimes you are able to play with your friends for hours and then do your homework. Other times you need to rest after school. Why do you think that is?

Try This! What activities can you do when you have a lot of energy? Act out one of these activities. How do you act when you feel like you don't have much energy? Act out something you do during these times.

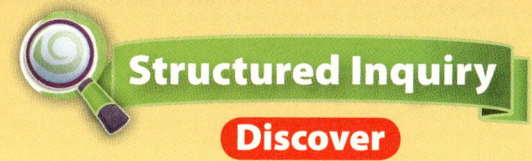

Record your work for this inquiry. Your teacher may also assign the related Guided Inquiry.

Make It Move

Why do some objects help make a car move better than others?

Your Group Needs
- box of objects
- metal toy car

Step 1 Observe the objects in the box. Think about how they can be used to move the car.

Step 2 Communicate how to use each object to make the car move. Use words such as *push* and *pull*.

Step 3 Experiment with each object to make the car move. Record how you used each object to move the car.

Step 4 Compare how well the objects moved the car.

Create Explanations

1. Why do some objects help make a car move better than others?

2. Which objects were the most helpful? Which were not very helpful? Why?

You Use Energy Explain

Energy is all around you. You use it all day long. Energy is stored in food and in your body. How do scientists define energy? **Energy** is something that can cause change and do work. You use energy to play, learn, and move things by pushing or pulling them. In science, all these activities count as work—they all use energy.

Things you plug in use energy, too. If you unplug a lamp, for example, it cannot get the energy it needs. It will not work. Other devices, such as remote-controlled cars, work without being plugged in. Their energy is stored. You will learn more about this kind of stored energy later in this lesson.

Do you use more energy running or walking? Why do you think this?

Imagine you are playing kickball. The ball rolls toward you. It has energy because it is moving. You kick the ball, and it moves away from you. Your body uses energy to kick the ball. Your body is doing work.

Your body needs energy to do work. The energy in your body comes from the food you eat. Fruit, vegetables, and whole-grain cereals are foods that come from plants.

Think About It

Do you think eating candy or sugary snacks would be a good source of energy? Why?

Think About It

Think about the activities the energy stored in your body helps you do. How do these activities help keep you healthy?

Plants get energy from the Sun. Plants use that energy to make food. You eat food made from plants. The food gives energy to your body. Your body uses the energy to move and to stay alive.

Sometimes you get hungry. Hunger can make you feel tired and out of energy. After you eat, you have more energy. You can run and play again.

123 Math in Science

We use *calories* to measure how much energy is stored in food. An apple has 75 calories. A granola bar has 110 calories. How many more calories does the granola bar have than the apple?

How is this girl getting more energy to play?

Forms of Energy Explain

God created many forms of energy, such as light and sound. Light is a form of energy you can see. The Sun gives off light that makes the sky bright in the daytime. Fireflies give off light at night to find other fireflies. You use your eyes to see light.

Another form of energy is sound. Sound is a form of energy you can hear. People talk to each other, and children laugh as they play. Ocean waves crash on the shore, and birds sing to each other. You use your ears to hear these sounds.

Scripture Spotlight
Read **Genesis 1:1–5**. When did God create light?

What can give off light energy in this picture? What can give off sound energy?

Energy can change from one form to another form. Your body stores the energy it gets from food. When you move your body, the energy in your body changes. It changes into energy that moves your muscles and energy that warms your body.

There are two main types of energy. All the forms of energy are one or both of these two main types.

- Energy of Motion—When something is moving, it has energy.

- Stored Energy—Some things that are not moving have energy, too. Portable devices, such as flashlights, have stored energy in their batteries. Objects that are still, but about to fall, such as a boy or girl at the top of a slide, also have stored energy. Stored energy can be released and used.

A ball at the top of a hill has stored energy. Suppose the ball rolls down the hill. The stored energy is changed to the energy of motion. When the ball stops, it has neither energy of motion nor stored energy.

Think About It

Think about the objects in your home. What kinds of energy do objects in your home use?

The roller coaster has stored energy at the top of the hill.

❓ What happens as gravity pulls the roller coaster down the hill?

Using Stored Energy Explain

Think About It
How are a battery and gasoline alike?

You just saw how a roller coaster uses stored energy. Other objects use stored energy, too.

A **battery** is an object that stores energy. A flashlight has a battery inside it. When you turn on the flashlight, it uses the battery's stored energy to give off light.

Gasoline for cars has stored energy that makes cars move.

Explore-a-Lab
Structured Inquiry

❓ **When will the elastic band have more stored energy?**

⚠️ **SAFETY:** Wear safety goggles. Never point the elastic band at anyone.

Gently stretch an elastic band between your fingers and shoot it. Now stretch the elastic band harder and shoot it. How far did the elastic band travel each time?

Make a Connection Extend

Make a chart. In one column, make a list of different objects in your home or classroom. In the second column, decide whether the object has energy of motion or stored energy. Compare your chart with a classmate's choices.

Lesson Review Assess/Reflect

Summary: What is energy? Energy can cause change and do work. Energy can be changed from one form to another. Energy can be stored, or it can be in motion.

1. **Graphic Organizer** Make a chart about changes caused by energy. List causes and effects.

2. **Vocabulary** How do you know if a battery has any stored energy?

3. **Test Prep** Which of these is energy of motion?
   A. gasoline   C. food
   B. sound   D. batteries

4. Explain how you use energy when you ride a bike.

5. Where do people get energy from?

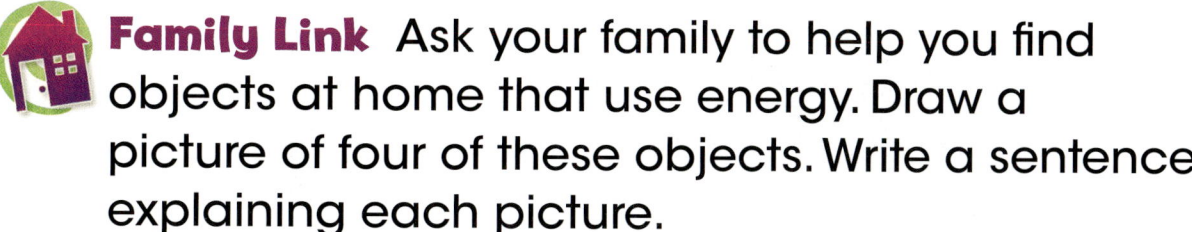 **Family Link** Ask your family to help you find objects at home that use energy. Draw a picture of four of these objects. Write a sentence explaining each picture.

359

Lesson 2

Vocabulary
temperature p. 362
thermometer p. 363
thermal energy p. 364
heat p. 364
solar energy p. 368

Find out what these words mean as you study this lesson.

Essential Question
What Is Thermal Energy? Engage

Get Ready to Learn How are the children in this picture dressed? In winter, thermal energy is important to how we feel. How will they be dressed in a few months when it is summer? Why will they be dressed differently?

Try This! What is the weather like where you live? Draw a picture of what you wear when it is cold outside. Draw a picture of what you wear when it is warm outside.

Record your work for this inquiry. Your teacher may also assign the related Guided Inquiry.

Cool It
What causes the water temperature to change?

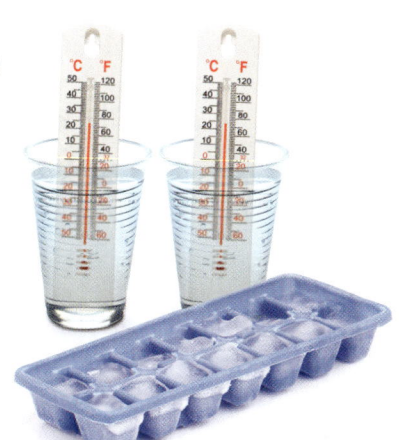

Your Group Needs
- two plastic cups
- two thermometers
- warm water
- ice cubes

Step 1 Put warm water and a thermometer into both cup A and cup B.

Step 2 Gather and record data about the water temperature of each cup.

Step 3 Put two ice cubes into cup B only. Then wait ten minutes.

Step 4 Gather and record data about the water temperature of each cup.

Create Explanations

1. What causes the water temperature to change?

2. Why were the temperatures different in Step 4?

Temperature Explain

Think about a time you touched an ice cube or ate a steaming bowl of soup. Ice is cold! Soup can be hot! **Temperature** is a measure of how hot or cold something is.

You learned that all the objects around you are made of matter. You also learned that matter is made of tiny particles, called atoms, that are too small to see.

Look at the bowl of hot soup. Its atoms are moving very fast, so its temperature is high. Now look at the ice cubes. Their atoms are moving very slowly, so their temperature is low.

❓ How do you know which object has a higher temperature?

Thermometers

Sometimes you want to know just how hot or cold something is. A **thermometer** is a tool that measures temperature. It has numbers on it and colored liquid inside a tube.

Think About It

How do you read a thermometer?

This thermometer has two scales. Most people in the United States use the Fahrenheit scale. The units are degrees Fahrenheit (°F). Scientists and most people in other countries use the Celsius scale. The units are degrees Celsius (°C).

Suppose you put a thermometer into hot water. The liquid in the thermometer moves up the tube. It stops at a higher number. That number is the water's temperature.

 **Math in Science**

The temperature on thermometer A is 30°C (86°F). The temperature on thermometer B is 24°C (75°F). Complete the number sentence. Use <, =, or >.

30°C (86°F) _____ 24°C (75°F)

Which thermometer is in a warmer place? How do you know?

363

Thermal Energy and Heat Explain

Thermal energy is the energy of moving atoms, the tiny particles that make up matter. Sometimes you run and play for a long time. Some of the energy in your body changes to thermal energy. You can feel this energy. It moves away from your body as heat. **Heat** is the movement of thermal energy from warmer places to cooler places.

Thermal energy is trapped by the warm clothes this child wears.

❓ What benefits did God create by making thermal energy?

Suppose you fill a bathtub with warm water. You get into the tub, and the water feels warm. Later the water feels cool. Some of the thermal energy moved as heat from the warm water to the cooler air. God's natural laws control how energy moves. He designed these laws so that thermal energy always moves from a warm place to a cooler place.

Think About It

Suppose thermal energy stayed in one place and did not move from a warm place to a cooler place. How would you feel after bike riding on a hot day? Why?

Rub your hands together fast. Do you feel the heat? Some of the energy made by rubbing your hands together changes to thermal energy. The energy moves away from your body as heat.

Heat is essential to everyday life. Heat from the Sun warms Earth. Without the Sun, Earth would be too cold for living things to stay alive.

Thermal energy moves from the hot fireplace into the cool room. You feel the movement of the energy from the fireplace as heat.

Why are these people warm?

You use heat every day. Heat in your toaster changes bread to toast. Heat from your hair dryer makes your wet hair dry. Heat from a fire helps keep your house warm.

Think About It

Why does a cup of hot tea get cooler?

? **How are these people using heat?**

Solar Energy Explain

Solar energy is energy from the Sun. It keeps Earth warm because it changes into heat when it hits objects.

People use solar energy in many ways. They build houses with windows. Sunlight goes through the windows and warms the air inside. People grow plants in greenhouses with see-through roofs and walls. Sunlight goes through the roofs and walls. This warms the air inside. The warm air helps the plants grow faster.

Scripture Spotlight

Read **Revelation 16:8–9**. Use the term *solar energy* to describe what you read about.

Explore-a-Lab
Structured Inquiry

 What effect will sunlight and shade have on temperature?

Measure the temperature outdoors in the Sun. Measure the temperature in the shade at the same time. Compare the two temperatures.

Make a Connection Extend

Solar energy can damage your skin if you stay outside in sunlight too long. Interview an adult to find out how to protect your skin from damage from the Sun. Make a list of suggestions, and share them with your class.

Lesson Review Assess/Reflect

Summary: What is thermal energy? Temperature is a measure of how hot or cold something is. Thermal energy is the energy of the tiny moving parts of matter. When it moves from warmer to cooler places, it is heat. Solar energy, energy from the Sun, warms Earth.

1. **Graphic Organizer** Make a chart that compares heat, thermal energy, and solar energy.

2. **Vocabulary** What units describe temperature?

3. **Test Prep** A thermometer is used to measure which type of energy?
   A. light   B. heat   C. sound   D. solar energy

4. What would happen to living things if the Sun stopped shining?

5. What natural laws did God make for thermal energy?

Family Link Decide which room in your house is the warmest during the day. Ask your family to help you figure out why it is the warmest. Record your ideas.

Lesson 3

Vocabulary

wave p. 372
pitch p. 374
loudness p. 375
shadow p. 377

Find out what these words mean as you study this lesson.

Essential Question

What Are Sound and Light? Engage

Get Ready to Learn What wakes you up in the morning? If it is dark, is it harder to wake up? Many people use an alarm clock to wake them up. Some people wake up with the sunlight.

Try This! What sounds do people, animals, and objects make? Write a list of things that make sounds. Then describe or imitate the sound each thing makes.

Record your work for this inquiry. Your teacher may also assign the related Guided Inquiry.

Shine a Light
How does light travel?

Your Group Needs
- three index cards, prepared by your teacher
- masking tape
- flashlight

Step 1 Tape masking tape to a desk to make a straight edge. Line up index cards along the edge of the masking tape, about 3 centimeters (1.2 inches) apart so that the holes of the cards line up.

Step 2 Predict what will happen when you shine the flashlight into the first hole.

Step 3 Observe and **record** what happens.

Step 4 Move the middle card out of alignment slightly. Use the flashlight and repeat Steps 2–3.

Create Explanations

1. How does light travel?
2. Did you correctly predict the results in both trials? Explain.

Sound and Light Waves Explain

Both sound and light travel in waves. A **wave** is movement that takes energy from one place to another.

Light waves, such as sunlight, can travel through space. Sound waves, however, need matter to travel. They can pass through solids, liquids, and gases. But they cannot move through space because space has no matter. Some kinds of matter, such as wood, block light waves.

Light waves travel faster than sound waves. Think about a thunderstorm. Lightning and thunder happen at the same time. But you see lightning before you hear thunder.

Scripture Spotlight

Read **Psalm 119:105**. What do you think it means?

Think About It

How are sound and light alike and different?

Light waves from lightning reach your eyes quickly. Sound waves from thunder reach your ears a few seconds later depending on the distance from you.

Sound Energy

The bark of a dog, the ring of a bell, and the voice of a friend are all sounds. God designed your ears so you could hear. When a sound reaches your ears, your brain tells you what sound you are hearing.

Sound is made when something vibrates. *Vibrate* means to move quickly back and forth. When someone plays a guitar, the strings vibrate. That makes the air vibrate and travel to your ears as sound.

Think About It

Why do you think that people with hearing impairments can often still enjoy music?

When someone knocks on your door, the wood in the door vibrates. That makes the air vibrate and travel to your ears as sound.

One way to tell one sound from another is pitch. **Pitch** is how high or low a sound is. Air that vibrates slowly makes a sound with a low pitch. Air that vibrates quickly makes a sound with a high pitch. The rumble of thunder has a low pitch. The buzz of a mosquito has a high pitch.

When this boy shouts, the air vibrates and travels to his friend's ears.

❓ How do you change the pitch of your voice?

Another way to tell one sound from another is loudness. **Loudness** is how strong or weak a sound is. The siren on a fire truck makes a loud sound. The purr of a cat makes a soft sound. Some sounds are so loud that they can harm your ears. When you listen to music, be careful not to play it too loudly.

Explore-a-Lab
Guided Inquiry

How can you make a high and low pitch?

Use a shoebox and rubber bands to make a model of a guitar. Experiment by trying to make a high-pitched sound and a low-pitched sound.

The sound the large bell makes has a low pitch. The sound the small bell makes has a high pitch.

Light Energy Explain

Some natural objects, such as the Sun and fireflies, give off light. Some objects made by people, such as light bulbs and candles, also give off light.

Most objects do not give off light. You see these objects only when light bounces off them and travels to your eyes. God designed your eyes so you could see. Without light, you would not see anything.

Scripture Spotlight
Make a connection with **John 8:12** to what you learn from this page.

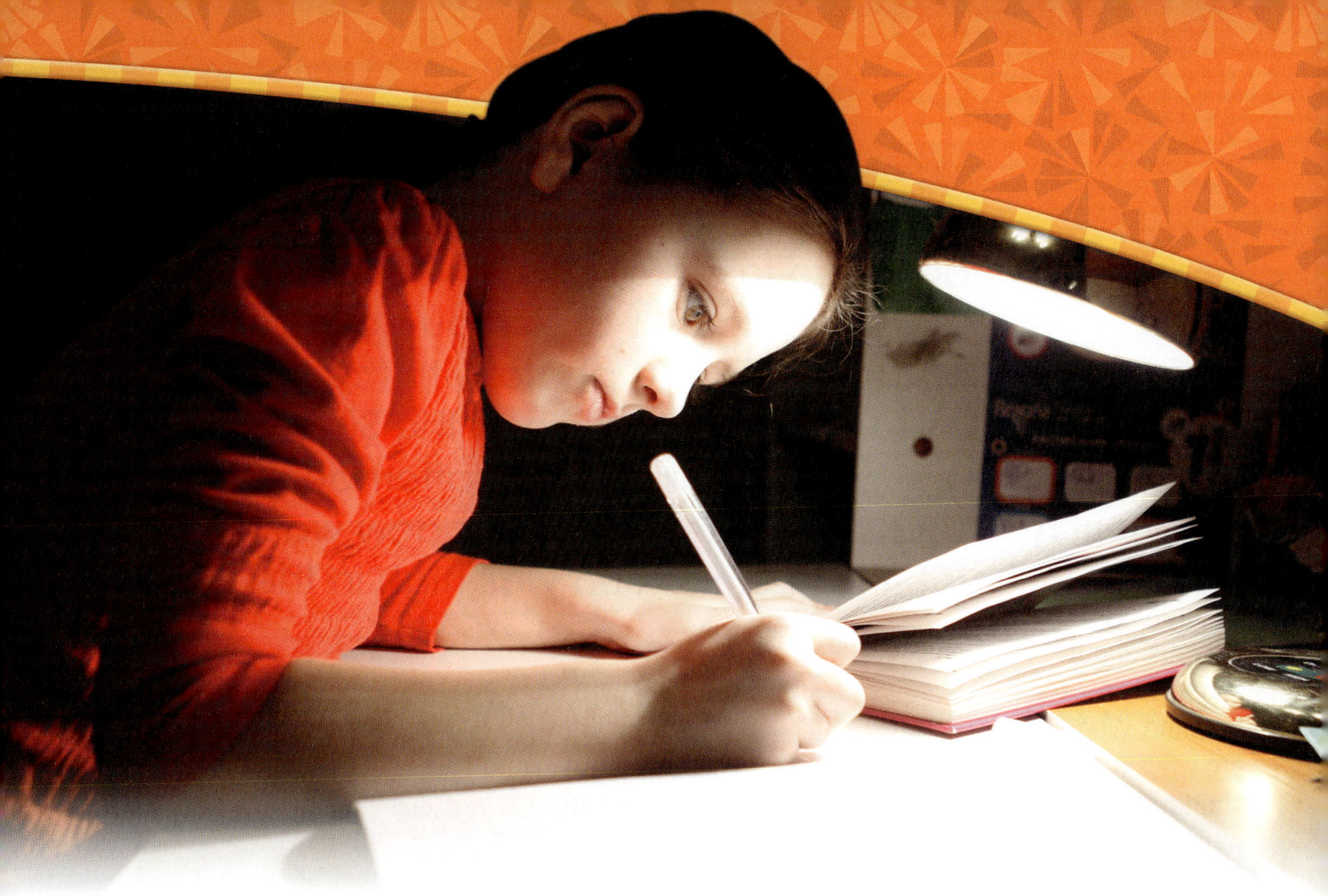

In this picture, light from a light bulb shines on each object. Then the light bounces off each object to the girl's eyes. She sees the objects because of the light.

A **shadow** is a dark or shaded area that appears when light is blocked. When a flagpole blocks the sunlight, you see a shadow in the shape of the flagpole on the ground. When your hand blocks the light from a lamp, you see a shadow in the shape of your hand on the wall or desk.

What is the source of light in this room?

Check out your *Science Journal* for a Guided Inquiry that helps you find your lost shadow.

Discover

Think About It

Sometimes children are nervous about shadows at bedtime. What are ways to make shadows smaller or make them disappear?

These two photos of the same golf ball were taken at different times on the same day. What do you notice about them? The photo with the longer shadow was taken when the Sun was low in the sky, in the late afternoon. The photo with the shorter shadow was taken when the Sun was high in the sky, close to noon.

Math in Science

Record the length of your shadow outside in the morning. Record it again at noon. How much did the length of your shadow change?

Make a Connection Extend

With a partner, discuss what life would be like without sound or light energy. Research how people with hearing or visual impairments are able to do day-to-day tasks, such as walking to school or answering the telephone.

Lesson Review Assess/Reflect

Summary: What are sound and light? Sound and light are forms of energy. Sound and light energy travel in waves that carry energy. You see most objects when light bounces off them. Vibrations cause sounds.

1. **Graphic Organizer** Make a Venn diagram. Compare and contrast sound energy and light energy.

2. **Vocabulary** What causes shadows?

3. **Test Prep** Which refers to how high or low a sound is?
   - A. loudness
   - B. wave
   - C. vibrate
   - D. pitch

4. Name something that gives off light. Tell whether the source of the light is natural or made by people.

5. Why did God design our eyes and ears to work together?

Family Link Ask each family member to name an object that makes sound and tell which part vibrates.

Lesson 4

Vocabulary

simple machine p. 382

inclined plane p. 383

screw p. 383

wedge p. 384

lever p. 385

wheel and axle p. 386

pulley p. 388

Find out what these words mean as you study this lesson.

Essential Question

What Are Simple Machines?

Engage

Get Ready to Learn Why do people like to ride bikes or scooters? The wheels and pedals are tools that make it easier for you to move faster and travel farther. And riding is fun, too! What are some other things that make it easier for you to move faster?

Try This! What are four tools that make doing work easier? With a partner, take turns using modeling clay to make models of tools you use in daily life. Then, have your partner guess what the tool is.

Lift It

How can you lift a textbook with a ruler?

Your Group Needs
- textbook
- pencil
- ruler

Step 1 Put the textbook on the end of the ruler. Use the ruler to try to lift the book. **Observe** whether it is easy or hard to do.

Step 2 Put the pencil under the ruler at the 15-cm mark. Push down on the other end of the ruler. **Observe** how easy or hard it is to lift the book.

Step 3 Move the pencil closer and farther away from the book. Each time you move the pencil, **observe** and **record** where it is placed under the ruler. Is it easier or harder to lift the book? **Compare** your observations.

Create Explanations

1. How can you lift a textbook with a ruler?
2. What would you have to do to lift two textbooks? Explain.

Simple Machines Explain

Imagine that you used your allowance to buy a new toy. You want to play with it, but first you have to remove the plastic case that protects it. You push it and pull it, but the case will not come off. You need a tool to help you. What tool will you use?

When you move something by applying a force, you are doing work. If you push or pull and nothing moves—no work is done. **Simple machines** are tools that make it easier for you to do work. They do not have many moving parts. A knife is a simple machine that can help you cut through a material or its wrapping.

❓ How is a paint can opener a simple machine?

Inclined Planes, Screws, and Wedges

Did you ever play on a water slide? A water slide is a simple machine called an inclined plane. An **inclined plane** is a slanted surface that joins a lower level to a higher level. An inclined plane makes it easier to move objects up or down.

A screw is a simple machine. A **screw** is an inclined plane wrapped around a rod. It holds objects together. A cap fits on a water bottle. The threads of the cap are what hold the cap onto the bottle.

Think About It

How do inclined planes and screws make it easier to do work?

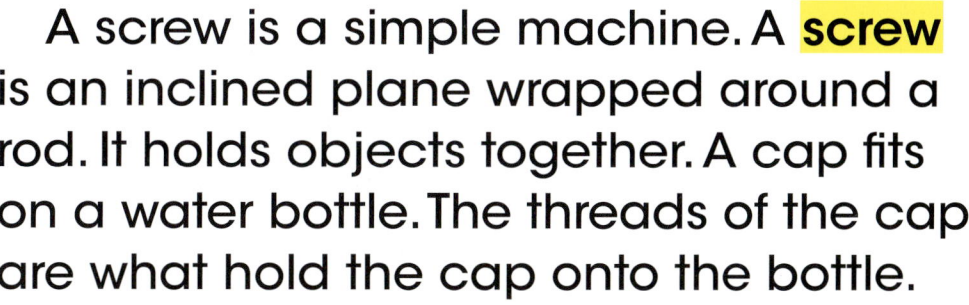

▼ A water slide is an inclined plane.

◀ Screws help hold things together.

Think About It

Give an example of how a wedge makes work easier.

A wedge is a simple machine that you use every day. A **wedge** is used to push two objects apart. It is made up of two inclined planes. Where the inclined planes meet, they form an edge that cuts things apart. A knife is an example of a wedge.

Wedge →

A hatchet or an axe is a wedge that makes it easier to chop wood.

Levers Explain

Another simple machine is a lever. A **lever** is a bar used to lift objects. The bar rests on a support called a *fulcrum*. The object is on one end. You push on the other end to lift the object. A lever often helps make it easier to lift objects.

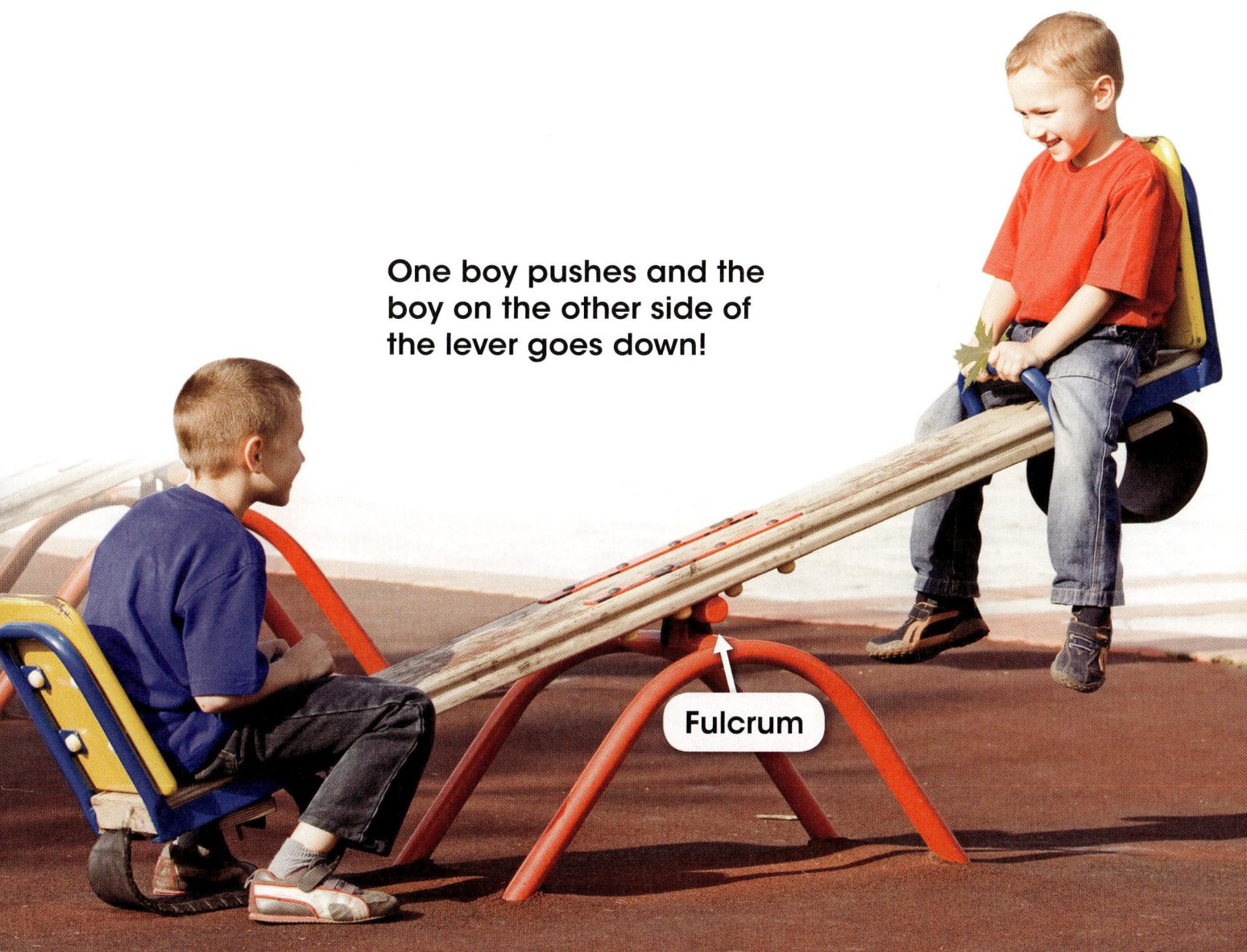

One boy pushes and the boy on the other side of the lever goes down!

Fulcrum

Wheels and Axles Explain

Wagons have wheels and axles. A <mark>wheel and axle</mark> is a simple machine with a rod, or axle, through the center of a wheel. The axle, or rod, makes it easy to turn the wheel.

The wheel and axle are similar to a lever. The axle is the fulcrum and the wheel is the lever. Together, they make it easier to move objects over distances.

Think About It

What might happen if the axle on this boy's bike was bent?

How are the wagon and the bicycle alike?

Wheel

Axle

Explore-a-Lab

Structured Inquiry

How far can wheeled objects roll?

Use a book and blocks to make a ramp. Roll different wheeled objects down the ramp. Measure how far each goes. Change how steep the ramp is and repeat.

387

Pulleys Explain

A **pulley** is a simple machine similar to a wheel and axle. It uses a grooved wheel on an axle with a rope or cable wrapped around the wheel to move an object. A flagpole has a pulley at the top of the pole. The top of the flagpole is too high to reach, so a person uses the pulley to help. The flag is hooked to the rope. The rope runs through the pulley. A person pulls down on the rope, and the flag goes up to the top of the pole.

Think About It

What kinds of work can pulleys do?

A pulley changes the direction when you pull. You pull down, and the flag goes up.

Make a Connection Extend

Imagine that you built a tree house. It is not easy to get into a tree house. How could you use a simple machine to help? Draw a picture. Write about how the machine would help you.

Lesson Review Assess/Reflect

Summary: What are simple machines? Simple machines are tools that make it easier for you to do work. They include the inclined plane, screw, wedge, lever, wheel and axle, and pulley.

1. **Graphic Organizer** Make a chart that lists the simple machines, how each helps, and an example of each.

2. **Vocabulary** How do simple machines make it easier to do work?

3. **Test Prep** Which simple machine is used to hold things together?
   - A. wheel and axle
   - B. pulley
   - C. inclined plane
   - D. screw

4. A knife is an example of a wedge. Why does a sharp knife cut a slice of bread better than a dull knife?

Family Link Ask your family to find objects at home that use simple machines. Draw a picture of the objects, and label the simple machines.

389

Careers in Science
Extend

Physicist

Physicists are scientists who study tiny bits of matter. They also study the Universe and energy. Physicists wants to know how our world works. They help make better computers, cell phones, and microscopes.

Energy Engineer

Energy engineers find ways to make energy work better. They want to find ways to use less energy.

Energy engineers study the cost of energy. They study how much and what kinds of energy we use.

Most of our energy comes from oil and coal. Someday, these kinds of energy may be used up. Energy engineers look for ways to use wind, water, and solar energy. These kinds of energy will not get used up.

Concept Check
1. In what ways do you see the work of physicists in your life?
2. Why is it important that scientists find new ways to save energy?

Science and Technology
Extend

Solar Energy Panels

Solar panels use sunlight to make electricity. Sunlight is free, and it never runs out.

You may have seen a calculator that has a solar panel. The panel collects light and turns it into electricity. The electricity makes the calculator work.

Scientists and engineers want to find new ways to use solar energy to power things like cars and homes.

Robonaut2

Robonaut2 (R2) is a robot that looks like a human. NASA can use robots like R2 to help astronauts safely explore space.

NASA sent R2 to the *International Space Station* in February 2011. R2's job is to help the astronauts working on the space station. It can give the astronauts a helping hand. It can also do jobs astronauts cannot do.

Concept Check
1. Why are solar energy panels a good idea?
2. What do you think astronauts must have in space that Robonauts do not need?

Unit 4 Review — Assess/Reflect

Vocabulary

Use the words below to complete the sentences.

energy   solid   simple machines
volume   mass   chemical
sound   atoms

1. When you want to move objects that are too heavy to lift, you can use _____ _____ to help you.

2. The tiny particles that make up all matter are _____.

3. When we measure how much space an object takes up, we measure _____.

4. An object that vibrates back and forth produces _____.

5. Heat, sound, and light are three forms of _____.

6. The shape of a(n) _____ does not change to fit the shape of a container.

7. A heavy object has a large _____.

8. A change in matter can be a physical change or a(n) _____ change.

Describe What You See

9. Look at the picture. Use the words *matter, mass, property,* and *energy* to describe the boy on the swing.

Use Science Practices

10. Kendra mixes a blue liquid and a green powder. She **observes** bubbles forming and **measures** an increase in temperature. After five minutes, the powder is gone and the liquid is red. What kind of change—chemical or physical—can Kendra **infer** happened? Why?

Multiple Choice

11. Which property tells how high or low a sound is?
 A. pitch   **C.** loudness
 B. volume   **D.** temperature

12. Which is not a form of matter?
 A. gas   **C.** mass
 B. liquid   **D.** solid

Short Answer

13. A worker needs to get a box of tools to the roof of a house. What simple machine would make this task easier?

14. What physical change could happen to an iron nail? What chemical change could happen to it?

15. What happens when you tap a drum with your hand? How do you know this?

16. During a thunderstorm, you usually see lightning before you hear thunder. Why is this true?

Using the Glossary

The Glossary is like a small dictionary. It lists important science terms from your book. The words and terms are listed in alphabetical order. Each word is followed by its meaning. Some words have more than one meaning. This glossary gives the scientific meaning. That is how the word is used in this book. After the meaning is a page number that tells on what page the word is first used.

abyssal plain The flat area in the deep part of the ocean. (p. 223)

acid rain A mixture of rain water and acid caused by pollution. (p. 96)

anemometer A device that measures the wind's speed. (p. 263)

antibiotic Medicine that kills or slows down some germs. (p. 182)

astronaut A person who goes into space or has trained to go into space in a spacecraft. (p. 308)

astronomer A person who studies stars, planets, and other things in space. (p. 306)

atom A tiny particle that is too small to see that makes up all matter. (p. 320)

autumn The season between summer and winter. Autumn is also called *fall.* (p. 279)

B

basic need What a living thing must have to stay alive. (p. 22)

battery An object that stores energy. (p. 358)

behavior Something an animal does or a way it acts. (p. 60)

brain The part of the nervous system that controls all the other body systems. (p. 142)

C

calorie A unit that describes how much energy is stored in food. (p. 354)

canines The sharp teeth next to the incisors that help tear food. (p. 114)

canyon A long, narrow valley with steep sides. (p. 219)

cavity A hole that germs make in a tooth. (p. 189)

cell The basic unit of all living things. Living things are made up of many different kinds of cells. (p. 112)

checkup A visit with a doctor to check on your health. (p. 178)

chemical change A change that makes a new kind of matter. (p. 343)

coast Where an ocean or a sea meets the land. (p. 220)

communication The sharing of ideas, thoughts, feelings, and information. (p. 152)

condense To change from a gas to a liquid by cooling. (p. 271)

constellation A pattern of stars. (p. 301)

core The center of the Earth. (p. 241)

crosswalk A marked place on a road so that people can get from one side to the other safely. (p. 202)

crust The outer layer of Earth. (p. 241)

dentist A person whose job is to take care of people's teeth. (p. 189)

desert A very dry place. Many deserts are hot, but some are cold. (p. 76)

diabetes A disease in which the sugar level in the blood is too high. (p. 131)

diet The type of food and drink a person takes in. (p. 122)

digestive system All the parts of the body that break down food and absorb nutrients. (p. 112)

dinosaur A large reptile that lived on Earth long ago and is now extinct. (p. 250)

doctor A person who treats sick people and helps them get well. (p. 177)

drought A very long time without rain. (p. 24)

Earth The third planet from the Sun and the home God created for us. (p. 292)

earthquake The movement of Earth's surface. (p. 241)

edible Able to be eaten. (pp. 38, 123)

emotion A feeling or a mood. (p. 163)

enamel The hard outer layer of a tooth. (p. 188)

endangered At risk of dying out. (p. 100)

energy Something that can do work and cause change. (p. 352)

equator An imaginary line that runs around the middle of the Earth. It divides Earth into a northern half and a southern half. (p. 278)

erosion The movement of rocks and soil caused by wind, water, ice, and gravity. (p. 238)

esophagus The tube that food passes through from your mouth to your stomach. (p. 116)

evaporate To change from a liquid to a gas. (p. 270)

extinct Gone forever. Extinct kinds of plants and animals have died out. (p. 252)

first aid Fast help for someone who is sick or hurt. (p. 200)

fissure A large crack in Earth's surface, usually caused by an earthquake. (p. 242)

floss A string used to clean between teeth and gums. (p. 189)

flower Part of a plant that has petals and produces seeds. (p. 32)

food ad A notice from a company that tries to get people to buy their food. (p. 131)

food chain A diagram of how food energy goes from one living thing to another (p. 86)

food group Different kinds of food that have similar properties. (p. 124)

food guide An eating plan designed to help people have a balanced diet. (p. 124)

food label A notice on food packaging that lists information about a type of food. (p. 132)

food web A diagram that shows how a number of food chains are connected. (p. 88)

forest An environment with many tall trees. (p. 79)

fossil The remains of a living thing that died long ago. (p. 248)

freeze To change from a liquid to a solid. (p. 336)

fulcrum The point where a lever rests. (p. 385)

galaxy A very large group of stars, planets, their moons, asteroids, comets, dust, and gases. The Solar System is part of the Milky Way galaxy. (p. 300)

gas A kind of matter that fills its container. It does not have a definite volume or shape. (p. 334)

germ A tiny living thing that can make people sick. (p. 176)

germinate To sprout, or start to grow. (p. 31)

gill A body part that fish use to breathe oxygen from the water. (p. 50)

grassland An environment filled with grasses. (p. 78)

grooming Caring for your body and the way you look. (p. 190)

H

habitat The place where a plant or an animal finds the things it needs to live. (p. 74)

hail Precipitation that falls as large pellets of ice. Hail forms inside a cloud. (p. 274)

head lice Tiny insects that live in hair and make a person's head itch. (p. 191)

heat The movement of thermal energy from warmer places to cooler places. (p. 364)

hurricane A very large storm that forms over warm waters with damaging winds, heavy rains, and large waves. (p. 266)

hygiene Keeping yourself and the things around you clean and healthy. (p. 186)

I

igneous rock A rock formed when melted rock cools and becomes hard. (p. 230)

incisors The teeth in the front of the mouth that are used for biting and cutting through food. (p. 114)

inclined plane A simple machine that has a slanted surface. It joins a lower level to a higher level and makes it easier to move objects up and down. (p. 383)

intestine A long tube in the body through which food passes after it is broken down in the stomach. It is divided into the small intestine and the large intestine. (p. 116)

invertebrate An animal that does not have a backbone. (p. 58)

lake A large body of water that has land all around it. (p. 224)

landform A natural shape, or feature, of Earth's surface. Landforms include mountains, plains, canyons, rivers, and lakes. (p. 214)

landslide When large amounts of rock and dirt slide quickly down mountains and hills. (p. 240)

larva A young animal that does not look like the adult. A caterpillar is a larva. (p. 64)

lava Melted rock that flows from a volcano. (p. 244)

lever A simple machine made of a bar that is pushed against a fulcrum to lift heavy objects. (p. 385)

life cycle All the stages a living thing goes through during its lifetime. (p. 30)

light A form of energy you can see. (p. 355)

liquid A form of matter that does not have its own shape and takes the shape of its container. (p. 333)

litter Garbage that is thrown away outside and not recycled. Paper and bottles laying on the ground or in water are litter. (p. 98)

living thing Things that grow and change, make more living things like themselves, and respond to things around them. (p. 18)

loudness How strong or weak a sound is. (p. 375)

mantle The middle layer of the Earth. (p. 241)

mass The amount of matter that is in an object. (p. 322)

matter Anything that has mass and takes up space. (p. 320)

melt To change from a solid to a liquid. (p. 336)

metamorphic rock A rock formed when heat and pressure change older rock into a new kind of rock. (p. 232)

meteorologist A scientist who studies weather. (p. 258)

mid-ocean ridge A long, underwater mountain range. (p. 222)

migrate To travel back and forth between two places. Some animals migrate to find food or to lay eggs or have their young. (p. 60)

mineral A substance you need in small amounts for growth, activity, and good health. (p. 123) A natural solid not made by living things that is the same all the way through. (p. 228)

molars The wide flat-surfaced, strong teeth in the back of the mouth that crush food. (p. 115)

moon A large object that revolves around a planet. (p. 293)

mountain A landform that is much higher than the land around it. (p. 216)

nerve A long fiber that carries messages between the brain and other body parts. (p. 145)

nerve ending The tip of a nerve that reacts to temperature and pressure, and senses smell, light, sound, and taste. (p. 145)

nervous system The body system that controls the body and senses what is happening inside and outside the body. (p. 142)

nonedible Something that is not fit to be eaten. (p. 123)

nonverbal communication Facial expressions, posture, gestures, and eye contact that convey information, ideas, thoughts, or feelings. (p. 156)

nutrient Substance that a living thing needs to grow. (pp. 23, 112)

obese Over a healthy weight. (p. 131)

observatory A special building used by scientists to study space using large telescopes. (p. 306)

ocean A very large and very deep body of salt water. (p. 220)

orbit The path an object takes as it moves around another object. (pp. 280, 293)

oxygen A gas found in air that animals need to live. (p. 49)

peak The top of a mountain. (p. 216)

personality Thoughts, feelings, and behaviors that are special to you. (p. 162)

physical change A change in the size or shape of matter. (p. 340)

pitch How high or low a sound is. (p. 374)

plain A large, flat area of land. (p. 217)

planet A large ball of gas or rock that travel around a star. (p. 292)

plant A kind of living thing that makes its own food. (p. 21)

poison A substance that can make you sick if you eat it, drink it, or breathe it. Many poisons are deadly. (p. 198)

pole A location on the "top" or "bottom" of Earth. The top location is called the North Pole, and the bottom location is called the South Pole. (p. 278)

pollen A powder made by the male parts of a flower. (p. 32)

pollution Harmful substances that are added to the air, water, or ground. (p. 95)

precipitation Water that falls to Earth as rain, snow, sleet, or hail. (p. 273)

premolars The teeth next to the canines that help grind food. (p. 114)

property A quality you can use to describe things. Color, shape, and size are properties. (p. 321)

pulley A simple machine that uses a grooved wheel and a rope to move an object. (p. 388)

pulp The soft tissue that reaches from the top of each tooth to the root. (p. 188)

pupa An insect that is changing from a larva to an adult. (p. 64)

R

receiver In communication, the person who gets a message. (p. 152)

reflex A body's response to something that the brain does not need to think about. (p. 146)

relationship How you get along with another person. (p. 162)

resource A material found in nature that people use. (p. 40)

response In communication, how the receiver reacts to a message. (p. 152)

revolve To move around another object. (p. 293)

rock A natural solid made from minerals. (p. 229)

rocket A spacecraft that uses burning fuel to push it forward. (p. 308)

S

saliva The liquid in your mouth that mixes with food and helps break down food. (p. 113)

sand Tiny broken pieces of rock and other solid materials. (p. 231)

satellite An object in space that orbits a larger body such as a planet or a star. A satellite can be natural or human-made. (p. 265)

screw A simple machine that holds objects together. It is an inclined plane wrapped around a rod. (p. 383)

seamount An underwater mountain peak. (p. 223)

sedimentary rock A rock formed when bits of broken rock, soil, and shells are pressed together. (p. 231)

seed The first stage of the life cycle for most plants. It has stored food and a tiny plant inside. (p. 31)

seedling A young plant that has just started to grow. (p. 31)

sender In communication, the person sending a message. (p. 152)

serving The amount of food in one portion. (p. 133)

shadow A dark or shaded area that appears when light is blocked. (p. 377)

shelter A place where an animal can go to be safe or to stay out of the heat, cold, or other bad weather. (p. 52)

simple machine A tool without many moving parts that makes it easier for people to do work. (p. 382)

sleet Precipitation that forms as rain freezes and becomes tiny pellets of ice. (p. 274)

smoke detector An alarm that sounds when it senses smoke. (p. 197)

snack A small amount of food or drink between meals. (p. 130)

solar energy Light and thermal energy from the Sun. It keeps Earth warm. (p. 368)

Solar System The Sun and the group of objects that orbit it. It includes the planets, moons, asteroids, meteors, and comets. (p. 293)

solid A form of matter that has its own shape. (p. 330)

sound A form of energy you can hear. (p. 355)

space probe A device sent to space that collects and sends information back to Earth. (p. 307)

spinal cord A bundle of nerves that runs from your brain down your back, through your vertebrae. It carries messages between your brain and most of your body. (p. 146)

star A huge ball of hot gases in the sky. (p. 291)

stomach A sac-like body part that produces acid to break down food and absorbs nutrients from food. (p. 116)

Sun The closest star to Earth. The Sun is the center of our Solar System. (p. 291)

symptom A sign of being sick. (p. 176)

telescope An instrument used to view objects far away. (p. 306)

temperature A measure of how hot or cold something is. (p. 362)

texture How something feels. (p. 325)

thermal energy The energy of motion of the atoms that make up matter. (p. 364)

thermometer A tool that measures temperature. (p. 363)

thunderstorm A type of weather with heavy rains, lightning, and thunder. (p. 266)

tornado A powerful windstorm that may form within a thunderstorm; its winds form a funnel shape. (p. 266)

Universe Everything that exists, including all the galaxies, stars, solar systems, planets, and moons. (p. 302)

vaccine Weakened or dead germs that teach the immune system how to fight a germ. (p. 181)

valley The low area between two mountains. (p. 216)

value An idea or belief a person tries to live by. (p. 165)

verbal communication Spoken or written words that give information, ideas, thoughts, or feelings. (p. 155)

vertebrate An animal that has a backbone (p. 58)

vitamin A substance that is needed in small amounts for growth, activity, and good health. Living things make vitamins. (p. 123)

volcano An opening in Earth's surface from which gas, volcanic ash, and lava flow. (p. 244)

volume How much space something takes up. (p. 323)

waste Any food not used by the body. (p. 117)

water cycle The moving of water from Earth's surface into the air and back again. (p. 272)

water vapor Water in the form of a gas. (p. 270)

wave The way that energy travels from one place to another. (p. 372)

weather The conditions of the air around you. (p. 260)

weathering The breaking up of large rocks into smaller pieces by wind, water, and ice. (p. 238)

weather map A map that shows weather information for a large area during a certain time. (p. 263)

weather satellite A human-made object that travels around Earth and gives information weather forecasters use. (p. 265)

wedge A simple machine with slanted sides that pushes or cuts things apart. It is made up of two inclined planes. (p. 384)

wetland An area of land that is usually wet. Swamps, marshes, and bogs are types of wetlands. (p. 80)

wheel and axle A simple machine with a rod, or axle, through the center of a wheel. (p. 386)

Index

A

abyssal plain…223
acid rain…96
air…22
amphibian…58
anemometer…263
animal…46–55, 56–67, 100–101, 149
    basic needs…22, 46–55
    behavior…60–61, 66
    body parts…54–55
    care for young…47
    endangered…100–101
    life cycle…62–63, 64–65
    movement…57
    nervous systems…149
    shelter…46, 50
    types of…58
antibiotic…182
astronaut…308, 309, 391
astronomer…303, 306, 311
atom…320
autumn…279

B

basic need…16–25, 22, 46–55
battery…358
behavior…60
Big Idea…15, 71, 109, 139, 173, 211, 257, 287, 317, 349
bike helmets…196
bird…52, 58, 60, 61, 62, 67, 100
brain…142, 142–143
bully, dealing with…153
butte…218

C

calorie…354
canine…114
canyon…219
cavity…185, 189
cell…112
checkup…178
chemical change…339, 343, 343–344, 345
chemist, organic…347
child abuse…153
cloud…262, 269
coast…220
communication…150–151, 152, 152–159
    abuse…153
    emergencies…154
    health information…158
    nonverbal…150, 151, 156–157, 159
    verbal…155
    with a bully…153
condense…271
cone…34
constellation…301
core…241
crater…244
crosswalk…202
crust…241

D

dentist…189
desert…76
diabetes…131
diet…122

digestive system…110–119, 111
    caring for…118
    esophagus…116
    intestines…116
    mouth…113
    saliva…113
    stomach…116
    teeth…113, 114–115
dinosaur…250, 250–252, 253
doctor…177
drought…24

E

Earth…241, 292
    core…241
    crust…241
    mantle…241
earthquake…241, 241–243, 255
edible…38, 123
emotion…163–164
enamel…188
endangered…100–101
energy…350–359, 352, 360–369, 370–379
    energy paths…86–87, 88
    energy transfers…356–357
    heat…364–367
    light…355, 371, 372, 376–378, 379
    solar energy…368, 391
    sound…355, 372, 373–375, 379
    stored energy…356
    thermal energy…360–369
    waves…372
energy engineer…390
environment…92–93
    human's effect on…90–101

equator...278

erosion...237, 238–240

esophagus...116

evaporate...270

exercise...124

Explore-a-Lab...24, 30, 38, 51, 52, 75, 100, 146, 179, 189, 214, 231, 243, 250, 265, 271, 280, 296, 300, 326, 323, 335, 342, 358, 368, 387

extinct...252

F

fats...129

first aid...200–201

fish...50, 56, 58
   gills...50

fissure...242

float or sink...326

floss...189

flower...29, 32–33

food ad...131

food chain...83, 86–87

food group...120, 121

food guide...124–125

food label...132

food web...88

foods and nutrition...38–39, 82, 84–85, 110, 120–127, 128–135, 136–137
   food group...120, 121
   food guide...124–125
   food label...132

forest...79

fossil...246–249, 248, 253

freeze...336

fulcrum...385

G

galaxy...300

gas...334, 337

Genesis Flood...215, 239, 252

geologist...254

geophysicist...284

germ...174, 175, 176, 179–180, 181–182, 183

germinate...31

gill...50

grassland...78

gravity...240

grooming...190–191

gums...188

H

habitat...74, 72–81, 99
   desert...76
   forest...79
   grassland...78
   loss...99
   wetland...80

hail...274

head lice...191

health and safety...174–183, 184–193, 194–203
   antibiotics...182
   checkup...178
   dental hygiene...185, 188–189, 193
   fire safety...194, 197
   first aid...200–201
   germs...174, 175, 176–180, 183
   hygiene...184–193
   poisons...198–199
   safety hazards...194–203
   safety rules...196
   traffic safety...195, 202
   treating sickness...177–178, 181–182
   vaccine...181, 183

heat...364

hurricane...266

hygiene...184–193, 186

I

incisor...114–115

inclined plane...383

igneous rock...230

insect...64–65, 66
   head lice...191
   life cycle...64–65, 66

invertebrate...58

J

junk food...134

L

lake...224

landform...213, 214, 214–215, 222–223, 225
   canyon...219
   mountain...216
   plain...217
   underwater...222–223
   valley...216

landslide...240

larva...64

lava...230, 244

leaf...28–29

Lesson Activity...59, 85, 117, 124, 134, 148, 154, 158, 163, 165, 200, 201, 306

Lesson Review...25, 35, 45, 55, 67, 81, 89, 101, 119, 127, 135, 149, 159, 169, 183, 193, 203, 225, 235, 245, 253, 267, 275, 283, 297, 303, 309, 327, 337, 345, 359, 369, 379, 389

lever...385

life cycle…30, 30–35, 64–65
   adult…65
   butterfly…64–65, 66
   egg…64
   larva…64
   plant…30–35
   pupa…65
light…355, 371, 372, 376–378, 379
liquid…333
litter…98
living things…18, 282
   animal…46–55, 56–67, 100–101, 149
   basic needs…16–25, 48–53
   plant…16–25, 21, 26–35, 36–45, 100–101
   seasons and…282
loudness…375
lungs…50

M

machine…380–389
   inclined plane…383
   lever…381, 385
   pulley…388
   screw…383
   simple…380–389, 382
   wedge…384
   wheel-and-axle…386–387
   work…380
mammal…58
mantle…241
mass…284, 322, 324
Materials scientist…347
Math in Science…21, 28, 41, 53, 65, 87, 99, 132, 142, 219, 229, 240, 264, 274, 282, 301, 308, 332, 341, 354, 363, 378

matter…318–327, 320, 328–337, 338–346
   changes in form…335–336
   chemical change…339, 343, 343–344
   gas…334, 337
   liquid…333, 337
   physical change…339, 340, 340–342
   properties of…321–326, 327
   solid…330–332, 337
melt…336
mental health…160–169
   decisions…161, 166–167, 168, 169
   emotions…163–164
   personality…160, 162
   relationships…162
   values…165, 169
mesa…218
metamorphic rock…232
meteorologist…258
mid-ocean ridge…222
migrate…60, 66
mineral…123, 228
molar…115
mountain…217

N

nerve…145
nervous system…140–149, 141
   brain…142–143
   injuries…148
   nerve endings…145
   nerves…145
   reflex…146
   senses…140, 141, 144
   spinal cord…146

nonedible…123
nonverbal communication…150, 151, 156–157
nutrient…23, 112, 123, 126
nutrition…123, 124–126, 128–135, 137

O

obese…131
observatory…306
ocean…215, 220–223
ocean landforms…222–223
   abyssal plain…223
   mid-ocean ridge…222
   ocean trench…223
   seamount…223
   volcanic island…222
oceanographer…284
orbit…280, 293
oxygen…49

P

paleontologist…254
pass…216
peak…216
personality…160, 162
physical change…339, 340, 340–342
physicist…390
pitch…374
plain…217
planet…292

plant…16–25, 21, 26–35, 36–45, 100–101
   basic needs…16–25
   cones…34
   endangered…100–101
   flower…29, 32
   germinate…31
   life cycle…30
   parts of…26–35
   pollen…32
   resources…36–45
   seed…31
   seedling…31
   types of…16, 20–21
plateau…218
poison…198–199
pole…278
pollen…32
pollution…91, 95–98
precipitation…262, 272, 273, 274
premolar…114–115
property…228
pulley…388
pulp…188
pupa…65

R

rain gauge…259, 263
receiver…152
recycle…41, 45, 98
reduce…37, 41
relationship…162
reptile…58
resources…40
response…152
revolve…393

rock…229, 229–232, 239
   description…226, 229
   igneous…230
   metamorphic…232
   resources (uses)…233–234
   sedimentary…231, 239
rocket…308
root (plant)…27, 28–29, 36
roots (tooth)…188

S

saliva…113
sand…227, 231
satellite…265
screw…383
Scripture Spotlight…20, 31, 33, 48, 75, 86, 112, 122, 155, 156, 158, 168, 186, 197, 214, 220, 228, 233, 241, 250, 262, 270, 273, 292, 301, 320, 336, 342, 355, 368, 372, 376
seamount…223
season…276–283
   Earth's tilt…280–281
   living things and…282, 283
seat belt…196
sedimentary rock…231, 239
seed…31
seedling…31
seismograph…255
sender…152
serving…133
shadow…377
shelter…52
simple machine…380–389
sleet…274
smoke detector…197
snack…130
soil…23

solar energy…368, 391
Solar System…288–297, 293
   Earth…289, 294–295
   moon…289, 293
   planet…292, 294–295, 296
   Sun…289, 290–291
solid…330–332, 337
sound…355, 372, 373–375, 379
   hearing…373
   loudness…375
   pitch…374
   vibrate…373
sound wave…372
space…302, 304–309
   exploring…304–309
   space probe…307
   spacecraft…304, 308
   star…291, 298, 306
   telescope…306
space probe…307
spinal cord…146
spring…279
star…291, 298
   description…291
   patterns…299, 305
stem…28–29
stomach…116
Structured Inquiry…17, 27, 37, 47, 57, 73, 111, 121, 129, 141, 151, 161, 175, 185, 213, 227, 237, 247, 259, 269, 277, 289, 299, 305, 319, 339, 351, 361, 371, 381
summer…278–279
Sun…261, 270, 273, 280–281, 283, 289, 290–291, 291
   and seasons…280–281, 283
   description…290–291
   weather…261, 270
   water cycle…273
sunlight…22, 24, 280–281, 283, 370
symptom…176

teeth…113, 114–115
   canine…114–115
   enamel…188
   gums…188
   incisor…114–115
   molar…115
   premolar…114–115
   pulp…188
   root…188

telescope…306

temperature…362

texture…325

thermal energy…360–369

thermometer…263, 363

Think About It…18, 19, 23, 24, 30, 33, 34, 39, 40, 43, 44, 50, 54, 58, 59, 61, 62, 64, 66, 74, 76, 80, 84, 87, 88, 93, 96, 98, 99, 113, 114, 116, 118, 123, 125, 126, 131, 133, 134, 144, 147, 148, 154, 157, 158, 164, 167, 168, 176, 180, 181, 182, 187, 189, 190, 192, 196, 197, 199, 201, 202, 216, 219, 222, 224, 229, 232, 234, 240, 243, 244, 249, 251, 252, 261, 264, 265, 266, 271, 273, 274, 278, 281, 282, 291, 293, 294, 295, 300, 302, 307, 308, 322, 324, 325, 332, 333, 334, 336, 341, 344, 353, 354, 356, 358, 363, 365, 367, 372, 374, 378, 383, 384, 387, 388

thunderstorm…266

tornado…266

undersea exploration…285

Unit Review…104–105, 206–207, 312–313, 392–393

universe…298–303
   constellations…299, 301, 303
   galaxy…300
   stars…291, 298

vaccine…181, 183

value…165

verbal communication…155

vertebrate…58

vibrate…373

vitamin…123

volcano…230, 244, 245
   crater…244
   eruption…244
   fissure…244
   lava…230, 244

volume…323

waste…37, 98, 117

water…17, 204, 213, 215, 223, 224, 238, 268–275

water cycle…268–275

water features…213, 215, 220, 221, 222–223, 224
   lake…213, 215, 224
   ocean…213, 215, 220, 222–223
   pond…215
   river…215, 221
   stream…215, 221

water vapor…270, 271, 273

wave…372

weather…258–267
   balloon…255
   causes…261, 272–273
   precipitation…262, 272, 273, 274
   radar…264
   reports…260–262
   satellite…265
   storms…264, 266
   tools…259, 263–265
      anemometer…259, 263, 264
      barometer…259, 263
      rain gauge…259, 263
      thermometer…259, 263
      wind vane…263

weather map…258, 263, 265

weather satellite…265

weathering…238

wedge…384

wetland…80

wheel and axle…386

wind…261

wind turbine…285

wind vane…263

winter…278–279

work…380

Photo Credits

Cover Digital Media Pro/Shutterstock, (banner l to r) Fotorich01/Shutterstock, Janprchal/Shutterstock, Courtesy of Larry Blackmer, Steshkin Yevgeniy/Shutterstock, Lucarelli Temistocle/Shutterstock, NASA Images/NASA, Matej Pavlansky/Shutterstock; **SS 0–SS 1** Dorling Kindersley Rf/Thinkstock; **SS 2** Comstock Images/Thinkstock; **SS 3** (inset) Lee Prince/Shutterstock, (bkgd) Igor Kovalchuk/Shutterstock; **SS 4** Jupiterimages/Brand X Pictures/Thinkstock; **SS 5** Andrea Danti/Shutterstock; **SS 6** Shanta Giddens/Shutterstock; **SS 7** Noam Armonn/Shutterstock; **SS 8** (t) Agorohov/Shutterstock, (b) TSI Graphics; **SS 9** (tl) Zedcor Wholly Owned/Thinkstock, (tr) Istockphoto/Thinkstock, (bc) R. Gino Santa Maria/Shutterstock; **12–13** Fuse/Thinkstock; **14–15** Cathy Keifer/Shutterstock; **16** Andre Nantel/Shutterstock; **17** Iwona Grodzka/Shutterstock; **18** Anan Kaewkhammul/Shutterstock; **19** krosbona/Shutterstock; **20** Phb.cz (Richard Semik)/Shutterstock; **21** Kenneth Sponsler/Shutterstock; **22–23** inacio pires/Shutterstock; **24** TSI Graphics; **26** Filipe B. Varela/Shutterstock; **27** Olga Popova/Shutterstock; **28** pbsubhash/Shutterstock; **29** matt/Shutterstock; **30** (l) Hydromet/Shutterstock; **31** Andrea Danti/Shutterstock; **32** (l) Steve Bower/Shutterstock; **32–33** (cl) dmiskv/Shutterstock, (cr) Subbotina Anna/Shutterstock; **33** (tr) Rob Stark/Shutterstock, (br) Studio 1231/Shutterstock; **34** (l) Brian Maudsley/Shutterstock, (c) Arkady/Shutterstock; **35** (tr) ULKASTUDIO/Shutterstock; **36** (l) Ann Worthy/Shutterstock, (r) Peter Zijlstra/Shutterstock; **37** Olga Lyubkina/Shutterstock; **38** Viktor1/Shutterstock; **39** Tischenko Irina/Shutterstock; **40** Steven Frame/Shutterstock; **41** Mike Flippo/Shutterstock; **42–43** (bkgd) Ales Liska/Shutterstock; **43** (inset) Alexander M. Omelko/Shutterstock; **44** (l) Homeart/Shutterstock, (r) Peter Ploskonka/Shutterstock; **46** Durden Images/Shutterstock; **47** (tr) JinYoung Lee/Shutterstock; **48–49** Manamana/Shutterstock; **49** (tr) Graca Victoria/Shutterstock; **50** (inset) Photographer/Shutterstock, (bkgd) Ruslan Nabiyev/Shutterstock; **51** Tom C Amon/Shutterstock; **52** FloridaStock/Shutterstock; **53** Vatikaki/Shutterstock; **54–55** iStockphoto/Thinkstock; **56** Krasowit/Shutterstock; **58** (1) Andreas Gradin/Shutterstock, (2) Image Source/Thinkstock, (3) Matt Jeppson/Shutterstock, (4) Istockphoto/Thinkstock, (5) Courtesy of Larry Blackmer; **59** pr2is/Shutterstock; **60** Tomatito/Shutterstock; **61** Bull's-Eye Arts/Shutterstock; **62** Trevor Kelly/Shutterstock; **63** Svetlana Valoueva/Shutterstock; **64–65** Jens Stolt/Shutterstock; **65** (tr) Vladischern/Shutterstock; **66** Map Resources/Shutterstock; **68** (b) Kenneth Keifer/Shutterstock, (r) Bain News Service/Prints & Photographs Division, Library Of Congress, Lc-B2-6512-13; **69** (l) Istockphoto/Thinkstock, (r) Andrea Danti/Shutterstock; **70–71** Royalty Free/Masterfile; **72** Jouke van Keulen/Shutterstock; **73** TSI Graphics; **74–75** (c) Pashin Georgiy/Shutterstock; **75** (r) Elena Butinova/Shutterstock; **76** Imagix/Shutterstock; **77** (t) Design Pics/Thinkstock, (b) Chee-Onn Leong/Shutterstock; **78** Jim Parkin/Shutterstock; **79** Marcin Niemiec/Shutterstock; **80** FloridaStock/Shutterstock; **82** Monkey Business Images/Shutterstock; **83** TSI Graphics; **84** Clint Cearley/Shutterstock; **85** Sam DCruz/Shutterstock; **86** (l) Alexander Kalina/Shutterstock, (r) D. Kucharski & K. Kucharska/Shutterstock; **87** (l) P.schwarz/Shutterstock, (r) P.schwarz/Shutterstock; **90** kldy/Shutterstock; **91** Katrina Leigh/Shutterstock; **92–93** Gary Whitton/Shutterstock; **94** Val Thoermer/Shutterstock; **95** Martin D. Vonka/Shutterstock; **96** Mary Terriberry/Shutterstock; **97** Cheryl Casey/Shutterstock; **98** plazas i subiros/Shutterstock; **99** Christopher Halloran/Shutterstock; **100** Bob Blanchard/Shutterstock; **102** (t) Gary Whitton/Shutterstock, (b) Mikeledray/Shutterstock; **103** (l) Kirsanov/Shutterstock, (r) Istockphoto/Thinkstock; **104** Filipe B. Varela/Shutterstock; **106–107** Royalty-Free/Masterfile; **108–109** Monkey Business Images/Shutterstock; **110** Kellynelson/Shutterstock; **111** TSI Graphics; **112** Thomas La Mela/Shutterstock; **113** Vladimir Wrangel/Shutterstock; **117** Leonello Calvetti/Shutterstock; **118** (br) Barbaradudzinska/Shutterstock, (tl) Nikola Bilic/Shutterstock, (bl) iStockphoto/Thinkstock; **120** Monticello/Shutterstock; **121** TSI Graphics; **122** Sean D/Shutterstock; **123** (l) Zoonar/Thinkstock; **124** Isaxar/Shutterstock; **125** (t) courtesy of USDA, (c) Marco Mayer/Shutterstock, (b) Hemera/Thinkstock; **126** Shah Rohani/Shutterstock; **128** Spotmatik/Shutterstock; **129** TSI Graphics; **130** Magone/Shutterstock;

131 Littlemiss/Shutterstock; **132** Monkey Business Images/Shutterstock; **133** TSI Graphics; **134** (br) Nils Z/Shutterstock, (c) Sarsmis/Shutterstock, (t) Oznuroz/Shutterstock, (bl) Sevenke/Shutterstock; **136** (t) Creatas/Thinkstock, (c) Olga Miltsova/Shutterstock; **137** (l) Liquidlibrary/Thinkstock, (r)Monika Wisniewska/Shutterstock; **138–139** Royalty Free/Masterfile; **140** Geanina Bechea/Shutterstock; **143** Alex Mit/Shutterstock; **144** Royalty Free/Masterfile; **147** (l) Alxhar/Shutterstock, (r) Alex Mit/Shutterstock; **148** Lavigne Herve/Shutterstock; **150** Huntstock/Thinkstock; **151** Doglikehorse/Shutterstock; **152** Royalty Free/Masterfile; **153** Karen Roach/Shutterstock; **154** Nicholas Moore/Shutterstock; **155** Darren Baker/Shutterstock; **156** Carlos E. Santa Maria/Shutterstock; **157** Esbobeldijk/Shutterstock; **158** Kurhan/Shutterstock; **160** Peteri/Shutterstock; **162** Rob Marmion/Shutterstock; **164** Royalty-Free/Masterfile; **165** Mangostock/Shutterstock; **166–167** Igor Bulgarin/Shutterstock; **168** Rob Marmion/Shutterstock; **170** (t) Dmiskv/Shutterstock, (b) Monkey Business Images/Shutterstock; **171** (l) Iofoto/Shutterstock, (r) Jupiterimages/Thinkstock; **172–173** (bkgd) Khafizov Ivan Harisovich/Shutterstock, (inset) Royalty Free/Masterfile; **174** Catalin Petolea/Shutterstock; **175** 3445128471/Shutterstock; **177** Fuse/Thinkstock; **178** Blaj Gabriel/Shutterstock; **180** Stephanie Frey/Shutterstock; **181** Sura Nualpradid/Shutterstock; **182** Jupiterimages/Thinkstock; **184** Wavebreakmedia Ltd/Shutterstock; **186** Akva/Shutterstock; **187** Boris Sosnovyy/Shutterstock; **188** Stockshoppe/Thinkstock; **189** Anna Hoychuk/Shutterstock; **190** Michaeljung/Shutterstock; **191** (t) Goodluz/Shutterstock, (cr) iStockphoto/Thinkstock; **192** Royalty Free/Masterfile; **194** (l) Digital Vision/Thinkstock, (r) Stockbyte/Thinkstock; **195** TSI Graphics; **196** Royalty Free/Masterfile; **197** Magicoven/Shutterstock; **198** (b) Rayuken/Shutterstock; **199** (t) Children's Hospital of Pittsburgh, (b) Suzanne Tucker/Shutterstock; **200** Elena Elisseeva/Shutterstock; **202** Losevsky Pavel/Shutterstock; **204** (t) Bananastock/Thinkstock, (b) Lee Prince/Shutterstock; **205** (l) Darren Baker/Shutterstock, (r) Keith Brofsky/Thinkstock; **207** Courtesy of USDA; **208–209** Ipatov/Shutterstock; **210–211** Michael William/Shutterstock; **212** Natalia Bratslavsky/Shutterstock; **213** (inset) Yesaulov Vadym/Shutterstock; **215** Junker/Shutterstock; **216** Royalty Free/Masterfile; **217** kavram/Shutterstock; **218** Amy Nichole Harris/Shutterstock; **219** iStockphoto/Thinkstock; **220–221** (bkgd) Andrei Dumitru/Shutterstock; **221** (inset) Aridocean/Shutterstock; **224–225** (b) EastVillage Images/Shutterstock; **226** cameilia/Shutterstock; **227** Maksim Toome/Shutterstock; **228** TeplouhovJurij/Shutterstock; **229** Yury Kosourov/Shutterstock; **230** (c) TSI Graphics, (t) Josemaria Toscano/Shutterstock, (b) TSI Graphics; **231** (c) TSI Graphics, (t) Lucie Danninger/Shutterstock, (b) TSI Graphics; **232** (l) TSI Graphics, (r)TSI Graphics; **233** Royalty-Free/Masterfile; **234** (t) TSI Graphics, (b) sootra/Shutterstock; **236** Jhaz Photography/Shutterstock; **237** (l) Bepictured/Shutterstock, (r) Lana Langlois/Shutterstock; **238–239** Iain Frazer/Shutterstock; **240** Nick Stubbs/Shutterstock; **241** United States Geological Survey; **242** FEMA/Kevin Galvin; **244** (inset) Beboy/Shutterstock; **246** bocky/Shutterstock; **247** charles taylor/Shutterstock; **248** Mike Brake/Shutterstock; **249** Wellford Tiller/Shutterstock; **250** Posztos (Colorlab.hu)/Shutterstock; **251** (t to b) Linda Bucklin/Shutterstock, (2) JCElv/Shutterstock, (3) Computer Earth/Shutterstock, (4) Vaclav Volrab/Shutterstock, (5) Vaclav Volrab/Shutterstock, (6) Ralf Juergen Kraft/Shutterstock; **254** (l) Robert Gubbins/Shutterstock, (r) Department of the Interior/USGS; **255** (l) Iladm/Shutterstock, (r) Michael Blann/Thinkstock; **256–257** Juriah Mosin/Shutterstock; **258** (inset) Lisa F. Young/Shutterstock, (bkgd) Map Resources/Shutterstock; **259** Gavel of Sky/Shutterstock; **260–261** MaszaS/Shutterstock; **262** Royalty Free/Masterfile; **263** (cl) Sebastian Knight/Shutterstock, (cr) iStockphoto/Thinkstock, (l) Darryl Brooks/Shutterstock, (r) Evgeny Tomeev/Shutterstock; **264** pjcross/Shutterstock; **265** (inset) Athanasia Nomikou/Shutterstock; **266** (t) Alexey Stiop/Shutterstock, (c) Iafoto/Shutterstock, (b) Ramon Berk/Shutterstock; **268** Lisovskaya Natalia/Shutterstock; **270** BlueOrange Studio/Shutterstock; **271** Royalty Free/Masterfile; **272–273** Andrea Danti/Shutterstock; **274** (l) HABRDA/Shutterstock, (r) Steve Collender/Shutterstock; **276** Royalty-Free/Masterfile; **277** Gavel Of Sky/Shutterstock; **279** (b) Orla/Shutterstock; **282** photobank.kiev.ua/Shutterstock; **284** (l) Sam Dcruz/Shutterstock, (r) Istockphoto/Thinkstock; **285** (l) Istockphoto/Thinkstock, (r) Captain Albert E. Theberge, NOAA Corps (Ret)/NOAA/Department of Commerce;

286–287 Royalty Free/Masterfile; **288** (l) Sailorr/Shutterstock, ®Robert Gendler/NASA; **289** (l) David Koscheck/Shutterstock, (c) Ivana Rauski/Shutterstock, (r) Edgaras Kurauskas/Shutterstock; **290** Olegusk/Shutterstock; **291** (tl) K13 ART/Shutterstock, Olegusk/Shutterstock; **292–293** Lunar And Planetary Institute/NASA; **294** Revenant/Shutterstock; **295** Lunar And Planetary Institute/NASA; **296** (t) Photodisc/Thinkstock, (b) NASA/Jpl/NASA; **298** Viktar Malyshchyts/Shutterstock; **299** TSI Graphics; **300** Spitzer Space Telescope/NASA; **301** (l) Nikm/Shutterstock; **302** Catmando/Shutterstock; **304** Hubble Telescope/NASA; **306** (c) NASA, Steve Lee University of Colorado, Jim Bell Cornell University, (r) NASA/NASA, (t) Dja65/Shutterstock; **307** NASA/NASA; **308** NASA/NASA; **310** (t) Suec/Shutterstock, (b) Peresanz/Shutterstock; **311** (l) Uniquelight/Shutterstock, (r) Edwin Verin/Shutterstock; **312** Natalia Bratslavsky/Shutterstock; **314–315** Maska/Shutterstock; **316–317** Dmitriy Shironosov/Shutterstock; **318** Jordache/Shutterstock; **319** TSI Graphics; **320–321** Bienchen-s/Shutterstock; **322** (l) Xpixel/Shutterstock, (r) Dcwcreations/Shutterstock; **323** TSI Graphics; **324** (t) Prism68/Shutterstock, (b) Ekaterina Pokrovsky/Shutterstock; **325** (l) Sari Oneal/Shutterstock, (r) Denisnata/Shutterstock; **326** Joe Belanger/Shutterstock; **328** (bl) Dmitriy Shironosov/Shutterstock; **329** (tr) BonD80/Shutterstock, (b) Royalty-Free/Masterfile; **330** (b) Royalty-Free/Masterfile; **331** (l) Alex James Bramwell/Shutterstock, (r) Nick Pavlakis/Shutterstock; **332** (t) Marie C Fields/Shutterstock, (c) kak2s/Shutterstock, (tl) Madlen/Shutterstock, (b) Fotoline/Shutterstock; **333** Tim Scott/Shutterstock; **334** (b) Gelpi/Shutterstock; **336** (l)Royalty-Free/Masterfile, (r) Monkey Business Images/Shutterstock; **338** (b) Royalty-Free/Masterfile; **339** (r) liza1979/Shutterstock; **340** Rafa Irusta/Shutterstock; **341** (l) Anna Sedneva/Shutterstock, (r) Elena Blokhina/Shutterstock; **342** (tr) iStockphoto/Thinkstock, (bl) Jiri Hera/Shutterstock, (br) Violetkaipa/Shutterstock; **343** Yuri Arcurs/Shutterstock; **344** (l) Josh Resnick/Shutterstock, (r) iofoto/Shutterstock; **346** (t) Photos.com/Thinkstock, (b) Ivanagott/Shutterstock; **347** (l) Rangizzz/Shutterstock, (r) Istockphoto/Thinkstock; **348–349** Royalty Free/Masterfile; **350** Catalin Petolea/Shutterstock; **351** jgl247/Shutterstock; **352–353** iStockphoto/Thinkstock; **354** Royalty Free/Masterfile; **355** Manzrussali/Shutterstock; **356–357** John Foxx/Thinkstock; **358** Royalty Free/Masterfile; **360** Royalty Free/Masterfile; **361** (t) Simplegraphic/Shutterstock, (b) Arena Creative/Shutterstock, (inset) Evgeny Tomeev/Shutterstock; **362** (l) Julija Sapic/Shutterstock, (r) Royalty Free/Masterfile; **363** Evgeny Tomeev/Shutterstock; **364–365** Oliveromg/Shutterstock; **366** Neeila/Shutterstock; **367** Royalty Free/Masterfile; **368** (bkgd) Khafizov Ivan Harisovich/Shutterstock, (inset)Monika Hunácková/Shutterstock; **370** (bkgd) Royalty Free/Masterfile, (inset) Neveshkin Nikolay/Shutterstock; **371** TSI Graphics; **372** Costazzurra/Shutterstock; **373** (l) Zoulou_55/Shutterstock, (r) Sebastian Kaulitzki/Shutterstock; **374** (l) Istockphoto/Thinkstock, (r) Catalin Petolea/Shutterstock; **375** (l) Paul Maguire/Masterfile, (r) Virginija Valatkiene/Shutterstock; **376** Fer Gregory/Shutterstock; **377** Samson Yury/Shutterstock; **378** (l) Royalty Free/Masterfile, (r) Royalty-Free/Masterfile; **380** Jupiterimages/Thinkstock; **381** TSI Graphics; **382** Royalty Free/Masterfile; **383** (l) STILLFX/Shutterstock, (r) karnizz/Shutterstock; **384** Tr3gin/Shutterstock; **385** Sergey Lavrentev/Shutterstock; **386** Royalty-Free/Masterfile; **387** Spotmatik/Shutterstock; **388–389** Courtesy of Piqua SDA Christian School; **390** (l) Alan C. Heison/Shutterstock, (r) Goodluz/Shutterstock; **391** (l) Istockphoto/Thinkstock, (r) Stocktrek Images/Thinkstock; **392** Maska/Shutterstock.